Oct '14

To Carolyn —
For whom the Cold War was fraught. With lots of love and best wishes always,
Don

Thomas C. Reed

The Reagan Engima
1964-1980

Thomas C. Reed

FIGUEROA
PRESS

THE REAGAN ENIGMA: 1964-1980
by Thomas C. Reed

Published by
FIGUEROA PRESS
840 Childs Way, 3rd Floor
Los Angeles, CA 90089
Phone: (213) 743-4800
Fax: (213) 743-4804
www.figueroapress.com

Figueroa Press is a division of the USC Bookstores
Cover, text, and layout design by
USC Design Studio

Produced by Crestec, Los Angeles, Inc.
Printed in the United States of America

Library of Congress Cataloguing-in-Publication Data
Thomas C. Reed
THE REAGAN ENIGMA
ISBN-13: 978-0-18-218169-8
ISBN-10: 0-18-218169-3
Library of Congress Number: 2014951425

To Kay Riddle Reed, who helped make every moment of this history and who now encourages my writing the story.

CONTENTS

ACKNOWLEDGEMENTS

An author's words are but cold kindling. His editor lights the fire that illuminates the dark corners of history. Sandy Baker served as the tireless editor for this work. Without her, this book would have been only a recitation of places and dates, a catalog of observations and vignettes.

I am indebted to the University of Southern California and its unique President Max Nikias for the encouragement and subsequent release of this work. USC's Tiffany Quon managed the publication process. Jorge Negrete, Danny Byerley and their associates at the USC Design Studio created the cover. JoEllen Williamson served as the enveloping link to all corners of my graduate alma mater.

Cris Wanzer served as copy editor; Phil Schwartberg provided the electoral maps.

Stuart Spencer, identified in what follows as the Steven Spielberg of Reagan's political life, opened his entire mental filing cabinet to provide the hitherto undisclosed details of Reagan's political persona.

Both Michael Reagan, in person, and Maureen Reagan in conversations prior to her death a decade ago and subsequently in her memoirs, provided key insights into their father's thinking during the mid-Sixties.

Nancy Clark Reynolds, Don Hodel, and Leslie Reed were deeply involved with Reagan and his Los Angeles peers during the politically formative years. Their recollections filled in many of the blanks. Long-time Hollywood producers Ray and Chris Wagner explained the divergent social structures of Hollywood and the Los Angeles Establishment during the Sixties.

Colleen McAndrews, the controller of Reagan's 1970 gubernatorial re-election campaign, did much document research at the Reagan Presidential Library and then elsewhere into the psychology of adult children of alcoholics. Gene Kopelson documented Reagan's relationships with Dwight Eisenhower and Robert Kennedy.[*] Paul Haerle and Norman Watts were key staffers and/or political office holders during the entire span of this book's years. Their recollections provided needed confirmations.

Reagan biographer Lou Cannon and Civil War historian George Bradley repeatedly read and improved the manuscripts. Book reviewers Sarah Davies and Charles Ball identified aspects of the Reagan persona often missed by others.

The book's first draft focused on Reagan's denial of his presidential run in 1968. Paul Golob, Sandy Dijkstra, Elise Capron, and Roz Foster urged the expansion of this story into an examination of Reagan's immense mind along with its flaws plus coverage of all of Reagan's campaign years, 1964 to 1980.

The Sacramento Old Hands, Ed Meese, Bill Clark, and Lyn Nofziger, are credited in the manuscript, but there are not enough words to express my appreciation for their diverse insights, collected over the past decade.

Karen McDonald, P.J. Lenz, and Joanne Clark provided the archiving help and secretarial support that is indispensible to a history covering decades long past.

The www.reagan68.com web site, along with its displayed video clips, was created and edited by Andrew Reed.

Garrett Civian provided intellectual property counsel.

If this book captures the attention of you, the reader, it could well be due to the efforts of publicist Diana Banister.

But at the end, I most appreciate the patience and support of my dear wife Kay who also first met Ronald Reagan a half century ago. From the beginning Kay understood the man's potential. As our peers disappeared from history's stage, she was the one who insisted on my writing this memoir.

Healdsburg, CA
October, 2014

---

[*] Kopelson has submitted details to a variety of historical journals.

Introduction

Ronald Reagan's political career has been scrutinized and mythologized more than most. But Reagan, the person, has seldom been understood by journalists or biographers.

Thomas C. Reed, one of USC's most distinguished alumni, was one of the few in a position to understand the man behind the historic headlines and the world-shaking events. Tom managed and lived with Reagan during the enigmatic leader's politically formative years. This allowed Tom to penetrate the Reagan veneer in a way others never did.

The Reagan Enigma is a fascinating insider account of Reagan's development as a person and a leader. It allows us to better understand the presidential years that followed.

The University of Southern California is pleased to present *The Reagan Enigma, 1964-1980*, as an important contribution to the scholarship surrounding our 40th president.

Max Nikias
President of the University of Southern California

PROLOGUE

In the opening weeks of Reagan's first presidential term, Clark Clifford, a senior Democrat, captured his party's expectations when speaking with his peers in Georgetown.

"Reagan is an amiable dunce," he declared.

Many American politicians laughed Reagan off as a lightweight movie star; they lost all the elections to which they brought that outlook.

The Soviet Politburo found Reagan to be "unsophisticated."

Their empire is now gone.

What aspects of Reagan's mind did these experts not understand?

In 1965, I was invited to Reagan's home for a crystallizing personal conversation. Two decades of close association followed, from campaign planning to Cold War termination. During those years, decoding Ronald Reagan's mind was a constant challenge.

Subsequent journalists and profilers, even the former president himself, have churned out reams of analyses and memoirs, but all are two-dimensional. They fit nicely on the printed page, but none answer the central question: "What made Ronald Reagan tick?"

Even Edmund Morris, Reagan's chosen but failed biographer, had to admit, "Nobody understood him."[1]

My journals and film clips from the Reagan years remained sequestered for decades. I sought invisibility as the best shield for family and friends. I staked no claims, sought no credit, and avoided all commemorations while returning to a high-tech professional life far from the Washington hothouse.

---

1   CBS *60 Minutes*, 9 June 2004

But with the all-too-frequent passing of those who knew Reagan quite well, a parade of well-meaning historians has appeared at my door. Some seek files, others want insights.

The golden anniversary of Reagan's "Time for Choosing" speech seemed like the right time to open these archives, to collect the insights of my surviving peers, and to weave all of this into an unexpected but accurate explanation of Reagan's mind.

What follows may provide the perspective that many have sought, but few have found.

CH. 1   THE SPEECH

Fifty years ago, an aging movie-actor-turned-TV-host was relaxing after a performance at Hollywood's Coconut Grove. As he peeled an orange, three admirers joined him.

"Great job, Ron!"

The target of that ovation, Ronald Reagan, was the son of an alcoholic father. He was also the victim of a grim Hollywood divorce, but by that autumn of '64, Reagan had reassembled his life with a steady if mundane job and a happy second marriage.

On that evening in mid-October, Reagan had just spoken to a live California audience in support of Barry Goldwater's collapsing presidential candidacy.

A gruff Henry Salvatori had barked the opening plaudit.

Auto dealer Holmes Tuttle proposed specific action. "Ron, the whole country needs to hear that talk." Turning to Cy Rubel, the third Reagan booster at the table, Tuttle unknowingly proposed to revamp the twentieth century. "Cy, let's the three of us put up the cash needed to broadcast Ron's talk on national TV."

Rubel nodded; Salvatori grinned. A week later[2] Ronald Reagan delivered his "Time for Choosing" address to tens of millions of viewers. It soon came to be known as "The Speech."[3]

"Time for Choosing" was an articulate and well-integrated talk, one that Reagan had given often to individual audiences. It was professionally delivered with no disconnects or *non sequiturs*. The digestible statistics, the memorable anecdotes, and the humorous

---

2   On October 27, 1964
3   See Appendix A for a summary of The Speech, or go to <reagan68.com> to view it.

one-liners would relax audiences for decades to come. Reagan's talk was filled with historical references, from ancient Greeks to colonial revolutionaries to more recent American heroes. Those analogies gave the Speech a classic tone, and the Speech, in turn, electrified a discouraged electorate.

The line that grabbed my attention: "We are faced with the most evil enemy mankind has known in his long climb from the swamps to the stars."

Those words resonated with the writings of former communist Whittaker Chambers, describing why one of his former colleagues had converted from Soviet dogma to implacable anti-communism.[4] "One night, in Moscow, I heard screams."

With the Speech, much of America's weary political class awakened. Dave Broder of *The Washington Post* described the Speech as, "The most successful national political debut since William Jennings Bryan's 'Cross of Gold' speech at the Democratic Convention in 1896."

A curious nation wanted to know more. Electronically, Reagan had been blasted into political orbit. Upon returning to earth, he landed in the heart of America's Vietnam-poisoned civil desert.

I watched that speech from a Pittsburgh hotel room strewn with schedules and coffee cups. I was there as an advance man, working the Goldwater campaign. Reagan's well-chosen words, warning us of "a thousand years of darkness," struck a chord. They jolted much of America's body politic. Many viewers, from professional politicians to concerned amateurs, all wanted to know more.

"Who is this man?" they asked. "What makes him tick?"

"Is he just an actor, a movie star reciting well-learned lines for a pal? Or does he have a mind of his own?"

"Who are his friends? Where does he get his ideas? They make sense, but where do they come from?"

"Does Reagan live in some right-wing cave? Or does he come from a community of working people with hopes and fears of their own?"

---

4   *Witness*, Whittaker Chambers, 1952, Regnery Gateway

More active political observers wanted to investigate Reagan's flaws. "We all have them," they noted. "Does he have quirks that will disable a political career? Will he self-destruct? Is he willing to learn?"

I reflected on those same questions. Upon my return home, I wrote a letter urging Reagan to seek public office. I closed with an offer to help.

Some time before, my father had given me a copy of Whittaker Chambers' memoir; an account of his association with, and then his breaking from, the Communist Party during the thirties. In his opening, a memorable letter to his children, Chambers warned that, "In this century it will be decided for the generations to come whether all mankind is to become communist, or whether the whole world is to become free."

That one sentence connected all the dots for me.

It turns out they did the same for fellow-reader Reagan. Thirty years later, as I unwound in the Oval Office with President Reagan,[5] we recited those lines to each other, verbatim and from memory, as we set in motion our plans to end and win the Cold War.

Viewing my children's prospects at the end of 1964, I feared for their well-being. Lyndon Johnson had just been elected to the American presidency in his own right. Living in Texas, home to the LBJ cognoscenti, my neighbors and I knew what to expect during the mid-sixties to come: an ego-driven entanglement in Vietnam and a foolish inflation of the American economy, all promoted with little presidential reliance on truth.

Many of my peers would soon protest the Johnson incursions into Vietnam, but I did not think shouting in the streets would accomplish our goal, which was getting rid of LBJ. Article One of the US Constitution defined a better route.

Given LBJ's ego, he would surely seek re-election in 1968. There were no credible opponents on the horizon, only a defeated former vice president and a passel of tired senators. If Reagan would step forward, enter the political arena and then win, he could be the vehicle for defeating Johnson in '68.

---

5   At that time I was serving as a special assistant to President Reagan for National Security Policy

Such were the thoughts of the young, but that is why I posted my letter to Pacific Palisades at the end of '64.

Reagan received that note during the holidays. He put it in the "worthwhile" stack for future reference.

Ch. 2 Opening Moves

The first serious "let's get started" call originated with Neil Reagan during April of 1965. It was directed to Stuart Spencer, a political pro and a personal friend of Neil's.

"Hi, Stu. Interested in my brother's campaign?"

Spencer was a child of the Depression. He enlisted in the US Navy at age 17, boarding AGS-3, the *USS Rocky Mount*, during the early summer of 1945 as it prepared for the invasion of the Japanese homeland. The *Rocky Mount* was a communications and command post ship, the flagship for the Marines' Fifth Amphibious Force. Seaman First Class Spencer had trained to operate the newfangled radars, nursed daily by freshly-minted ensigns from MIT. The *Rocky Mount* was at sea, en route to the invasion of Kyushu, when it got the news of Japan's surrender. The fireworks, gunfire, and hilarity lasted through the night. The crew had heard about the Kamikaze attacks on US ships off Okinawa. They were not looking forward to a repeat experience in the East China Sea.

Spencer returned home to find another Navy man, Richard Nixon, sitting at his father's kitchen table.

That young lieutenant's opening words were, "Nice to meet you, Stu. I need your Dad's help." Nixon, fresh out of the Navy, had just won the Republican nomination for a congressional seat in Orange County. "I hope your father will help raise some money."

The senior Spencer agreed. The son's handshake with Nixon in the summer of '46 laid the first strand of a web that was to make history.

Young Spencer went to work for the City of Alhambra; in time the locals wanted him to run for city clerk. He knew early on that being a candidate was not his calling, although for years he and his good friend Bill Roberts had been active in the Young Republican organization. In 1960, they organized their own firm to focus on Republican candidates, not ballot measures as other new political consultants were doing.

In '62, Senator Tom Kuchel (R - CA) asked the Spencer-Roberts partners to run his re-election campaign. They did so, winning by 13 percentage points. Two years later, as Nelson Rockefeller was planning his California presidential primary drive, he sought Senator Kuchel's advice.

"Call Spencer-Roberts," was the senator's immediate and unqualified response. By then the firm had three partners: Stu Spencer, Bill Roberts, and San Franciscan Fred Haffner.
Rockefeller hired the firm, but he lost that primary to Barry Goldwater. In the process, however, Rockefeller's campaign managers earned the Arizona senator's respect.

In Los Angeles, the three men who had underwritten Reagan's "Time for Choosing" speech[6] were having thoughts parallel to those of Neil Reagan's. They noted that California's governorship would be the next first-string opening on the ballot. The Democratic incumbent, Pat Brown, was a two-term favorite of the labor unions. If he sought a third term, that aging beneficiary of the Republican collapse of 1958[7] would offer an exposed target.

How different history might have been if a Senate seat had been open in '66. In retrospect, I believe Reagan was, at that time, more qualified to become an orating and policy-making US senator rather than the chief executive of the nation's most prosperous state, but the governorship of California was the only

---

6   As noted earlier, Rubel, Salvatori, and Tuttle were the core of the Funding Fathers, a group so identified in a book of that name: *Funding Fathers: The Unsung Heroes of the Conservative Movement*, by Nicole Hoplin and Ron Robinson, 2008, Regnery
7   During that mid-century year, California was comfortably Republican, but US Senator William Knowland (R-CA) was both dangerously ambitious and hopelessly inept. To gain control of the California delegation to the 1960 GOP convention, Knowland needed control of the California statehouse. In 1958 he entered the governor's race, forcing the incumbent Republican Governor Goodwin Knight to run for the Senate seat Knowland would vacate. The "Big Switch," as it came to be known, offended most Californians. Both men lost. Democrat Brown won the governorship. A decade of Democratic control of California ensued.

game in town. Thus, Reagan's political life was channeled into the administrative branch of government.

As Reagan weighed the possibility of a political run, he sought Barry Goldwater's advice.

"If you're gonna run for office, Ron," the senator responded, "hire those Spencer-Roberts SOBs. They're good."

A week later, Holmes Tuttle weighed in with his call to Spencer.

"Stu, we'd like to talk about a possible Reagan campaign. Can you drop by? I'm on La Brea."

Spencer examined this business opportunity with care. Others were courting his firm, and Reagan was an unknown, though he had done well with the Speech. As the winter of '64-65 turned to spring, Spencer gathered his partners for some brainstorming.

"How rigid is this guy?" they asked each other. "How far right is he? What's inside his head?"

San Francisco's Mayor George Christopher, another Republican candidate for governor, was also wooing Spencer-Roberts.

By the end of March, the partners had agreed to take a careful look into Reagan's mind. They were not under contract, just performing due diligence.

In April, the three Spencer-Roberts partners began their investigations while seated in the Reagan living room. They posed open-ended questions for hours on end, invading Reagan's private life, prying into his belief system. They were not looking for answers, just testing RR's mental acuity, his understanding of real-world issues. Nancy Reagan sat quietly by.

"We found him to be pretty solid. A conservative, but thoughtfully so," Spencer told me later. "A motion picture professional."

During the weeks that followed, Spencer took time to meet with Reagan's contemporaries, some of the other players in his life.

The first meeting was with US Senator George Murphy (R - CA), a Hollywood peer and a Reagan political ally of long standing. Spencer and Murphy lunched at a Hollywood watering hole where deals and dreams bloomed.

"Ron's a dependable guy, a good performer," the senator said. "All of us in the business like him. He shows up on time with his lines down pat. Incredible mind. Directors love him; no retakes."

"OK," Spencer responded. "But can he cut it as governor?"

"Well, Stu, not many of us think he's heavy enough for that job. Governor? He's never run anything other than a stable. But then, he's a helluva negotiator," Murphy concluded. "Ron did a great job at SAG. If he runs, Stu, I'm with him. Let me know how I can help."

Spencer's next conversation was with Reagan's agent and financial angel, Taft Schreiber, Vice President of MCA.[8] Those two lunched in professional surroundings outside the Universal Studios' "Black Box" office building. Schreiber and MCA president Lew Wasserman had already compared notes.

"We're 100 percent for him," Schreiber advised. "I've been his agent for 25 years. I know him, his wife, even his former wife, inside and out. He's bright. He'll do well."

But then Schreiber added, "You'll have to fire a lot of people, Stu. Ron has never fired anyone, ever."

Schreiber's comment was prescient. In later years, Spencer got the job of notifying Reagan cabinet members they were no longer needed, then negotiating their golden parachutes.

Spencer next shared morning coffee with Jane Wyman, the first Mrs. Reagan, at her Spanish architecture home outside Beverly Hills. Wyman knew why Spencer had come, and she was forthcoming about her private life with "Ronnie."

"We parted company because I was doing well in motion pictures. He had moved on, into politics and speech-making."

Wyman was more concise in her separate comments to June Allyson. "Don't ask Ronnie what time it is. He'll tell you how the watch is made."[9]

---

8   A talent agency once known at the Music Corporation of America
9   *Nancy Reagan: The Unauthorized Biography*, Kitty Kelley, 1991, Simon & Schuster, page 84

Wyman bore Ronnie no ill will. She seemed glad he was in such good hands, meaning Spencer-Roberts. She wished her former husband well.

"What about the press?" Spencer asked.

"I'll stay out of it, Stu," Wyman agreed. "I want nothing to do with Ronnie's campaign, though I hope he wins. I'll never talk to the press."

She never did. Her word was good.

§§§

At the end of April, the Reagans travelled to Phoenix to visit Nancy's family. While there, Reagan checked back with Spencer by phone.

"When are you guys gonna make up your mind?" he queried.

Apparently Reagan had already made his decision, but Spencer's response was more cautious.

"We'll be ready to talk when you get home," Spencer said.

During that same week, when I visited a Hudson Valley hunting lodge, I crossed paths with Ralph Cordiner, the recently retired Chairman of General Electric. Cordiner had served as Reagan's mentor within that company.

"Reagan is going to run for governor," Cordiner confided over a glass of whiskey. "He's good. He'll win."

In early May '65, when the Spencer-Roberts partners returned to the Reagan home for a closing meeting, their host was dressed in blindingly white slacks riding above iridescent red socks. This fiery show was topped by a floral golf shirt. Reagan was smiling broadly, daring the men from Spencer-Roberts to miss the show.

They did not. On May 15, Spencer-Roberts signed a contract with Holmes Tuttle to look into, and perhaps manage, Reagan's first campaign.

This was not to be a renewal of the '64 internecine fights. It was to be the birth of a new, unified Republican approach to government. Conservative policies would be at its core, but the target audience would be a new constituency, in time to be known as Reagan Democrats.

Soon after that meeting, Reagan handed his stack of "worthwhile" fan mail to the new managers. In time, their partner in San Francisco, Fred Haffner, got in touch with me. Over coffee in his Kearney Street office, he told me of his partners' assessment of Reagan.

"He'll make a sound candidate," Haffner confirmed. "He's a real professional."

We then discussed my experience as an advance man and my commitment to what I perceived as the Reagan cause.

"OK," Haffner ordered. "Get yourself down to Modesto, do the advance work for Ron's upcoming appearance there. When done with that, start organizing Friends of Reagan committees. Go screen and recruit a broad base of volunteers all across northern California. In time we'll want you to meet some legislators."

Haffner meant *liberal Republican* legislators, those who were suspicious of Reagan's political credentials. In effect, I was being given my preliminary exams.

Apparently, I passed. At the end of the month I was invited to meet with Reagan at his home in Los Angeles.

§§§

A network of narrow, tree-lined streets led me to the Reagan home in Pacific Palisades, a sprawling, single-story ranch house with minimal parking, but a maximum view.

A butler in a white jacket met me at the door, but the man I had come to see, movie star Ronald Reagan, soon stepped forward. It was our first personal encounter. Reagan's good-natured welcome was augmented by a broad smile, twinkling eyes, and a firm handshake. As other guests milled about in the immediately adjacent living area, Ron (as I was to call him) presented his wife Nancy and their two children, 13-year-old Patti and 7-year-old Ronnie. I found all four to be congenial, not conceited, but certainly glamorous.

Ron and I chatted about the audio scrapbook he was keeping for his children.

Nice idea, I thought.

He then introduced his older brother, Neil, a vice president of the McCann-Erickson advertising agency that handled much of Ron's movie publicity. Other arrivals included Bill Roberts and Fred Haffner of the Spencer-Roberts firm, along with Denny Carpenter, Orange County Republican Chairman. Carpenter was my volunteer counterpart from the South. Dr. Stewart McBirnie, Reagan's evangelical pastor, filled out the guest roster.

Some of us failed to notice that the businessmen bankrolling the exploratory part of this campaign, Rubel, Salvatori, and Tuttle et al. were absent from this gathering. Those men, whom I now call the Los Angeles Elders, were meeting regularly downtown at the California Club to develop their version of Reagan's political career. The prospective candidate seldom joined those conversations; few actors were welcome within those walls.

The Reagans' spacious living room featured a large stone fireplace on the south wall with an elevated concrete bench built in. That hearth was framed, left and right, by glass windows disclosing a well-planted pool area in the foreground and a superb view of the city as a backdrop. There were no antiques, no collectibles in the house, just an imposing sofa resting against the opposite wall with armchairs at each end. This is where the Reagan children slumped until withdrawn by Nancy once we all had arrived.

With the family's departure, Reagan's political audience settled into those vacated spaces. That's how it all began for me on that Thursday before Labor Day in 1965.

The ensuing discussions were wide-ranging. The plan was for Reagan to take the pulse of the state in '65, with a decision on his gubernatorial candidacy to come at year-end. But as we wound up our business that evening, Reagan jumped the gun.

"I've made up my mind," he told us all. "I'm going to run."

The Roberts and Haffner faces took on a startled look. Their company had not yet signed on for a full campaign, but there it was. Ronald Reagan had made a decision, just as he told Ralph Cordiner six months earlier.

The volunteers were ready to get to work; Spencer-Roberts had been drawn into the web.

I had spent the previous year in the losing Goldwater campaign; this one felt like a winner. All of us were exhilarated.

CH. 3 SCREEN TESTS

Ith Reagan's political auditions done, the screen tests came next.

During the September visit to the Reagan home, our group reviewed the potential hazards. The professionals worried about early money, while Reagan was unconcerned. He left that problem to "the boys."

Unspoken, we shared a greater concern: "Can Reagan take the heat?"

Once the campaign started, we knew Reagan would no longer be worshipped as a movie star. He would be seen as a maverick bull charging a herd of sacred cows. The picadors, i.e., an inherently antagonistic press corps, were sure to emerge at every stop.

At the end of September '65, we set off to face these adversaries. Nominally, we were to help the Republican parties of Connecticut and Massachusetts raise money. Bill Roberts and I accompanied Reagan on this trip.

After gathering substantial funds at a small luncheon in Greenwich, Reagan moved on to New Haven. This is a college town, home to Yale University. We were astonished when 4,500 Republicans filled a hall to wildly cheer this new voice on the American scene. There were no adverse demonstrators outside.

I then witnessed Reagan's first contested press conference. I had seen him speak, even answer complex questions from diverse audiences back in California, but New Haven was something else. Suspicious stringers from all across New England augmented local reporters. They expected a hollow performance by a newly prominent, right-wing celebrity. Instead, they got an overpowering, professional performance with comprehensive and convincing responses that left many of those reporters in the intellectual dust.

This man is a marvel, I wrote in my journal. *Most impressive. Handled all the curve balls very well. He's a pro!*

I was not the only one reaching those conclusions. National reporters had come up from New York to check Reagan out. NBC sent a film crew to get material for a Reagan show that Frank McGee aired in October. Reagan played well on that national stage.

We then moved on to Boston, where Reagan performed flawlessly at a successful Republican finance luncheon. In the evening he brought down the house at the National Federation of Republican Women's windup banquet. These were skeptical, middle-of-the-road worker bees, but hundreds rose for a standing ovation when Reagan finished his talk.

Between these events, Roberts and I took RR over to the state capitol to meet not only the governor, Republican John Volpe, but the new Attorney General of Massachusetts, Edward Brooke.

Volpe first won election in 1960, lost the seat in '62, but reclaimed the statehouse in '64. Potential candidate Reagan and survivor Volpe opened their conversation with small talk, but in time, they turned to political mechanics: how to exploit fratricide within an incumbent Democrat's political family. That had been the key to Volpe's return to office in Massachusetts. Reagan saw Pat Brown's run for a third term as fuel for similar discontent within the Democratic Party of California.

"Interesting," RR quietly observed as we left the governor's office.

We then moved down the capitol's hallways to meet with Ed Brooke, the first African American Republican officeholder in the history of the Commonwealth.

The half-hour conversation was short on specifics, long on drama. As we left the attorney general's chambers, Reagan issued a professional verdict.

"Wow, quite a charmer."

The two men connected at once. Reagan had just encountered another master of the political stage.

In our later conversations, RR never mentioned the remarkable elevation of an African American to top-level political office in Brahmin, Massachusetts. Reagan was politically and personally color-blind. Accepting people for what they were, he was the most inclusive politician any of us ever met.

In November, our tours took the Reagans, and my wife and me, to Squaw Valley, nominally for a legislative fundraising event. But there was a broader agenda. Spencer-Roberts had seen the need for a final dialog between the candidate and his potential chairman. The Reeds and the Reagans shared a condominium complex for a couple of nights. As an engineer, I talked about campaign organization; as an actor, Ron talked about movies. We exchanged humorous anecdotes about politicians and movie stars, but there was little substance. Neither baseball, whiskey nor women ever entered the conversation.

We got along with much laughter, and apparently I once again passed, but there was another dimension to those days. On November 7, Paul Laxalt came by for a visit.

At the time, Laxalt was the lieutenant governor of Nevada. In '66 he would seek the governorship on the other side of the state line. It was a first meeting for these two men. They hit it off at once, perhaps because both were ranchers, if not cowboys. The Laxalt family was Basque, his father a serious sheepherder. Ron loved horses. Conversation in the early afternoon revolved around their mutual annoyance with cattlemen, their empathy for both sheep and stallions.

In time, the two shifted to the California and Nevada gubernatorial contests. Neither wanted to talk about campaigning. Both wanted to explore their post-election plans; neither envisioned defeat.

We were meeting in the Tahoe watershed. Reagan and Laxalt were outdoorsmen who treasured the beauty of Lake Tahoe. On that autumn afternoon, as the two prospective governors surveyed that lake from their glass-enclosed aerie, the Tahoe Regional Planning Agency was conceived, if not born.

Both men won their gubernatorial races. In the seventies, Laxalt was elected to the US Senate. During the eighties he served as Reagan's presidential campaign chairman and close confidant. It all started there in Squaw Valley in November '65.

§§§

On a cold Sunday evening in early December of that year, as I sat by the fire at home with my family, the phone rang. A familiar voice was on the line.

"Hi, Tom. This is Ronald Reagan."

After a brief exchange of pleasantries, the lead player in the drama now unfolding got to the point. "I'd like you to be my northern California chairman,[10] Tom. Could you do that?"

No hesitation on my part. All in.

"Of course, Ron." I had expected the offer, but not this call.

"Thanks," was his only response. "See you down here for the kickoff."

That was it. I spent the evening in rumination, surprised for several reasons.

First because Reagan, or more accurately his Spencer-Roberts advisors, were willing to entrust campaign leadership to this 31-year-old novice. During the autumn months since my first meeting with Reagan, I had been given organizational assignments. I had travelled with the man, and I had begun the recruitment of talent, but I was still quite unknown to any of the San Francisco Establishment. My counterpart in the Christopher campaign, Arch Monson, embodied that Establishment. He was the president of the most prominent men's club in San Francisco, an organization with an enclave in the redwoods to the north.

On the other hand, my invisibility would be a blessing. We would be able to work the city's surrounding counties and California's Central Valley while the Christopher team lunched in town.

---

10   Most campaigns in California have Northern and Southern chairs. For our purposes, Northern California consisted of 46 counties, mostly-agricultural except for those surrounding San Francisco Bay, home to about one-third of California's population. Southern California consisted of 12 counties centered on Los Angeles and San Diego, with about two-thirds of the state's population. The cultures and media markets for North and South are quite different, and they are hundreds of miles apart. Thus, the need for separate leadership and campaign offices.

Secondly, I was taken aback by the mere fact of a Reagan phone call. I had never heard of Reagan calling any campaign volunteers.

During the years that followed, I came to understand that as governor, he seldom used the phone to ask anyone to do anything. When a serious need arose, his emissaries usually contacted, importuned, or sometimes browbeat me with the intended message. In later-year meetings, over coffee or jellybeans, Reagan often asked questions and provided guidance. But during those decades, RR rarely called me or anyone else, either to be filled in on current projects or to direct some specific action. Whether I was down the hall, accessible by intercom, or in my campaign office far away, Reagan seldom used the phone to stay in touch.

This remained his *modus operandi* for the rest of his career. During the heat of Reagan's 1980 presidential campaign, RR did not voluntarily phone George Bush, his running mate. The first two weeks of that campaign went by with nary a "let's stay connected" call from Reagan. Their respective managers had to schedule those links.

Reagan's invitation of December '65 also put me on Nancy Reagan's call list, a dubious honor heretofore sloughed off on those closer at hand. Nancy was a very active candidate's wife, supportive and protective of RR, but incessantly injecting her views and personal demands on anyone who would listen—along with many who did not wish to do so.

This was not a newly developed trait. Upon her marriage to the president of the Screen Actors Guild, Nancy endlessly sought visibility. Dick Powell, head of Four Star Television, told his exec, "For God's sake, give Nancy Reagan something so I can stop the calls." In later years, Mrs. Reagan rang up the headmaster at her children's school every night at 6:30 p.m., intruding on the man's dinner hour to discuss daughter Patti's behavior problems.

Nancy's political calls, directed at any who would listen, usually came first thing in the morning as soon as RR left the house. She wanted to discuss her perception of the campaign, garnered from her dinner companions of the night before. These women were hardly a cross-section of working-class California.[11]

That December's call from Ronald Reagan moved me to the center of his somewhat congested inner circle.

By the end of December, the stage was set. As a professional, Reagan understood his role. His announcement of candidacy was to be the curtain raiser. It would be the beginning of the show (the campaign), but for the show to work, all the props needed to be on stage, and all the characters had to know their lines before the drapes were drawn. In the countdown to the '66 kickoff, Reagan neither touched the props nor tampered with the script. He was a pro. Other, less professional candidates announce first, and then try to get organized in real time. That does not work. Reagan played it perfectly.

---

11   For an illuminating survey of Nancy Reagan's social network, see Vanity Fair, July 1998, "Ronnie and Nancy" by Bob Colacello, pg 76.

CH. 4 NEW VENUES

O n January 4, 1966, Ronald Reagan announced his candidacy for the governorship of California. That declaration was well orchestrated: a half-hour TV show, a massively attended press conference, and a noisy, exuberant rally, all at the Ambassador Hotel in Los Angeles. I attended that event, but thereafter I confined my activities to northern California, where I had challenging responsibilities along with a little locally provided cash to carry them out.

Much of our northern California campaign was run at the retail level. We wanted to connect with the local civic leaders and press as best we could. On January 22, I met Reagan in San Francisco for the hour-long drive north to Healdsburg, a small town then known as the Buckle of the Prune Belt. Our target was the *Healdsburg Tribune.*

Sonoma County is an agricultural community. It is highly dependent on water for apples and grapes, along with a host of other crops. As an eager young volunteer, I had done extensive research on the north coast's water supply, on plans to flood Round Valley, and on the Corps of Engineers' plans to reverse the flow of the Eel River. Environmentalists were up in arms; longtime resident Native Americans were in anguish; but the farmers needed water. As we entered the wine country, I gave our candidate my briefing on Sonoma County's water supply. Reagan knew all about ranches and water.

As we pulled into the *Tribune's* rain-soaked parking lot, that paper's sturdy editor greeted us at his door with an extended hand and a wide grin. He had his own agenda. The wooden floor of his one-room office was spattered with blood. Two pieces of a dismembered reptile were still in motion.

Let's get out of here, I thought. *That man has just killed a rattlesnake!*

Our infectiously charming candidate showed no concern. He was right at home. He laughed, then launched into a tale about a rattlesnake that once made his horse bolt out on the trail. Both men chuckled, trading stories for half an hour about the best, or the least dangerous, ways to deal with rattlesnakes. No discussion of the Eel River or Round Valley. As the sun was setting, they exchanged warm handshakes. We left Healdsburg after trading mutual pledges of support.

It was a typical performance by the Great Communicator, an appellation that applied to more than oratory. Reagan was able to connect wherever he went.

We kept touring. Reagan appeared on horseback at rodeos. The audiences and the local press loved those displays, but he also appeared in the cities, wearing a coat and tie for tradeshow talks.

On March 11, Reagan spoke to the Western Wood Products Association meeting in San Francisco. As part of his text, on cards none of us ever saw, he made his memorable remark, "A tree's a tree; if you've seen one you've seen 'em all."

That was another example of the Great Communicator at work: exactly the right phrase—for *that* audience. Reagan's lumber industry fans laughed and cheered, while the metropolitan press took a more skeptical view.

During our after-speech decompression time, Reagan gleefully repeated the line, savoring the response it had drawn. Between sandwich bites, he then began discussing the Redwood National Forest, a federal proposal of concern to the timber industry.

"It only needs to be a mile wide," he remarked to his hosts. "A half mile on each side of the freeway. That's all the folks look at."[12]

---

12   In 1987, the 11-mile-long, but only a few-hundred-yards-wide Navarro River Redwood State Park was established in Mendocino County astride California's Route 128.

Reagan was not serious, but in private he could not resist a catchy punch line, even if it made little sense. Communicating introspectively was what Reagan did at every opportunity.

When the press reported the "seen one, seem 'em all" story, a political firestorm ensued. The environmental community had problems with that statement for decades to come.

In the real world, Reagan displayed serious environmental dedication. Once elected to the governorship, he made his cabinet join him on horseback to ride parts of the John Muir Trail in the High Sierras. He blocked the flooding of Round Valley because of early agreements with the Native Americans. "A deal's a deal," he observed to his gratified parks director and horrified water superintendent when announcing the decision.

On April 21, we took Reagan to the Mendocino County Fairgrounds. After a rousing speech to more timber people (and perhaps marijuana growers), a highly inebriated lady approached our candidate. Reagan was charming as always, but in time we had to forcefully remove the woman from the hall. The next day we learned she was the newspaper editor's wife.

"You never know," was Reagan's only rejoinder.

§§§

I write of these travels with Reagan not out of nostalgia, but because our after-speech interludes and our conversations with visitors offered an unparalleled insight into the Reagan mind.

Stage performers all understand the decompression mandate. Musicians, dramatic performers, or political speakers all leave the stage as hyperkinetic, adrenalin-filled performance junkies. They do not go home for a good night's sleep. Rock bands drink and smoke until dawn. Actors need an hour or two to relax, perhaps with a drink or a sandwich, but always with others with whom they can simply unwind.

That is exactly the way it was with Reagan. After performances in Los Angeles, RR went home to Nancy. She often joined him in San Francisco. But in the small-town motels, from Modesto to Stockton to Eureka, he and I shared a suite, once even a room, as we recovered from the evening's performance. Those were the times when a fully relaxed Reagan spoke with his travelling troupe informally and in confidence.

§§§

By the spring of '66, though well into a campaign for a Republican nomination, none of us really knew the source of Reagan's political beliefs.

"Wasn't he an FDR-supporting Democrat?" we asked each other. "Where did all this conservatism come from?"

It took a half year of these after-speech decompression chats to map Reagan's partisan DNA.

He and his older brother Neil were children of the Depression. They were appreciative of FDR's New Deal, but soon after World War II, Neil was the first to change party affiliation. He feared Soviet encroachment into central Europe and did not trust the Soviet sympathizers known to be in the US.

RR's views changed more slowly. His earliest eye-openers came from his wartime experience while making Air Corps training films.

"We had to deal with 'business-as-usual' bureaucrats while our boys were getting shot down over Berlin," he complained.

After the war, RR spent several months making a movie in Laborite, Britain.

"Nothing worked very well over there," he mused one evening. "They were still recovering from the war, rationing food, and yet the government was spending time and money nationalizing things. Pretty stupid."

Reagan's more serious revelations came at home during the late forties. Communists in Hollywood were seeking control of the film industry. Reagan allied himself with the performers and producers resisting those inroads. One consequence was an anonymous call threatening an acid-in-the-face attack if Reagan continued to oppose the communist penetration of his union. The Burbank police offered protection along with a shoulder-holstered firearm. Reagan began to understand that lofty socialist ideals could be enforced only by conspiracy and terror.

Even so, during the forties, Reagan remained an enthusiastic supporter of President Harry Truman. But with that president's irresolute conduct of the war in Korea,[13] RR's respect began to wane. By the spring of '51, with Chinese forces joining the fight, the war in Korea had become a relentless yet inconclusive meat-grinder. Truman relieved an insubordinate Douglas MacArthur, the Allied Commander in the Pacific, of his command. In response, the general returned to the US to speak to the Congress. On April 19 he warned those lawmakers, along with a huge national radio audience, "There is no substitute for victory."

MacArthur's speech was broadcast into our high school cafeteria during lunchtime. My draft-age classmates and I took careful note. So did Ronald Reagan, listening from his between-marriages bachelor pad north of the Sunset Strip. MacArthur's warnings sank in, triggering the dissolution of Reagan's support for Democrat Truman.

In early '52, with no plan for victory and no war's end in sight, Reagan wrote to Dwight Eisenhower, urging the retired general to run for the presidency. That note may have been enclosed with Ron and Nancy's wedding announcement sent to the Eisenhowers in March of that year.[14]

In the autumn of '52, Reagan campaigned vigorously for General Eisenhower. With those actions, Reagan changed his political allegiance if not his formal affiliation.

Some claim that Nancy and her strongly conservative stepfather were the cause of Reagan's partisan conversion, but I think that confuses cause and effect. By the time of Ron's wedding to Nancy in March '52, he had already crossed the political divide. At best, the Davis family provided affirmation for decisions already made.

In the mid-fifties, Reagan began his TV run as host of The General Electric Theater. The company's CEO, Ralph Cordiner, became Reagan's mentor, while Reagan's speaking tours[15] exposed him to the real world of industrial America. He did not just

---

13   Initiated by North Korea's invasion of the South on June 25, 1950.
14   Source: Mamie Eisenhower archives, Eisenhower Library.
15   To well over a hundred factories and research labs, speaking to and with over a quarter-million GE employees.

speak and sign autographs; he drank coffee and listened. Reagan repeatedly told me those conversations opened his eyes to the costs of intrusive government and the merits of free markets.

In 1956, though still a Democrat, Reagan actively supported Eisenhower's candidacy for re-election. Four years later, despite importunings from Democratic leaders in California, Reagan helped Richard Nixon in his unsuccessful run for the presidency. Two years after that, Reagan buttressed the former vice president in his race for the governorship of California.

By then it was time for Reagan to formally change party affiliation. As he was speaking at a Republican fundraiser in his Pacific Palisades hometown, a woman in the audience asked, "Have you registered as a Republican, Mr. Reagan?"

"No, not yet," he responded.

a declaration of Republican belief
DWIGHT D. EISENHOWER / RICHARD M. NIXON
BARRY M. GOLDWATER / NELSON A. ROCKEFELLER
narrated by Ronald Reagan

"Well, I'm a registrar." The inquisitor stepped to the front of the room. "Sign here," she ordered.

With that, Reagan made the formal transition.

During that same campaign, he hosted a recording that featured Dwight Eisenhower along with other prominent Republicans in promoting their party's beliefs. (See album jacket above.)

§§§

The most emotional event of the '66 primary campaign took place on May 12 at a structure once known as the San Francisco Livestock Pavilion, a cavernous hall lying south of San Francisco. When under construction, late in the 1930's Depression, the local paper complained about its cost.

"Why, when people are starving, should money be spent on a palace for cows?"

The name stuck. For half a century this gigantic auditorium was used for large gatherings and stock shows. Today there are modern, upscale convention centers in downtown San Francisco, but in '64 the Cow Palace was it—the site of the Republican National Convention, the place where Barry Goldwater seized control of the Republican Party. It was a holy place to the Goldwater people.

By now, our Reagan campaign was firmly centrist in character, but we needed those dedicated Goldwater volunteers for the Election Day activities to come. I decided to let them hold a Reagan rally at the scene of the '64 convention. Trevor Roberts, a young Goldwater volunteer, organized the event. For the Goldwater partisans and to RR it was a haj, the equivalent of a return to Mecca.

Reagan rose to the occasion. He prepared for his appearance in Room 17, the Eisenhower Suite. As we awaited the curtain call, Reagan spoke of his appreciation for Ike, of hoping to meet the general's standards.

When show time came, the rafters resounded with cheering and applause. It was Reagan's best primary-election performance.

The primary election should have been a sure thing, but it was not.

§§§

One of the participants in our September '65 gathering at the Reagan home was his older brother Neil. He was a short, chunky, but well-dressed advertising man. I paid him little attention; I should have known better.

McCann-Erickson, Neil's firm, handled RR's movie publicity. As a consequence, they acquired the Reagan campaign's TV account by default. Half-hour specials built around a Reagan speech were easy to produce, but during the weeks leading up to the June primary we needed shorter, punchier spots. Neil Reagan's presence proved ominous.

The Reagan campaign had not been allowed to hire the most creative, reliable, or dedicated advertising agency. We were stuck with McCann-Erickson. It was a big company, and many of its employees did not agree with Ronald Reagan's political philosophy.

This matter came to a head in May when we received our first shipment of 30- and 60-second TV spots. They were to run statewide during the weeks just before the June 7th primary. Those commercials opened with several RR "talking head" performances, all filmed in an empty studio. Then the camera cut to a supposedly live audience. The producers had selected stock footage of a 1940's movie theater crowd: ladies in hats, gentlemen in double-breasted suits, ushers in uniforms with flashlights, all applauding respectfully. The subliminal message: RR is your grandfather's candidate, not a man for the sixties.

"We cannot run this junk," I protested at the first in-house viewing.[16] "Look at your faces. What will our volunteers think of this stuff? The undecided voters will laugh, then flee in droves."

"We can make our own," Haffner offered. "We've got time."

With the help of a local TV production house,[17] we spent a hectic few days building new spots. We started with clips from the emotional Reagan appearance at the Cow Palace a week earlier. To those we added some spontaneous-looking audience shots of youngsters and old-timers; Blacks, whites, and Asians; men and women, all wildly cheering as they poured into the Cow Palace. In truth, this stock footage came from a religious revival held months before, but that dubbed-in crowd looked just right. We got the new ads on the air by June 1. The enthusiasm they engendered was just what we needed.

Unfortunately, these actions also precipitated storms in the Southland. Our demands for quality, our determination to win every northern California county, our refusal to accept what we viewed as substandard McCann-Erickson junk, offended Neil Reagan and thus, in time, Ronald Reagan's Los Angeles financiers. Their irritation was amplified by Nancy before transmission to RR, a man who eschewed angst. I had annoyed the wrong people.

---

16   Decades later, a retired McCann employee confirmed the humor they saw in their election-year prank.
17   Snazelle Productions Inc. on San Francisco's Columbus Avenue

§§§

On June 7, Reagan won his party's nomination by a 2:1 margin. Of greater personal satisfaction, we carried northern California with 51 percent of the vote, losing only San Francisco and its two adjoining counties to Mayor Christopher. We then moved quickly to broaden our base.

On Election Day, we had mailed Reagan-signed personal letters to all party leaders, office holders, and Christopher chairmen throughout the state. In those letters, Reagan asked for the recipient's help if he prevailed, while pledging his support if Mayor Christopher won the nomination.

In Los Angeles, our calls focused on the supporters of Mayor Sam Yorty, the unsuccessful Democratic candidate who tried to defeat Pat Brown in their primary. Yorty joined our crusade.

I took some of the San Francisco assignments myself. The Christopher leadership was gracious, although the mayor himself disappeared. When I visited with San Francisco attorney Cap Weinberger, I asked him to serve as chairman of the Reagan campaign's executive committee. He accepted at once, beginning a relationship with RR that continued for a quarter century.

On Wednesday, June 8, I travelled to Los Angeles for meetings with candidate, staff, and volunteers at the Ambassador Hotel. The celebratory tone was gone; the grim business of winning an election against an entrenched governor, strongly supported by the unions, now faced us.

Though we talked about budgets and schedules, the emphasis was on people. How could we assemble the coalition needed to win?

It was also the day I experienced my first Reagan hallway downgrade.

The foyer outside one of the Ambassador's breakout rooms was carpeted and well lit. I was en route back to the meetings at hand when Reagan approached, walking purposefully down a subdued access hall.

"Tom, we need a more efficient campaign structure." It was Reagan's most modulated stage voice. "You've noted the need for a state chairman. I'm asking Phil Battaglia[18] to take that job." With that, he continued down the passageway.

Reagan hated bad news and confrontations, so when he had to deal with either, he did so in passing, facilitating an escape as soon as possible. This was a stratagem Reagan used often. In 1983, when replacing his National Security Advisor, Reagan changed nominees during an encounter in the West Wing hallway with Bill Clark.

I had no problem with the selection of a statewide chairman; I had tried to accomplish this earlier, without success. We should have sought a big name; a man or woman whose very appearance would demand attention, whose endorsement would count.

Dwight Eisenhower had been corresponding with Reagan for some time, offering advice while urging him to run for office. Because the former president had a residence in Palm Desert, California, he had a logical interest in this campaign.

Cap Weinberger, a former Republican State Chairman and prominent Rockefeller supporter, would have broadened our appeal.

Frank Sinatra's formal support for RR came only in 1970, but he would have been a great draw four years earlier. *No harm in asking*, I thought.

But visibility and stature were not the criteria. The only issue was control.

Bill Roberts was annoyed by the emergence of a second power center to the north. The candidate did not like hearing complaints from his unhappy brother about our self-produced TV ads. Nancy was annoyed by my "disrespect," i.e., unanswered phone calls.

Campaign results—carrying the North and earning a broad mandate—did not count.

I was stunned by Reagan's words. He had moved me to the back bench, not for poor performance, but simply to stop me from annoying his brother, his wife, and the L.A. Elders.

This was a basic clash of cultures: my highly-structured, results-oriented, weapons-physics standards versus Reagan's laid-back, problem-avoiding Los Angeles lifestyle. His was a unique

---

18   At the time my counterpart, the Reagan chairman in Southern California.

mind. Its speed and retentive skills apparently precluded the need for order. His inclusive nature could accommodate while also ignoring ineptitude.

RR wanted positive, stress-free people around him so he could focus on the message.

I continued to believe in Reagan's principles. I thought he was a national asset—the only credible alternative to LBJ—and I vowed to continue promoting his career as an important national figure. I intended to do what was needed to protect RR from himself. But on that day in June of '66, I learned a basic lesson about politics: there are few friends in that game, only acquaintances.

CH. 5   EISENHOWER THE MENTOR[19]

Dwight Eisenhower first met Ronald Reagan as a celebrity political ally in early 1952. At that time Reagan was urging an Eisenhower presidential candidacy. Their paths crossed often during the ensuing campaign year, again during the re-election drive in '56, and then during Nixon's failed presidential run in 1960.

In 1961, upon leaving the presidency, Eisenhower moved his winter golfing quarters from Augusta, Georgia, to Palm Desert, California. Thereafter, Reagan and Eisenhower, along with their golfing chums, connected often in the California desert.

During those years, John Kennedy, Ike's successor, occasionally sought the general's advice. Immediately after the Bay of Pigs fiasco, less than a hundred days into Kennedy's opening term,[20] the new president asked Eisenhower to come meet at Camp David.

As Ike prepared to leave his Gettysburg farm on that April morning, his son John asked what his father thought of that disaster.

The general's brisk rejoinder was, "I don't do bad invasions."

During the summer that followed, Ike went public with a criticism of Kennedy's "dreary record in foreign policy." Their antipathy mellowed in the aftermath of the Cuban Missile Crisis and Nixon's '62 defeat in California, but Eisenhower-Kennedy relationship was never close.

---

19   Eisenhower's conversations with other presidents, events where this author was not present, are drawn from *Going Home to Glory*, David Eisenhower, 2010, Simon & Schuster; and from *The President's Club*, Gibbs and Duffy, 2012, Simon & Schuster.
20   On April 22, 1961

Eisenhower had urged Nixon to run for the governorship of California. His former VP was not sure this was a good idea. As he wrote to Eisenhower in July '61: *"I continue to lean strongly against the idea."* But Ike was insistent. Eisenhower probably felt some responsibility for the resulting damage to Nixon's reputation, thus explaining Ike's cautious endorsement of Nixon's '68 presidential candidacy just prior to that year's convention.

In '63, however, Ike accepted his VP's post-election statements about quitting politics, moving to New York, and practicing law. With Kennedy's death and Johnson's accession to the presidency, the 34th president worried about his party's prospects for the upcoming '64 elections. He did not like Barry Goldwater, and the feeling was mutual. The senator from Arizona referred to Ike as "a dime store New Dealer."

Ike's preferred candidate in '64 was his university-president brother Milton. When that idea gained no traction, he turned to Bill Scranton, at the time the governor of Ike's then-home-state of Pennsylvania. Ike addressed the '64 convention, and he made a proforma campaign appearance with Goldwater, but when the election was over he journaled the experience as "the 1964 debacle."

The one bright spot, as it was to many Americans, was the Reagan Speech. As Ike watched "Time for Choosing" from his Gettysburg home, a light apparently flashed on.

§§§

During those same mid-sixties years, newly installed President Johnson began paying full attention to Dwight Eisenhower. Immediately following Kennedy's death, LBJ invited Ike to the White House. They met on the afternoon of November 23, and twice more during breaks in the Kennedy funeral proceedings.

Kennedy's successor faced an immediate and critical choice. Should "continuity" be his watchword? Should he conjure the ghost of the slain president? Should he wrap himself in the mystique of Camelot? Or should he declare a new beginning, a Texas-sized break from the Ivy League?

Ike urged a clean sweep. "Let a decent interval pass, but then clean house and appoint your own team," he advised.

As a part of this conversation, Eisenhower warned Johnson of the widespread fear of Bobby Kennedy he had found during his travels around the country. Ike noted that many citizens were disturbed by the arrogance of Kennedy's Justice Department as well as his use of the Internal Revenue Service to harass Kennedy adversaries. Any persons, corporations, or universities that gave Congress any testimony or took public positions unfavorable to the Kennedy Administration were fair game.

Johnson did not need this Eisenhower caveat; he was already on guard. "Robert Kennedy detested Lyndon Johnson with a ferocity that startled many observers, while Johnson harbored fears of Bobby Kennedy that bordered on paranoia."[21]

Despite Ike's advice, Johnson decided against any cabinet changes. Facing an election in less than a year and a chance to win the presidency in his own right, LBJ decided to stick with the cards he held.[22] That deck was stacked, not only with political enemies, but with the proponents of an interventionist Vietnam policy based on gradualism, not victory. By late '63, America's involvement in Southeast Asia was spiraling downward into a black jungle hole.

Once elected, Johnson continued to court Eisenhower at every turn. For three years, he sent General Goodpaster to brief the former president at Gettysburg, but even so, Eisenhower was looking for new blood, a fresh start for his party.

Ike had seen the "Time for Choosing" speech, and he knew Reagan personally. In early '65, Ike sought to learn more about this man's character. He turned to his longtime golfing buddy and travelling companion, Freeman Gosden,[23] one of Reagan's neighbors and peers in the Los Angeles movie industry.

---

21   *Mutual Contempt: Lyndon Johnson, Robert Kennedy, and the feud that defined a decade*. Jeff Shesol, 1997, W.W. Norton & Co.

22   Harry Truman, an earlier vice president who also ascended to the presidency by surprise, accommodated Franklin Roosevelt's cabinet for three months, but then, with the end of the war in Europe, Truman swept the slate clean. Three years later, he was elected to the presidency in his own right.

23   Hollywood radio performer, credited with being the inventor of the "situation comedy." For decades Gosden played "Amos" in the pre-WW II "Amos and Andy" show.

"Tell me about this fellow," Ike inquired by phone. "I liked his speech. What's Reagan all about?"

Those conversations began in July '65; they were followed by an exchange of letters wherein Ike asked Gosden about Reagan's standing out West. Ike then offered advice.

"I think Ron should make an unequivocal statement that he is a Republican. [He only re-registered three years ago.] Point out that our party is broad, interested in common sense solutions," he wrote. "We can, and often do, differ sharply on detail, but we want the support of all. Tell Ron he needs to reach out."

That was exactly the way Reagan saw the challenge.

During the winter of '65-66 Reagan, Gosden, and Eisenhower connected in person during their visits to Palm Desert. By spring, Gosden was sending along poll data he had received from Holmes Tuttle, while Ike and RR spoke directly and often by phone. Ike was urging RR to pay attention to the northern part of the state, even during the primary.

"We need Independents and Democrats on board,"[24] Ike said.

Eisenhower's first letters to Reagan thanked him for hosting the general's appearance on a '62 campaign radio show. He then turned to operational advice.

"State your philosophy clearly," Ike said. "Meet with newspapers to tell your story. Avoid labels and hyphenated voting blocs. Stress your basic beliefs." Ike endorsed California Republican Chairman Parkinson's Eleventh Commandment: "Do not speak ill of other Republicans."

In June of '66, I knew little of this background, but immediately after the California primary, Eisenhower called Reagan with an invitation to come visit. Three of us[25] accompanied Reagan on the flight to DC and then, the next morning, on the two-hour limo ride to the general's home in Gettysburg.

Despite his 77 years, Ike was effervescent and quite cordial to all of us. After a 45-minute chat in the former president's office,[26]

---

24   This correspondence, along with telecon notes, available at the Eisenhower Library.
25   Press Secretary Lyn Nofziger, State Campaign Chairman Phil Battaglia, and me.
26   Joined by Ike's aide, General Schulz.

we stepped outside for a press availability in the parking lot.[27] With a substantial turnout by the Washington media, Ike effusively endorsed the Reagan candidacy for governor. We welcomed Ike's approval of Reagan's broadly based campaign and his comments about the coattails RR could offer other Republicans in California. Ike identified RR as "a man of great integrity and common

Above: Former President Eisenhower's Gettysburg office, June 15, 1966. Seated, left to right: Dwight Eisenhower and Ronald Reagan; standing: Tom Reed

sense." But then, in closing, we got more than we anticipated.

Given the Eisenhower-Reagan correspondence over the prior years, Ike's words could not have been spontaneous or unrehearsed.

"You can bet [Ron] will become a presidential possibility."

I agreed with that objective, but all of us winced at the problems this proclamation might cause us back home. We did not want presidential prospects to cloud our immediate campaign.

Eisenhower's statement also offended his former VP, a defeated candidate in political rehab. By the spring of '66, Richard Nixon's eyes were fixed on a comeback.

After a few more comments to the press, the former and future presidents headed off for lunch at Ike's home. The rest of us dined at the local café.

From RR's comments during our return trip to DC, we learned that the two men covered a lot of ground during their lunch hour.

They first talked about political campaigning. Ike urged Reagan to run a broadly based, big tent campaign.

"You can't win without the Democrats," Ike said. "Include women on your staff; meet with the media."

Reagan agreed with all of that advice.

---

27 For video excerpts of this appearance, see <reagan68.com>

The Gettysburg conversation then turned to Vietnam, a new and complex minefield for Reagan.

Eisenhower repeated his often-voiced views about the folly of gradualism.

"Johnson's greatest error in prosecuting this war was not having used more power at the outset," the retired general said. He knew from personal experience that "gradual escalation will not work." In referring to the challenge of an enemy battalion holding a hill, the former five-star said, "Give me a division and I'll take it without a fight."

Reagan listened. The words from the man who ended the war in Korea were soon entered onto Reagan's vast internal hard drive. He would return to that principle of overwhelming force, when force was needed, during the years to come.

As our limo pulled up to the Madison Hotel, RR passed along Ike's concerns about Bobby Kennedy. This was not a subject Reagan cared to discuss.

§§§

Nine months later,[28] once elected to the governorship, Reagan made a more public visit to the aging general who was again wintering in Palm Desert. Two years before, LBJ had sent 3,500 Marines ashore at Da Nang. By the spring of '67, Vietnam resembled the bloody Korean impasse. The lessons learned in Ike's ending that war dominated the men's conversation.

"I'd mine Haiphong Harbor," the general confided. "Bomb hard. Hot pursuit of troops or aircraft into havens. If that means China, too bad, Ron. They're offering sanctuary; they're killing our boys; they're already in. Plan for amphibious landings on northern turf. Head for their capital; bomb the dams; flood the place. That's what worked in Korea."

Those words struck home. It was the Korean stalemate of 15 years before that inspired RR to abandon the Democratic Party, to urge Eisenhower to seek the US presidency. And there the two men were, confirming that lesson.

---

28   In March '67.

Reagan visited Eisenhower's El Dorado home for the last time in March '68. Ike's failing health slowed the conversation. LBJ was still sending emissaries to court the general, but a month later Ike suffered the heart attack that sent him on a one-way trip to Ward Eight in the Walter Reed Hospital.

Ike's early '68 views were broader than before. He discounted his role in World War II, noting, "It was the American economy, the Arsenal of Democracy that really won that war."

He went on to urge focus in defense planning, reminding Reagan of the New Look he instituted when entering the presidency. "Limit defense spending, expand the economy," Ike said. "Sooner or later, that's how we'll win."

Fourteen years later, as RR set in place his plan for closing down the Soviet Empire, I could read those thoughts in the 40th president's eyes.

During the following summer, Eisenhower endorsed Nixon's candidacy from his hospital bed. He addressed the '68 convention via closed-circuit TV from Ward Eight. But Ike and RR never connected again.

For more than a decade, Eisenhower had served as a model, then a mentor, to the man who, a dozen years later, would accede to the presidency. Ike's views on campaigning matched Reagan's all-inclusive style. Ike's cautions about military gradualism sank in. They agreed that the US economy would be the deciding Cold War weapon.

Those two made a great pair.

CH. 6   REIGN STORMS

Holmes Tuttle often joined Eisenhower's golfing foursomes in Palm Desert, but unlike many other winter residents of the desert, Tuttle spent most of his time in the real world. He was not involved with oil, movies, or inherited wealth. He sold cars, thousands of them, every day. Coming to Los Angeles as a young man, he built Holmes Tuttle Ford into the biggest dealership in the biggest automobile market in the world.[29] He understood his customers' hopes, dreams, and problems; he accepted those people for what they were. As with Eisenhower, Tuttle understood the need for a big tent, whether selling cars or candidates.

As with Reagan, Tuttle was drawn into the world of Republican politics by the Eisenhower possibility. As a successful businessman, not a celebrity, Tuttle became a serious fundraiser for the general's campaign.

During the fifties, Tuttle and Reagan developed a solid relationship. In part that was because they shared a world outlook. Both men believed in honest government at home and a firm resistance to the expanding communist terror abroad. In another dimension, both were low-pressure golfers who knew how to relax. Reagan often visited Tuttle's second home in the desert.

During the early sixties, these two men—one Republican, one Democrat—worked in Nixon's gubernatorial campaign. Tuttle came to appreciate Reagan's ability to connect with working-class Americans. In '64, Tuttle was one of the Funding Fathers, the trio who paid for the now-famous nationwide broadcast of Reagan's "Time for Choosing" speech.

---

29   He sold a Ford coupe to young Ronald Reagan in 1941

Cy Rubel, Chairman of the Union Oil Company, was the initial leader of this group. During World War I, he served in the Army Corps of Engineers, where he was awarded the Distinguished Service Cross for valor. Rubel was Reagan's kind of true American patriot. Sadly, he grew ill shortly after the Speech, so Tuttle then took over as leader of the Reagan finance team.

At the time, Tuttle was 59 years old. His low-overhead office was on the ground floor of a La Brea industrial building. Known to be direct and sometimes tactless, Tuttle could overstep the bounds of propriety or let his temper run wild, but when the storm subsided, he was not above telephoning the target of his ire to apologize.

To understand Reagan's success, one must understand the workings of the money machine that Tuttle created. It was an instrument of incredible integrity and anonymity. While Reagan had to appear at fundraising events, he never was involved in the details. He never asked people for money; he never made calls. In general, Reagan was unaware of who had given how much. That was not his job. Few political candidates have enjoyed such freedom from distraction. For as long as Reagan was a candidate for any office, Holmes Tuttle protected him from the third-party importuning that could have led to scandal.

On Labor Day of 1966, California's two-term governor, Pat Brown, kicked off his campaign at a union rally. He opened with an attack on extremism, then on stage professionals.

"Reagan's just an actor. An actor killed Lincoln, you know."

Brown went on to note Reagan's lack of government experience.

The governor did not talk about his own achievements, which were substantial, or why he deserved a third term. With those omissions, he ceded the initiative to the Reagan campaign.

On the Friday after Labor Day, Reagan did it his way. He began the fall campaign much as he had in January, with a press conference, rally, and TV show in Los Angeles. His opening theme: California had seen enough of professional politicians; two terms were adequate; it was time for a change in Sacramento.

When early critics tried to tie Reagan to oddball groups, from Hells Angels to the John Birch Society, Reagan responded with his classic smile and a masterful line. "They've bought my philosophy. I haven't bought theirs," he said.

As the fall unfolded, the Berkeley campus of the University of California, then others around the state, began to explode with anti-war, anti-establishment, and Black Panther rallies. Middle-class Californians were extremely displeased.

"We taxpayers are supporting these universities," some wrote to their newspapers. "Why is Governor Brown allowing this chaos to continue?"

That was an unfair question, but then politics is not always a fair game. Campus disturbances became a major arrow in Reagan's quiver.

On another front, however, the inexperience charge remained a problem.

One evening, during the decompression hour after an event in Stockton, Reagan and I began talking about this "no experience" issue.

"Wasn't Hiram Johnson one of California's great governors?" Reagan asked. "He was an outsider, wasn't he?"

"He was an annoyed private citizen," I responded. "I'm not that good on California history, but I think Johnson hated the railroads."

"Sounds familiar to me," RR mused. "Could you get me some details?"

In those pre-Google days, I spent the next morning at the Stockton Library. I found that Hiram Johnson, a young attorney, resented the stranglehold the railroads had gained over the people and the economy of California. In 1910, at age 44, and with no prior political experience, Johnson ran for governor of California as the reform candidate. He defeated the establishment interests in the Republican primary and went on to win the governorship itself, displaying amazing coattails in the process. His reform ticket won a majority of the legislative contests in both houses, and the accomplishments of the resulting legislative session of 1911 remain unparalleled.

Hiram Johnson was re-elected easily to the governorship in 1914. In '16 he went on to the United States Senate, where he served[30] until his death in 1945, at age 79. His remains are buried at Arlington National Cemetery. Most Californians who know their history consider Hiram Johnson to have been their greatest governor.

I gave Reagan my research report over breakfast the following morning.

A week later, at a well-attended press conference in Los Angeles, reporters asked Reagan the usual question: "How can you hope to get elected governor of California when you've had no experience at all in government?"

To my astonishment, my earlier briefing about the legendary Governor Johnson flowed from Reagan's mouth, almost word for word. Only the literary style had been improved.

"Hiram Johnson had no government experience," Reagan explained to the assembled reporters. "That was his strong suit. He beat the railroads and revamped our Constitution. He was our greatest governor. Experience in office was, and remains, the problem, not the solution. We need another Hiram Johnson."

It was a brilliant performance. "We need another Hiram Johnson" disposed of the experience issue once and for all.

To many of us, that was more than a campaign moment. It disclosed the full scope of Reagan's retentive and analytic mental powers. He knew what he wanted to know, he knew how he would use that information when the time came, and he had the mental capacity to store, and then retrieve vast libraries of fact and history as needed. He used his quiet time to think through the phrasing he would employ when show time came. Reagan's mind was unbelievably vast and fast. None of us had ever seen anything like it.

The public persona of Reagan could be quite deceiving: perfectly coiffed, always beaming unless the scene called for a relaxed scowl. He delivered his public lines quickly, often closing with a softening quip.

That's how actors on the world stage perform. Envision the smiling and California-costumed Reagan in November-cold Geneva two decades later, descending the steps of the Maison de

---

30   As a dedicated, anti-war isolationist Republican

Saussure to greet the dour and fur-capped Gorbachev as the general secretary emerged from his black limousine below. Reagan was always in command of the stage.

During the autumn campaign in the North, we needed to deliver candidate, press, and staff to some exceptionally remote locations. Reagan would get to the Bay Area by commercial aircraft or private jet, but once in our territory, we switched to the "Turkey Bird," an antique DC-3 used to deliver those birds to market. An enthusiastic turkey breeder[31] from Modesto donated the use of his plane, reasonably sanitized and with satisfactory seats installed, for the duration of the campaign.

Reagan, moving about without Nancy, loved this crate. He delighted in hazing the coat-and-tie reporters travelling with him from the big city. His jokes were unending, the odors tolerable.

There were more rodeos, Mexican American Independence Day rallies, "nationalities" meetings, and interviews with editorial boards. As the pressure mounted, so did the quality of Reagan's performances. He was at home with all those folks.

§§§

The polls closed at 7:00 p.m. on November 8th. By 7:30 p.m. the networks were predicting a Reagan victory, and by 8:30 p.m. it was clear that it would be a very big win indeed. At 10:30 p.m. Reagan called the northern California headquarters to again express his thanks.

"Great job, Tom. It looks like you folks carried northern California. You didn't even need Los Angeles," he cracked. "I want all of you to accept my heartfelt thanks."

I did not go to L.A. for these festivities, nor did I go the next day. We celebrated at the office and then at the Hilton Hotel with my team. All had done an exemplary job with no internal strife.

When the votes were counted, Reagan won by a million votes. He received 3.6 million, or 58 percent of the vote to Pat Brown's 2.6 million, 42 percent. We carried northern California with a 170,000-

---

31   Merv Amerine

vote margin, losing only three counties.[32] Republicans won all the statewide offices (lieutenant governor, etc.) with the exception of attorney general. We came within striking distance of controlling both houses of the state legislature. That was accomplished two years later. And, from the ranks of the campaign, there emerged a new generation of governmental leadership.

The victory was so broad and so complete that Reagan did in fact become California's undisputed leader. With that landslide, he also became a luminary on the national scene.

The reign of New Deal philosophy, the advocacy of more government as the solution to society's ills, was brought up short with the election of '66. All across America, expanded bureaucracies and unauthorized wars were repudiated by the voters.

We could not see it on that November morning, but one epoch had ended, and another had begun.

---

32   San Francisco (with 41 percent of the vote), Alameda (49.5 percent), and tiny Plumas County off in the mountains (49 percent)

CH. 7   FANNING THE PRAIRIE FIRE

On a Saturday morning in late October,[33] prior to the election, I shared a motel breakfast with candidate Reagan. Over coffee and fruit, he turned to the future.

"Tom, do you want to continue on this team?"

Reagan's campaign was on a roll. The published polls indicated success lay only weeks away.

"If you mean Sacramento, Ron, no," I replied. "I want to pursue the Prairie Fire."

That was a reference to the national political conflagration Reagan often projected in his speeches. Many of us hoped a decisive '66 Reagan victory in California would redress the national loss in '64 and burn away the protective shell surrounding LBJ.

RR closed out the conversation with, "OK. But I want your help before then, Tom."

Nine days after Ronald Reagan's landslide election to the governorship of California,[34] with no authority or approval from anyone, I invited Spencer-Roberts partner Fred Haffner to join me on a flight to Los Angeles. Our first stop was his firm's unkempt headquarters, located on an industrial side street in the city's downtown area. Stu Spencer and Bill Roberts were awaiting our arrival.

My opening bid was simple and direct: "I want to hire you guys for six months, from now until the legislature adjourns next summer."

"To do what?" Roberts asked.

---

33   In Concord, CA, October 22, 1966
34   On Thursday, November 17, 1966

"First of all, to help Ron in Sacramento," I responded. "He'll need to establish himself as a thoughtful governor and a national leader. I'd like your help with administrative and legislative strategy. On top of that, we'll need to build up our legislative candidates for '68. We're only one vote away from control in each house."

"That's fine," Spencer nodded. "We're already doing candidate support for the State Committee. That's it?"

"Not exactly," I laughed. "My core objective is to seek delegates to the Republican National Convention in '68, men and women pledged to nominating Ron for the presidency."

Roberts' eyes widened; his partners' jaws slacked.

"Outside of California," I went on, "I want your help in planning Ron's early appearances. You know, at governors' conferences, fundraisers, and major Republican Party events. For the moment, for '67, I just want to collect delegates. We'll decide what to do with them in '68."

"Intriguing," a cautious Roberts responded. "Who's in on this game?"

"As of this morning, just you guys. I've arranged an afternoon date with Ron and Nancy. The Prairie Fire is my agenda, although they don't know that...yet."

The business-oriented Spencer was the first to comment. "Well, we do need some work during the post-election dry spell. Ron's a helluva draw. So, what do you plan to use for money? Is Holmes buying?"

"I haven't discussed this project with Tuttle yet, but I will, within limits. I want his help in Sacramento and with candidate build-up, but I do not want his friends involved beyond the state line," I continued. "Those guys talk too much. Their allegiances run in a lot of different directions."

Spencer nodded his concurrence.

"Immediate cash will come from the Inaugural Committees I already control," I said. "For out-of-state work, I'll look to a national Reagan network. Some of the pieces are already in place."

"Are we supposed to corral and count delegates?" Haffner asked incredulously.

"Nope," I answered. "I have others in mind for that job. You're to do the strategy and PR."

By late afternoon, once we had settled on the details, we set out for the Reagan home in Pacific Palisades.

I had arranged for two of Reagan's prospective staffers[35] to join us in meeting with the Governor-elect and Mrs. Reagan. The first-couple-to-be knew only that my agenda involved political planning.

Once all eight of us were settled into the Reagans' comfortable living room, I got to the point: my plans for dumping LBJ.

"Ron, I want to talk about the Prairie Fire."

The governor's face hardened; he knew where I was going.

"Lyndon Johnson is a disaster. Vietnam and our economy confirm that. Even so, given Johnson's ego, he'll surely run again in '68," I said. "We cannot let him succeed. The Republicans on the horizon are all boring losers, Ron. You've got the talent and now the momentum to run and win two years from now. I want to start putting the pieces in place, to start collecting '68 delegates and to plan for your election to the presidency."

Reagan was absorbing every word; he uttered none in response.

I went on to discuss my proposed near-term agreement with Spencer-Roberts in support of strategic planning, legislative campaigns, and national travel. Spencer expanded on those ideas.

Now on more familiar ground, Reagan finally spoke. "Glad you'll still be aboard, Stu. You did a great job this year."

Battaglia and Nofziger, the two staffers present, concurred in the re-hiring of Spencer-Roberts.

As a welcoming afternoon fire blossomed on the Reagans' stone hearth, I then turned to the recruitment of national talent.

"Ron, I want to get in touch with O'Donnell, White, Milbank, and Rusher," I said.

I was referring to Texas Republican Chairman Peter O'Donnell, delegate-harvester Clif White, financier Jerry Milbank, and *National Review* publisher Bill Rusher.

---

35   Campaign chairman Battaglia, Press Secretary Nofziger

"Those are good people," Reagan observed. "I worked with Clif and Peter at the convention. I met Rusher at Buckley's apartment. Not sure I know Milbank, but yes, go ahead."

With those words, RR authorized my exploratory effort. Nancy Reagan was present and seemed to agree. She said little, but she, too, was absorbing it all.

Ronald Reagan had not initiated this meeting, nor had he specifically asked that a campaign be set in motion, but there can be no doubt that both Reagans were involved in the November 17 decision to plan for, and seek delegates to, the '68 convention.

Two hours later, as the sun set over the Pacific, the group scattered. I returned to San Francisco for a dinner meeting with Bill Rusher. That diminutive egghead had been an integral part of the Goldwater apparatus in '64. We carefully reviewed the reactivation of the sensible parts of the '64 machinery, and in particular how to get Clif White aboard. Rusher advised that George Romney had approached White, though he was not committed to the Michigander's campaign.

Rusher *was* committed. He was urging a Reagan run.

The next day I flew east to dine with Jerry Milbank at his home in Greenwich. Milbank had been one of the early and key financial backers of the Goldwater campaign. In later years, he became Chairman of the Republican National Finance Committee. I hoped he would provide leadership, at least in the greater New York area, for a national Reagan finance committee.

Milbank wanted to hear the details of Reagan's election in California.

"How did you do it?" he asked. "Is Reagan that good?"

On the other hand, Milbank was noncommittal regarding a 1968 campaign. "Too early," he warned, with prescience.

On the following day, Sunday, November 20, I had a working lunch with Clif White in Rye, NY. White was an academic. Born at the end of World War I in upstate New York, he served as a B-17 navigator in World War II, surviving 25 combat missions over Germany while earning the Distinguished Flying Cross. After the war, White attended Cornell, then stayed on to teach political science while organizing his own machine. White thought that "me too" liberal Republicanism was a sure loser. If voters wanted liberal programs with more government in their lives, they would go for the real thing, the Democrat on the ballot, every time. By 1962, White had assembled a national network of those who agreed with him. He had also studied and mastered every state's delegate selection process.

We first talked about the history of '64 and then about the fluidity that we should expect again in '68.

"The nomination is going to be decided at the convention," White claimed. "It's not going to be preempted by an early primary knockout. Ron better not make any overt moves until he establishes himself as a good governor in California."

To me, that meant a campaign to start around Labor Day 1967.

After White and I had evaluated all Republican candidates, once we confirmed the unfolding Johnson tenure as disastrous, and after we had dismissed Nixon as a loser, I popped the question.

"Clif, will you join a campaign to win the 1968 Republican nomination for Ronald Reagan?"

White had expected this query, probably tipped by my discussions with Bill Rusher.

"Yes!" he exclaimed.

Exactly the answer I wanted to hear.

I was both happy and relieved that White was willing to join the crusade. That evening, I returned to Los Angeles.

On November 21, I drove to the Palisades for breakfast alone with the Reagans. I wanted to relay the details of the Milbank and White conversations.

Reagan nodded his approval.   "Glad to know Clif wants to join up. I look forward to his never-missing, always-changing bow ties. Milbank would be good," RR added without further comment. As always, he was interested in substance, not campaign finance.

We then turned our attention to newly published Harris polls.

"They show LBJ as beatable," I offered, "at least by Romney."

RR scanned the demographics and then, with a studied look, voiced his verdict. "Johnson's on thin ice."

"Exactly."

In closing, I wanted to reaffirm my role as "captain of the adventure," as Teddy White later put it.[36]

"Yes, of course," was Reagan's prompt, but perhaps casual response.

I queried further, "Are you putting me in charge of this campaign? You want me to proceed, is that correct?"

Reagan's answer was an unambiguous, "Yes."

About a week later, on Thursday afternoon, December 1, I met Clif White's plane from New York. We wound our way up the narrow streets of Pacific Palisades to the Reagan residence for White's coming-aboard chat with Ron and Nancy. Both Reagans were there, and both were fully involved. Ron and Clif immediately connected as long-lost political wartime buddies. I was the only other person present. The meeting lasted for an hour and a half, and when it was over, White was satisfied that there had been a meeting of the minds, an agreement to campaign for delegates.

"Thanks, Clif," the governor-elect said at the door. "Go to it."

En route back to the airport, White and I settled on a system of compensation and expense reimbursement.[37] The campaign for Reagan's presidential nomination in '68 was underway.

Adopting a Strategy

Clif White, Stu Spencer, and I charted our plans telephonically over the 1966-67 year-end holidays. We settled on specifics at a lengthy meeting in Rye, NY, on Saturday, January 28.

"Romney's leading the pack right now," White announced as we started work. "As governor of Michigan, he may control about 320 delegates, including those from his home state. But even with 320, he's not halfway to the finish line. The winner needs 667; Romney can't get there from here."

White then continued with an analysis of the Nixon challenge. "Dick can count on about 310 votes right now," White said, "but

---

36   In his *Making of the President, 1968*, Theodore H. White, 1969, Atheneum Publishers. White confirmed my role as the designated leader of "an on-again, off-again campaign, ultimately derailed by accident and tragedy."
37   The source of funds would be gate-sharing at political events, augmented by my already-forming national finance committee.

he's working hard. He'll pick up more. He did a lot of good deeds for others last year. They owe him."

We then turned our attention to the governor of California.

"Reagan may be in the 200-300 range," White opined. "That assumes he controls California. Is that reasonable, Stu?"

"No doubt. Ron should win any California election held today," Spencer answered. "A year from now, who knows? Depends on how he does as governor. But I don't think Nixon will enter the California primary. Dick's done too much losing out there."

I added my thoughts. "How about the other states? Sooner or later we'll need tangible evidence of Ron's firepower at the ballot box. How are we going to do that? Last year's million-vote margin in California will soon be ancient history."

The three of us settled on a plan for a "favorite-son" slate in California, along with Reagan's entry in three "must opt-out" primaries during the spring of '68.

Favorite sons emerge when contending factions within a state let their leader form a slate of delegates to run under his banner. At the convention, those delegates then vote as the leader, or as a caucus of the delegates, think best. Their objective is to preserve that state's leverage. Reagan was to run as a favorite son in California. That would be unifying, would seem logical, and would give Reagan all 86 delegates from Nixon's home base.

In some of the other primary states, serious opponents (Romney, Nixon, or Rockefeller) would file. In others, locals would seek to control their own delegations via favorite sons. But in a few of the smaller states where the citizens wanted to get a piece of the action, the legislatures had hit upon the idea of an "opt-out" primary.

In those states, some official (usually the secretary of state) would select the names most mentioned in the local press as presidential hopefuls. He or she then decided which names should appear on that state's primary ballot. If an individual wanted his or her name removed, it was up to him or her to execute an affidavit confirming he/she was not a candidate.

As a result of this arrangement, no declaration of candidacy would be necessary to get on the Republican ballot in such opt-out states. Reagan's favorite-son status in California would provide the rationale for not executing an affidavit of non-candidacy elsewhere.

We decided to seek delegates in three of those opt-out states: Wisconsin, with its primary in April, and in Nebraska and Oregon with their primaries in late May. Our objectives would be a noticeable showing in Wisconsin with no campaign; a better-than-expected result in Nebraska with local support by Clif White's allies; then a victory in neighboring Oregon, where Spencer had strong political ties and where we hoped Reagan might actually campaign. A seemingly assured victory in California would follow in early June, a week after the Oregon primary.

Next, we turned our attention to top-down signals. Upon the conclusion of Reagan's first legislative session and immediately after the summer holidays of '67, Reagan would need to connect with the leaders of the Republican right. We wanted them to understand that while Reagan would continue to work Sacramento issues for the balance of that year, come '68 he would turn his attention to defeating Lyndon Johnson; he would willingly accept a draft.

We identified the five individuals who could send the signals and who, at the convention, would control the key votes.

The first, for protocol reasons, was Everett Dirksen, the Senate minority leader. He was not an "activist" and we did not expect him to solicit delegates. Dirksen was the pre-eminent party boss, well respected by his peers. The US Senate and the delegate-rich state of Illinois were his home grounds.

Illinois was also Reagan's home state. We wanted Dirksen to look favorably on the young émigré to California. We hoped the senator would spread the word that Reagan was a winner, that he had displayed coattails in California, and that, in '68, he could be equally helpful to other candidates all across the country.

The second target was Barry Goldwater, the '64 candidate. We would have to be careful here. Goldwater had lost, and lost badly in '64. His name was poison to many middle-of-the-road Republicans.

A greater difficulty was his strained relationship with Reagan. Even now I do not understand the reasons, but Goldwater never seemed to accept Reagan. They simply didn't connect. In part, it may have been Goldwater's jealousy; Reagan's star rose as the Arizona senator's campaign collapsed. In October '64 Goldwater had tried to use the TV time bought for Reagan's "Time for Choosing" speech to broadcast a Goldwater interview with Dwight Eisenhower taped at Gettysburg. Or perhaps these men's incompatibility may have arisen from Reagan's discomfort with Goldwater's abrasive *Götterdämmerung* approach to that campaign. The Arizona senator was not one to make Reagan feel comfortable. We did not expect to find Barry Goldwater in Reagan's corner; we wanted him to be neutral, to remain quiet.

The third key player was Strom Thurmond, first elected to the US Senate in 1954 as a Democrat from South Carolina. In 1948 then-Governor Thurmond ran for President of the US on a State's Rights ticket. In opposing Democrat Truman and Republican Dewey, Thurmond carried four states with 39 electoral votes.[38] In 1964, he bolted from the Democratic Party and joined Goldwater's Republican South at a rally in New Orleans. With that endorsement, the Republican candidate for president broke the Democrats' century-long hold on the Solid South.[39]

It was in New Orleans that I first met South Carolina's tireless advocate of conservative beliefs. Thurmond had been most courteous. When we next met, in the autumn of '67, he knew exactly who I was.

Goldwater went down to ignominious defeat in '64, but he did break the Democratic Party's hold on the Solid South by carrying five of those states.[40]   When that campaign was over, Strom Thurmond became the de facto trustee of Republican fortunes in the South. Thurmond's agent, South Carolina's Republican State Chairman Harry Dent, visited us early and often in Sacramento. We dined regularly at the picturesque Firehouse Restaurant. A deal was in the works.

---

38   AL, LA, MS, & SC plus one electoral vote from TN
39   See Appendix B, "The Solid South, 1865-1964"
40   AL, GA, LA, MS, & SC

Spencer, White, and I then planned to solicit the last-needed endorsements from Texans Peter O'Donnell (an earlier target for organizational help), and John Tower. Having family in his hometown of Wichita Falls, I knew Senator Tower quite well. A decade later, when I was nominated to serve as Secretary of the Air Force, it was John Tower who introduced me to the US Senate for confirmation.

With the backing, or at least the acquiescence, of Dirksen, Goldwater, Thurmond, Tower, and O'Donnell, Reagan might win the nomination. With their opposition, no chance.

On Friday, February 3, shortly after returning from my meeting with Spencer and White, I got together with RR in San Francisco. We met at his hotel prior to our separate dinner engagements. We talked shop (appointments to county fair boards), we talked about potential horse-friendly homes in the Sierra foothills, and I filled him in on my prior-week discussions with Spencer, White, and others. He seemed to approve, although his attention remained focused on the challenges facing him in Sacramento.

During the winter and early spring that followed, I regularly visited the Reagans' new Sacramento residence on 45th Street to continue those updates. I wanted to keep Nancy Reagan involved. I also kept the governor's office staff current with weekly breakfast meetings at Sacramento's Sutter Club.

Travels

During February, I accompanied RR on his first out-of-state political expedition as governor of California. Press aide Lyn Nofziger, security man Art Van Court, and I flew with him to Eugene, Oregon, for press and TV time, followed by an enormously successful Saturday night Republican fundraiser at the Lane County fairgrounds. The next morning we shared a Sunday brunch with the state's Republican leaders.

Oregon was one of the opt-out states where White, Spencer, and I planned to campaign for delegates. In our scheme of things, it was a "must-win" state. That Sunday brunch provided introductions to the important political and financial players in Oregon, many of whom soon joined our crusade.

During early March, Reagan moved up to the major leagues with travels into the heart of the Eastern Establishment. Again accompanied by Nofziger, Van Court, and me, joined by Spencer and White when once on the ground, RR starred at the annual Republican fundraising gala at the Hilton Hotel in Washington, DC. Several thousand of the more successful members of the party had parted with $500[41] each to start the countdown to '68. The featured speakers were three trend-defying governors: Volpe of Massachusetts, Romney from Michigan, and Reagan. Volpe and Romney had been re-elected in 1966 against strong odds in Democrat-stronghold states. Reagan was the landslide winner over a two-term Democrat favorite in California.

Volpe's remarks were lightweight; Romney's were ponderous and flat; Reagan stole the show. He was at his best. His lines cleverly mixed substance and humor with flawless timing.

After the show, Senator George Murphy hosted Reagan, Nixon, and Goldwater for drinks in his room. The atmosphere was formal, and Reagan was eager to leave. As soon as possible, we adjourned to RR's suite at the Madison, where Jerry Milbank and Goldwater treasurer Bill Middendorf came by for another drink. The atmosphere was much more convivial.

A week later, on March 8, Reagan, Nofziger, Van Court, and I, this time accompanied by Nancy Reagan and Phil Battaglia, flew to New York, checking in at the Waldorf for a good night's sleep. The next morning, I presided over a two-hour campaign update in RR's suite.

White provided a state-by-state delegate count.

"How do you know that?" RR asked often in response to White's delegate forecasts.

White credited personal insights, not hard data, in his responses.

---

41   About $3,500 in 2014 dollars

When we turned our attention to Ohio and its governor, Reagan noted his appreciation for Rhodes' early gubernatorial advice.

"Jim's a good friend. He's been of great help."

At lunchtime, Reagan moved on to meet with the publishers at *TIME-LIFE*. He did not think it went well. "Typical New Yorkers," was his later aside to me.

On Friday, March 10, we moved on to Washington. Reagan met with a roomful of Republican congressmen, then dined with California's two Republican senators, Murphy and Kuchel. RR was preparing for his tryout in the big leagues the next day. Not well enough, as it turned out.

Reagan was headed for the Gridiron Club.

CH. 8   SHAKING SACRAMENTO

Governor-elect Reagan was a 55-year-old man of enormous charm and mental agility, a fellow of vision and firmly grounded principles, but he was also a man with no experience in the top-down management of any large endeavor. Reagan's seven terms as the president of the Screen Actors Guild built superb negotiating skills, but the SAG operated from a small office with few employees.

One could expect a time of uncertain transition in Sacramento, but that quickly proved to be an understatement. With Reagan's million-vote victory, we needed to find out where the state capitol was and what went on there. Opening difficulties were intensified by Reagan's casual approach to selecting lieutenants.

During the closing days of the '66 campaign, RR had confided some post-election plans.

"If victory is in the cards," he said, "I want [State Campaign Chairman] Phil Battaglia to serve as my executive secretary."

On election night, Battaglia took the stage with Reagan. In his next-morning remarks, Reagan told the press he would look to Battaglia to "organize the state." This was not a sound choice. Lou Cannon described it as "an appointment by default."

My relationship with Battaglia was never good. At first, I attributed our difficulties to his lack of a philosophical compass. His June elevation to state chairman had been annoying, but it was of no practical consequence. It was his egomania, coupled with Reagan's inattention, that would create a crisis of historic importance.

Transition

Our first sortie to Sacramento took place on November 21 in response to a transition invitation from Governor Brown.

The governor's suite was well lit, laid out around a central atrium in contemporary California decor. We entered via an outer office of well over 1,000 square feet with walls paneled in bleached-blonde timber set to welcome the plaques and mementos that collect during any administration.

The chief executive's personal office—a cozy, but darker room perhaps 20 feet square—lay in the southeast corner of the first floor. Through bulletproof, green-tinged windows, the governor and his visitors enjoyed a lovely view of Capitol Park. The room itself had the feel of a masculine den or study featuring an ornate wooden desk surrounded by a half-dozen upholstered chairs. This is where Governor Brown received his successor.

During the campaign, Brown said some disparaging things about candidate Reagan. RR had responded with his Irish wit, turning Brown into a tragi-comic relic of yesteryear. Since both men were politicians skilled at putting others at ease, their transition meeting was quite amiable, but there was no substance. These were men from different political planets.

The incumbent governor wanted to talk mini-deals.

"I'll leave these judicial seats vacant if you will appoint so-and-so to the Youth Authority when the vacancy comes up in March," Brown offered.

Nodding and smiling, Reagan dodged. "Gee, Pat, I'm not familiar with those jobs. I'm sure you'll do what's right."

Reagan's chessboard mind had precluded Brown's efforts at downstream control.

The two men returned to the exchange of pleasantries and agreed their staffs would work together for a smooth transition. We did just that. The changeover was uneventful; the two never met again.

During the weeks that followed, Reagan worked out of his Pacific Palisades home or, if absolutely necessary, out of a bungalow at the Ambassador Hotel. The Los Angeles Elders had rented some cottages at that Hollywood campground, a venue that became another transition headquarters competing with the one we opened in Sacramento.

The internals of the Reagan changeover of late '66 were chaotic. Election-losers besieged the governor-elect. Hordes of hangers-on flooded the Sacramento office. There were no signs of a personnel plan, no appointments secretary designate.

The bright spot was Bill Clark, the former Ventura County Reagan chairman—a beacon of light whom Reagan tapped to serve as cabinet secretary. Amidst the chaos, Clark was designing the machinery needed to make Reagan's inner circle work. He did so against incredible odds, setting precedents and laying out procedures that Reagan would employ for years to come.

Holmes Tuttle was another source of strength. His finance team maintained its integrity throughout the inauguration season. There was no peddling of influence, no post-election fundraising that might cater to the special interests caught on the wrong side of the campaign.

The missing piece was an, the governor-elect's chief of personnel. By the end of November, no one seemed to have been chosen for this job, although later disclosures tell a different story.

Appointments

Without consulting Reagan, Battaglia, the chief of staff designate, had asked a lawyer friend from Los Angeles, Bill King, to take the appointments job.[43]   Battaglia's unilateral action was a glaring example of all that was wrong with this absurd transition system. King was a man who had participated only minimally in the Reagan primary campaign. During the general election, he helped organize Citizens for Reagan, a bipartisan shelter for Yorty Democrats who wanted to support Reagan. King had come to know Bill Roberts during their work together on the Rockefeller '64 campaign.

---

43   These details later provided by Mel Owen, a Reagan advance man and, earlier, Bill King's college roommate.

In later years, King moved to the Democratic Party, hoping to run Joe Alioto's campaign for governor in 1970. King's wife at the time was a dedicated liberal Democrat. Eventually, she went to work for Los Angeles Mayor Tom Bradley, twice the Democratic candidate for governor of California. King's only significant qualification for work in Reagan's office was his close relationships with Battaglia and Roberts.

King was an affable fellow, perhaps qualified to serve in a line job or board appointment in Sacramento, but his selection as chief of personnel in the Reagan Administration, its patronage boss, would have been a disaster.

I knew none of this at the end of November '66. I simply believed that the selection of people is the most important part of any chief executive's job. Competence and integrity were the primary criteria for our team, but on top of that, any policy-making individual recruited into the Reagan Administration needed to share Reagan's philosophic views, should understand the Goldwater legacy, and must have expended some effort in bringing the Reagan policies to power. This challenge was becoming critical, since Reagan himself was displaying a serious disregard for competence or compass in his approach to the personnel decisions that would shape his whole political future.

In early December,[44] despite my disinterest in joining the administration, I saw only disaster if someone—me—did not take hold of the appointive system.

I first met with Battaglia to tell him I wanted the job. He remained noncommittal, failing to mention his offer to Bill King. My next stop was at Reagan's side to tell the governor-elect I had been thinking about the problems of staffing up his administration.

"The process is a mess," I observed. "Your success hangs in the balance, Ron. The quality of your early appointees will be the key."

"I agree," he sighed.

"I've thought about your offer to come to Sacramento, Governor. I think I'd better take the job of appointments secretary before it's too late."

---

44   On December 5, 1966

A smile crossed his face. As always, one of "the boys" had identified a problem and made it go away.

"Fine," Reagan said, with no thought of crosschecks.

Within two hours, he announced my selection at a political dinner meeting.

Battaglia was not pleased. King was outraged when he got the news. By then, he was at the Los Angeles Airport en route to his promised job in Sacramento.

The next day, on December 6, Reagan's press aide released a confirming statement. I closed the deal by meeting with Nancy Sloss, Governor Brown's appointments secretary. She was most gracious and helpful.

The trials by fire began soon thereafter when I attended a meeting of the Major Appointments Task Force. These men were leftovers from the campaign finance committee; they were meeting within the wood-paneled walls of the California Club in Los Angeles.

Reagan had recognized this self-appointed group, assuring Tuttle that he would welcome their thoughts. Reagan's inclusive nature always accommodated the self-appointed.

Some of these gentlemen came from banking and oil industries; some were inheritors of family wealth; others simply orbited in the stratosphere of Los Angeles society. With the exception of auto dealer Tuttle, few had any sense of political reality.

As these conversations rambled on without end, I thanked the group for their invitation, noting that I had a pending return flight north.

Upon my arrival in San Francisco, I drove to the St. Francis Hotel where Reagan was staying in preparation for a speaking engagement. The two of us spent most of the afternoon discussing the transition in Sacramento, but in closing, I told RR of my concerns about the group meeting in Los Angeles.

"Ron, I don't think your appointments task force has any idea of what they are doing. You and I may be apprentices, but those fellows are utter neophytes. They have no idea of how Sacramento works, of what goes on there."

Reagan seemed indifferent. "Oh, come on, Tom, they're harmless. Just keep the boys happy, would you?"

"OK, I'll try."

I closed off our discussions by turning to a Clif White update, then by asking for a reconfirmation of my Prairie Fire authority. "When I finish with this appointments gig, Ron, am I to be directly in charge of your national campaign for the Republican presidential nomination? Are you happy with me hiring Clif White and Spencer-Roberts to assist in this effort?"

The governor-elect responded once again with an unequivocal, "Yes."

Inauguration

A vigorous motion picture professional assumed California's executive authority a little after midnight on January 2, 1967. On that Monday morning, Ronald Reagan took the oath of office, along with Lieutenant Governor Robert Finch, in the rotunda of the state capitol in Sacramento. Some report that hour was chosen to stop the flood of "deathbed" actions by outgoing Governor Brown. Others claim Mrs. Reagan's astrologer chose the date and time.

Inauguration, post-midnight, January 2, 1967. Ronald Reagan laughing with Gordon Reed. Nancy Reagan at left, Tom Reed (partially hidden) at far right.

In any case, the midnight show was good theater. It suited the group of Elders from Los Angeles quite well. Only a few hundred people could attend an event in such a cramped space, but the Elders were there, as were my wife, my father, and I. The three of us had bid my ill mother goodnight a few hours before prior to flying to San Francisco, at her urging, to take part in this historic event.

There was no grand oratory, but it was a great photo op. Every guest shook the Reagans' hands. We then walked down the hall to the governor's office to tour that citadel of bureaucratic power before heading off to bed.

Building a Personnel System

The next step in Reagan's assumption of power was more substantive. On the morning following the midnight formalities, I met with RR in the Governor's Mansion, a creaky multi-storied Victorian firetrap located on a busy commercial street in downtown Sacramento. The Reagan family had moved in after the formalities of the previous evening.

The Mansion's cramped and view-free rooms made that building the architectural antipode of the Reagan residence in Los Angeles. Nancy made this contrast clear, speaking in an imperious tone when I first walked through the mansion's front door.

"Tom, you've got to do something about this!"

I was there to conduct state business, my first personnel discussion with the new governor, so I slid past her into RR's bare and darkened den.

New hires into state government would receive their formal appointments on lovely parchment. Some machine would affix the governor's signature. But on that winter morning, my concerns were more immediate.

How do we make appointive decisions in the first place? How do I see to it that they stay made?

I hit upon a system of one-page memoranda very similar to the one-pagers Cabinet Secretary Clark was developing for policy matters. The document I generated on that January 3 set the precedent for a system that served RR well for 20-some years.

By early '67, I knew RR quite well. I understood the sort of people he was comfortable with, and his specifications matched mine. We wanted people of competence in their chosen field, men and women of absolute integrity, candidates who were compatible with the Reagan agenda. And we wanted all Californians to be pleased with their government. The job of the appointments secretary, along with his staff and volunteer network, was to listen to the recommendations of others on the staff, to legislators, and to the ideas of those outside the capitol. I also needed to be proactive, to reach out, to find and recruit the brightest and the best, the men and women who might not even apply for state jobs.

For that meeting in January, I prepared my first one-page template. It was headed by the date of our deliberations followed by the title of the job to be filled, a brief description of its duties, the names and two-sentence biographies of alternative candidates, a listing of who favored and who opposed each candidate, and my recommendation.

After opening humor, the governor and I got around to the matter at hand. We needed a Director of Emergency Services in place on day one. I handed RR my one-pager.

He read it, deployed his happy smile, and said, "I agree."

"Please put an "OK RR" next to the name you prefer," I countered. "That means the decision is made, Ron. We can issue a press release, and there will be no further reclamas."

Reagan was a decisive man. He liked this new system. It was the first of many such "OK RR's" that would launch or redirect countless careers.

Soon, others on the governor's staff were trying to revisit these decisions. The governor would have none of that. "OK RR" means what it says: "No looking back."

I felt some urgency in building this system. When left on his own, Reagan often turned to the next in line, the proximate person outside the door, to deal with the issue at hand; no searching for knowledgeable talent.

One early example is when Reagan's personal secretary,[45] who had served him for a year in Sacramento, had to move on for family reasons. RR turned to his outer office receptionist as the replacement. A nice young girl of no executive experience, she soon paralyzed the system by hiding any document that brought

---

45   Kathy Davis

bad news. Early on, she had noted RR's aversion to dark messages. Gloomy memos went unread into boxes in the office closet.

Such correspondence sometimes dealt with death sentence appeals, so we had to step in. Bill Clark's assistant, Helene Von Damm, implemented the rescue. She stuck with Reagan as his executive assistant until they reached the White House 14 years later. In 1983, she became Reagan's Ambassador to Austria.

Another example from Sacramento: In 1969, when Reagan learned of Bill Clark's planned departure from the chief of staff seat, the governor asked Clark's assistant, Mike Deaver, to take over. Deaver's principal turf had been the Nancy Account.[46] He was seldom involved in state government. Deaver had the good sense to decline the offer. Clark refocused Reagan's attention on attorney Ed Meese, who performed well as the governor's chief of staff for the rest of his term.

Nancy Reagan aggravated the personnel problems of every Reagan Administration with her simulation of *Alice in Wonderland's* Queen of Hearts. "Off with their heads" was Nancy's mantra toward any staffer or cabinet member who offended her, especially those responsible for "bad press" in the morning's news. She wanted such people gone, at once, often with little thought given to the replacement. Nancy badgered any who would listen until "something was done" about the alleged offender.

By the time of Reagan's second presidential term, her assaults had decimated the White House staff, leaving few experienced hands between the president himself and the energetic and well-meaning action officers like Oliver North.

As the years rolled by, Reagan's lack of management experience often led him to devolve perks and power to subordinates who had joined his team only in pursuit of those currencies, folks who saw RR as a political locomotive about to leave the station, men whose talents lay in making Governor and Mrs. Reagan "feel comfortable." Reagan had no idea how to establish chains of command or how to end the infighting that

---

46   i.e., dealing with Mrs. Reagan's daily telephonic outbursts

escalates as political careers progress. He was an upbeat man who did not like angst.

"Clark Kerr Fired by Reagan"—Really?

Early on, in January '67, a historic job opening appeared. I had nothing to do with it, and contrary to Berkeley folklore, Ronald Reagan was a bystander, as well.

A web search, even today, will produce a flood of headlines, e.g., "Clark Kerr fired by Reagan over campus protests."

The oral histories left by those who were there tell a different story.

In the autumn of 1964, Berkeley students seized and held a police car. They were protesting their inability to promote national political causes on campus. The regents of the university were not pleased. More to the point, they were appalled by university president Clark Kerr's weak response.

Edwin Pauley, a UC alumnus with 27 years of service on the Board of Regents, led others in demanding action. Pauley was a longtime Democrat. He had served as Treasurer of the Democratic National Committee in the late thirties. In 1940, Democrat Governor Culbert Olson appointed him to the regents. Governors Earl Warren and Pat Brown reappointed him.

Pauley was a major donor to the University of California, e.g., the Pauley Pavilion at UCLA.

By 1966, every public opinion poll echoed Pauley's words: "We're supporting this university. Obey the rules or get out."

In that election year, Reagan exploited this anger in his attacks on Governor Brown. During that same year, Regent Pauley, joined by Regents Canaday, Kennedy, and Hearst, sought to remove President Kerr because of his inaction in the face of campus violence. Pauley turned to fellow UC classmate John McCone, by then director of the US Central Intelligence Agency, to "get the goods" on Kerr.

At the December '66 regents meeting, Pauley tried to bring a Kerr-dismissal motion to a head. He had the votes, but with the '66 election results then in hand, others urged him to await the first meeting in '67 when two new ex-officio regents, Governor Reagan and Lieutenant Governor Finch, would replace Brown and his lieutenant governor, Glenn Anderson. A third ex-officio member as yet unnamed (the president of the Agriculture Board) was expected to be supportive as well.

Reagan had little knowledge of this plan to fire Kerr. In early January '67, as his appointments secretary, I was trying to discuss candidates for future membership on the regents. RR thought those queries irrelevant; there were no vacancies expected until summer.

Counselor Ed Meese, a former Alameda County assistant district attorney, says Reagan considered his attendance at the January 20 regents meeting to be pro-forma. Governors seldom attended those meetings. Since RR was new to the job, he decided to attend this first one only as a listener.

Alex Sherriffs, the governor's assistant for education policy, heard the same message.

The records of this January 20 meeting are embargoed by the university, although the UC libraries web site, CALISPHERE, provides some insight. Alex Sherriffs' interview is located there. But the best understanding comes from two oral histories, talks by those who were actually in the room on January 20, 1967.

Allan Grant, the newly appointed president of the Agriculture Board, spoke to the California State Archives in April '91. Grant was a staunch conservative eager to see Kerr go.

Elinor Heller spoke to the Bancroft Library Oral History Office much closer to the event, in November '79. Her husband Edward had served as a regent since 1940. Cuthbert Olson appointed him contemporaneously with Edwin Pauley. When Mr. Heller died in December '61, Pat Brown appointed Heller's Democrat-activist wife Elinor to the seat. She remained on the Board of Regents until the mid-seventies. Given Ms. Heller's reputation as a highly respected regent, along with her strong anti-Reagan credentials, her accounts of the regents' meeting of January 20 seem credible and accurate.[47]

The Heller and Grant oral histories match.

47   Elinor Raas Heller oral history, Bancroft Library, interviewed by Malca Chall, November 30, 1979.

When the regents convened in an executive session in University Hall on the Berkeley Campus, Ted Meyer was in the chair, but Pauley immediately set the agenda.

His demand to Kerr: "Resign or be fired."

When Kerr would not resign, he was excused from the room. Since he was a voting regent, an offsetting vote, arch-conservative Max Rafferty also left the room. Extended negotiations followed, some with Kerr seated in his office.

Two hours later, Lawrence Kennedy, a Brown appointee, made the motion to fire Kerr. William Forbes, a Los Angeles music industry executive appointed to the regents by Pat Brown in 1961, seconded the motion.

Ms. Heller notes that, "Reagan was taken by surprise and was upset" when this motion was made.

The vote was 14-8 in favor of firing. The "No" votes came from Regents Heller, Coblenz, Roth, Dutton, Unruh, Simon, Mahn, and Mosler. Reagan voted with the majority to fire Kerr.

In subsequent discussions with Ed Meese, Reagan said his position, in speaking to his fellow regents, was to "do what you would do if I were not here as governor."

At a press conference in Sacramento on January 24, Reagan said, "Firing Kerr was necessary but ill-timed." He stated (correctly) that he did not initiate the action, that the firing should *not* have been on the agenda for his first meeting as a regent, and that he was taken by surprise. Lou Cannon confirms this,[48] writing "Reagan did not maneuver behind the scenes to fire Kerr."

In personal conversation with Press Secretary Nofziger several years later, Kerr confirmed Reagan's minimal involvement.

"Reagan did not do me in," Kerr acknowledged.[49]

"Clark Kerr fired by Reagan" is not an accurate headline. Reagan was a bystander, preferring to proceed cautiously on the matter of violence at UC. He was attentive to the needs of the majority of students, their education blocked by tear gas and riot police.

---

48   *Ronnie and Jess*, Lou Cannon, 1969, Doubleday, pp 231-234
49   *Nofziger*, op cit, pg 64

Many of today's web headlines are simply not credible. The damage to coherent debate is unfortunate.

Fortune Cookies for All

Serving as Reagan's appointments secretary proved to be a tedious grind. When I accepted that hiring and firing responsibility, I agreed to serve for the classic hundred days. I would then return my attention to the '68 presidential race.

"Hiring" is not the right word for this process, since most of the governor's appointments are to unpaid boards or commissions that seem trivial when viewed from Sacramento. But they are positions of extreme importance to local communities and special interest groups.

One such body was the California Highway Commission. These men and women decide how and where gasoline taxes are to be spent, i.e., which freeways are built, widened, maintained, or abandoned. There was immense pressure to appoint a favorite of the Southern California Auto Club. Car dealer Tuttle had weighed in, but he did so properly, through channels, and then went quiet.

The more I reflected on this vacancy, the more I thought the Highway Commission ought to have representation from a rural county. After all, that's where most of the roads are. We also wanted appointees drawn from California's broad heritage; people who had given birth to our state.

I ended up preferring a Chinese American gentleman who had played a role in Reagan's campaign in Trinity County, a spacious but lightly populated district in California's far north. My decision memorandum to Reagan listed a variety of choices, including the Auto Club candidate from L.A. The stakes were enormous. The Highway Commission allocates billions of dollars every year.

The governor and I discussed the alternatives for some time. He was serious, mindful of Tuttle's wishes, but also attentive to his responsibilities to all Californians. He was pleased by the prospect of reaching into California's far north. I was delighted when an "OK RR" went next to my recommendation, Mr. Moon Lim Lee.

A week after his swearing-in, the new commissioner appeared in my office carrying a brown paper bag. He wanted to see me, saying he had a gift. When I heard that and saw the bag, I asked my secretary to stand in the doorway as a witness. The opportunities for impropriety in my job were enormous; I wanted to set a "clean as a whistle" example to my staff.

Mr. Lee took a seat, told me how much his appointment had meant to the rural counties of the far north and how the old-line Chinese Americans, whose ancestors had built the railroads, appreciated the gesture. He wanted to thank me and handed me the bag.

I opened it in trepidation, fearing the rustle of $100 bills. Instead, I found dozens of fortune cookies. The messages inside promised Tom Reed "a long life filled with happiness as the protector of California's rural Chinese American heritage."

§§§

Evidence of Reagan's Depression-era upbringing was ever-present. During his days as governor, RR asked the mailroom to let him see samples of the incoming personal correspondence. Much of it came from youngsters. He wanted to read and respond to as many such letters as he could. Some of that correspondence was later published by his secretary, Helene Von Damm,[50] but the most illuminating tale came from Reagan's assistant for electronic media, Nancy Clark Reynolds.

A middle-aged gentleman, down on his luck, had written to ask for a hand-me-down suit. The poor fellow was out of work, and had no garb for job interviews. He saw the governor as about his size.

"Could you send me one of your cast-offs?" he wrote.

Reagan's response to Ms. Reynolds: "Here's some cash, Nancy. Go buy him a suit. Don't tell Mrs. Reagan."

That was a regular refrain whenever Reagan reached into his own pocket to help others.

---

50   *Sincerely, Ronald Reagan*, Helene Von Damm, 1976, Green Hill Publishers.

A Hundred Days in Retrospect

I wound up my hundred days as appointments secretary in April '67. Dozens of cabinet jobs had been filled, and thousands of unpaid board members and local officials had been put in place. To evaluate this system, consider the top-level results; the five men chosen for Reagan's first inner cabinet. Since I was deeply involved on one side or another, I turn to Lou Cannon[51] for an appraisal of each man's record.

Meeting in Los Angeles, the Elders selected Gordon Paul Smith, a financial consultant, to serve as director of finance. This was an appointive disaster. Money is policy in government; the director of finance is the governor's key appointee. The gents in L.A. bungled the job. G.P. Smith was a bean counter, not a strategist. Cannon described the Elders Task Force as "operating with a blatant and ill-chosen exercise of power." He noted that "Smith did not understand the magnitude of the fiscal problems facing the state ... Democrats and Republicans in the legislature agreed that he was not up to the job ... His wanting to please his listeners ... would cost Smith his job."

A more thoughtful Cap Weinberger replaced Smith at the end of Reagan's first year in office.

Reagan was most comfortable with two of my recruits, Resources Administrator Ike Livermore and Agriculture Secretary Earl Coke. They were men of Reagan's age. Neither sought state jobs; I had enlisted them from a lumber company and a bank.

Livermore was a timber executive and a prominent member of the Sierra Club. At his opening press conference with the governor, Livermore called the head of the Sierra Club a "liar," adding that he was going to give the Pacific Lumber Company "a whack in the tail." The press loved Livermore; so did Reagan. Cannon uses the word "outstanding" to describe Livermore's tenure.

Earl Coke was an agri-businessman, Bank of America's Vice President for Agricultural Lending. In those days, the B of A was *the* lender to the farmers of California. They loved Earl Coke; he knew and understood every one of them. But to that camaraderie

---

51   *Governor Reagan: His Rise to Power*, Lou Cannon, 2003, PublicAffairs

he added government experience. He had served in Eisenhower's Agriculture Department.

Reagan welcomed both of these seniors, their grey heads standing in visible contrast to the younger, dark crania milling about. Livermore and Coke served honorably and well for Reagan's eight years in Sacramento.

The addition of Gordon Luce to the cabinet, to serve as business and transportation administrator, demonstrated the merits of recruiting from within the campaign. Luce had served as Reagan's campaign chairman in San Diego County. He had the right business credentials (running a savings and loan) and sweat equity (working in the campaign). Luce was sensible, never extreme, and always cool. Cannon notes that Luce was "incorruptible," important because all the business-regulatory departments fell under his purview. Luce stood up to the Los Angeles Elders, always doing what was best for California. "Effective" is the label Cannon used to describe Luce's work. I may have been the stationmaster in bringing Luce aboard, but he was everybody's choice, and he did an excellent job.

When Reagan decided on his own to appoint defeated attorney general candidate Spencer Williams to the Human Resources post, grave disappointment followed. Reagan was a product of the Depression; Williams was out of work and needed a job. As Cannon wrote, "Reagan felt obligated to find a position for him ... the only [cabinet member] whose hiring was instigated by the Governor." Williams was let go prior to the 1970 re-election season. A year later, with the assistance of Senator George Murphy, Williams was placed on the federal bench, a job more suited to his judicial temperament.

While these five appointments do not constitute a statistically valid sample, they did constitute Reagan's first cabinet. They suggest from whence came failure and success.

Reagan was easy to work for if you understood and agreed with his game plan. He neither micromanaged nor second-guessed. If you did your job as best you could, if you stayed within the basic Reagan belief system, and if he trusted you, then all would go well.

But even so, I was happy to move on, to return my gaze to the early retirement of Lyndon Johnson.

CH. 9   BOBBY KENNEDY: THE NEMESIS

During the weeks that followed John Kennedy's inauguration, the new president brought a playful sense of humor to the White House. When asked what he liked most about his new job, Kennedy responded without a pause, "The commute." But beneath the charm and *savoir faire* there lurked a darker side. The visibly married John Kennedy was bedding movie stars and Mafia molls, some within the White House itself. His electoral legitimacy was in serious doubt; he brought little executive experience to the presidency.

JFK also installed his hard-edged brother, Robert F. Kennedy, as attorney general of the United States. The consequences of that appointment resonate throughout the Reagan story to come.

§§§

On Saturday, March 11, Reagan appeared at the Gridiron Dinner in Washington.

This annual white-tie evening, hosted by the DC press corps, features humorous skits and then light remarks from a leader of each party. It is the ultimate insider's event.

The '67 dinner opened with a parody featuring the Delphic Oracle, a costumed man trying to identify next year's Republican nominee. With the end of this act, Reagan was introduced.

His performance was light and his jokes were good, but they were too California-oriented. They did not make much sense to the Washington insiders. Reagan tried to close with a short, serious pitch, but it fell flat. I stared into my coffee with a sense of unease.

The second parody took place in the Bounty Café, where the customers were plotting mutiny against President Johnson. At its close, the conspirators were scattered by "Sheriff" Hubert Humphrey.

Bobby Kennedy then responded. The New York senator was masterful; his jokes were self-deprecating one-liners about himself, his family, and his problems with President Johnson. His timing was excellent, and his humor was perfectly attuned to that in-crowd. In the eyes of the audience—me included—RFK won. Reagan was sent home as a country bumpkin not yet ready for prime time; a defeat that was intensely personal.

During the fifties, Kennedy had served as chief counsel to the Senate Labor Rackets Committee. While there, he fixated on organized crime.

Once installed as attorney general, Kennedy pursued corruption with a vengeance. As part of that hunt, he authorized[52] a grand jury investigation of MCA, at one time a talent agency, but by '62, a smothering Hollywood conglomerate.

A decade earlier a federal judge in Los Angeles found MCA guilty of violating anti-trust laws. In his decision, he described that company as, "the Octopus, with tentacles reaching out to all phases and grasping everything in show business."

MCA had been Ronald Reagan's agent since 1940. Jules Stein had organized the firm in 1924. In later pre-war years, he hired Lew Wasserman (at the time a theater usher), and Taft Schreiber (a saxophone player), to form the triumvirate later described as "the three smartest guys in Hollywood." As a team, they ran the firm for half a century.

During the forties, MCA assigned Schreiber to the Reagan account. Over the years, Schreiber came to play a substantial though sometimes obscure role in Reagan's financial life.

In 1952, Reagan, President of the Screen Actors Guild, negotiated and signed an unusual waiver agreement with MCA, giving that agency permission to enter the film production business. No one else had gotten such a deal. Nancy Davis, not yet married to Ronald Reagan, was a rubber-stamp member of the SAG board.

---

52   On August 25, 1961

In late '61, as Kennedy's federal investigators began to look into MCA's business practices, the MCA-SAG waiver of nine years earlier came to their attention. It did not smell right to them.

In February '62, Reagan was called before Kennedy's grand jury. Prosecutors wanted to know why, 10 years before, Reagan, as head of the Screen Actors Guild, had bestowed such good fortune on his own agent. That three-page waiver had exempted MCA from SAG rules, first adopted in 1939, that prohibited talent agencies from making movies. Such dual roles were thought to pose a serious conflict of interest.

Given little notice, Reagan was called[53] to testify before that grand jury. He showed up at the Los Angeles federal courthouse in his "work clothes," coming directly from the TV studio with no preparation time, no consultation with his lawyer. The interrogation lasted for half a day. The Feds quizzed RR at length about the SAG-MCA connection.

"Did you benefit personally?" they asked.

Reagan said he could not recall why he had settled on such an exclusive deal with MCA.

A week after his grand jury appearance,[54] the Justice Department subpoenaed the Reagan tax returns for 1952-1955. They were looking for evidence of compensation for the waiver.

In a memorandum to the attorney general, investigators spelled out their objective, "To prove that the grant of this blanket waiver was effectuated by a conspiracy between MCA and SAG." The latter meant Ronald Reagan.

Soon after receipt of the SAG waiver in '52, MCA acquired Universal Studios. Justice Department prosecutors claimed, correctly, that the '52 free pass enabled MCA to achieve "absolute dominance in the field of TV film production."

One of MCA's attorneys involved in securing this contentious waiver was Sidney Korshak, often described by federal investigators as, "the prime link between legitimate Hollywood business and organized crime."

---

53   On February 5, 1962
54   On February 13, 1962

The MCA case never went to trial, and Reagan was never indicted because, during the summer of '62, MCA settled with the Justice Department by divesting itself of its talent agency business. But there were broader consequences.

In May '62, the General Electric Company closed down the "General Electric Theater," an American anthology TV series that had run for nine years. Reagan had served as the show's well-paid host. The cancellation left him without a job.

Michael Reagan, Ronald Reagan's first son,[55] recounted for me the dinner in March '62 when the family first got this news. Michael was 17 at the time.

"We were having the occasional Sunday dinner with Dad at the San Onofre house. Just Dad, Nancy, Maureen,[56] and I. Nancy sat at one end of the table with her back to the kitchen. Maureen sat to her right, on one side; I was on the other; Dad was at the far end.

"Dad told us he had just lost his job with GE. He was very disappointed. The show had been cancelled. He said Ralph Cordiner[57] had called him earlier to report that he [Cordiner] had been contacted by Bobby Kennedy, who had said: 'If you want government contracts, get Reagan off the air.'"

Kennedy pressure may not have been the true reason for the cancellation of "The General Electric Theater." Some writers believe the cancellation was due to the "General Electric Theater" losing ratings to NBC's competing show, "Bonanza."[58]   But whatever the facts, Michael's clear recollection of that '62 dinner establishes RR's thinking at the time.

Reagan's oldest daughter, Maureen, also at that dinner, put it this way in her memoirs:[59]

"In 1961, after Dad had spent nearly seven years on the road for the company and just after John F. Kennedy took office, GE began receiving complaints from certain officers of the

---

55   Adopted by Reagan and Jane Wyman shortly after his birth in 1945.
56   RR's other natural child by Jane Wyman.
57   Chairman and CEO of GE at the time; RR's mentor within the firm.
58   See Lou Cannon's interview with Paul Wassmansdorf, a former GE executive, present at the company's cancellation discussions. *Governor Reagan*, Lou Cannon, 2003, Public Affairs, pg 113
59   *First Father, First Daughter*, Maureen Reagan, 1989, Little Brown, pg 110

federal government, informing them that the message of the GE spokesperson was not entirely appreciated...

"And then, one day in 1962, Dad got a call from a friend [at GE] informing him of a rumor that some agencies of the federal government had threatened to cancel millions of dollars' worth of GE contracts unless the company fired Ronald Reagan as its spokesperson.

"Dad checked out the story with his boss at GE [Ralph Cordiner] who admitted that the rumor was true. 'But don't worry,' [Cordiner] told Dad. 'We won't be blackmailed.'"

Turns out they were.

"I've always suspected," Maureen continued, "and I'm sure Dad agrees with me on this one, that Bobby Kennedy had a hand in all this. I think the Kennedy Administration saw in Dad's remarks a backhanded slur against their way of doing things."

Given these RFK-triggered disturbances of five years before, Reagan's Gridiron defeat at the hands of Bobby Kennedy called for a determined response from "the toughest competitor I have ever known," as Mike Deaver often put it.

Nancy Clark Reynolds unsheathed the weapon Reagan used best. Before the '66 election, Ms. Reynolds had worked as a newscaster for KPIX-TV (CBS) in San Francisco. After that election, she had been recruited to serve as Reagan's TV and radio press secretary. She often travelled as Nancy Reagan's press aide, but she never became Nancy's assistant. Reynolds was, and remains to this day, a true press relations professional.

In the early spring of '67, Reynolds cultivated an invitation from the CBS network to do an international news program utilizing the new communication satellite known as *Telstar*.

By then, *Telstar* was a generic name, like Kleenex. *Telstar-1*, launched in July 1962,[60] had been developed by AT&T's Bell Labs. It was the world's first communication satellite. There was a *Telstar-2*, followed by a variety of geosynchronous birds with different names, but for the rest of the sixties, the name *Telstar*

---

60   Soon disabled by another part of my life: the high altitude nuclear bursts we conducted over the Pacific in 1962.

remained attached to any satellite broadcasting news and photos across the Atlantic.

Reynolds and her CBS friends conceived a "Town Meeting of the World." The idea was for students, gathered in a London studio and utilizing the new satellite link, to ask questions of political leaders in the US.

Reynolds and her contacts at CBS settled on Ronald Reagan, working from Sacramento, and Bobby Kennedy, on that day seated in another US studio, to serve as the "bipartisan" responding panel.

What a misnomer!

Kennedy staffers later admitted that RFK "made no special preparations for the show,"[61] while RR brought intense focus to the opportunity.

During the entire week preceding the broadcast, Reagan studied notebooks covering Vietnam. He was already a master of American history.

On Sunday, May 14, RR rehearsed, grilled by staffers posing as students and a senior attorney playing the role of Senator Kennedy. By Monday morning, Reagan was ready for payback time.

The "Town Meeting of the World" ran for an hour on May 15.

The deck was stacked, of course. The "students" in London were officious and well-prepared left-wing activists, gathered from liberal Europe to anti-colonial Africa. Two rows of inquisitors sat atop a dais facing their camera. Some were establishment liberals; others were staunch defenders of the communist cause.

Bobby Kennedy was all smiles, sympathizing with the students' assaults on "past US mistakes," those to which the Kennedy Administration had contributed if not originated.

Reagan, for his part, was courteous but firm in his support of the US and its quest for freedom. He displayed an encyclopedic understanding of the war in Vietnam, its casualties and atrocities. He was a master of US history and the goals of our nation's founders. By the end of the show, Kennedy had little to say.

---

61   *Newsweek*, May 29, 1967

It was a brilliant Reagan performance, a nice recovery from the dismal Gridiron Club face-off just two months before, and it had been done before an audience of 15 million viewers. Virtually every pundit awarded RR first prize.

As *Newsweek* wrote, "It was political rookie Reagan who left veteran campaigner Kennedy blinking when the session ended."

Six years after Bobby Kennedy's lawyerly assault on Reagan's career, RR evened the score, but for the competitive Reagan, that was not enough. The spring of 1968 would offer an opportunity for massive retaliation.

Ch. 10   Summer Verdicts

During the spring of '67 Reagan built his gubernatorial record. He put an immediate freeze on new state hires, we recruited a broad array of department heads whose qualifications drew rave reviews from all segments of the political community, and the Reagan team won acceptance of a state budget that compensated for his predecessor's fiscal sleight of hand. Pat Brown, a desperate distributor of election-year treats, had spent a million dollars a day more than his administration was taking in. Upon inauguration, Reagan's California was insolvent.

These obligations dictated a tax increase as part of a spending-cut package negotiated with the opposition legislature. Reagan was, and always remained, a pragmatist. The tax increase was contrary to his belief system, but that was the price of avoiding a fiscal disaster.

Other attempts at financial restraint turned to ash. A swarm of senators and psychiatrists argued that the state's mental institutions were nineteenth-century snake pits—which they were. Some inmates were chained to their beds; others were harmless family members considered "inconvenient" by relatives or prior husbands. The concept of returning those patients to their communities was intended as a humanitarian gesture while saving the state money, but it put the burden on counties and cities with disastrous results to this day. Chief of Staff Battaglia urged and prematurely announced this tragic change of policy.

Of greater national interest, Reagan dealt with the Free Speech disturbances that had morphed into violent anti-war demonstrations on the campuses of the University of California. He withstood the heat from activist students, thus enabling continuing instruction for the majority. His call for tuition, a new concept for the state universities, and his university budget cuts brought more rancor, but his constituents, the vast majority of tax-paying Californians, approved.

Elsewhere in the capitol, Reagan needed to inspire the legislature to accept his other government-shrinking policies, e.g., abolishing bureaucracies and closing offices. He did that reasonably well in the face of determined opposition from Jess Unruh, a talented Assembly Speaker tenuously supported by slim Democratic majorities in both houses. Those battles were difficult; no one "won," but the budget was balanced, government shrank, and mutual respect emerged.

Reagan's environmental ideas, from protecting Lake Tahoe to removing lead from motor fuel, drew broader support.

On April 18, at the end of Reagan's first hundred days, the *Sacramento Union* headlined: "Governor Made Impact."

On May 22, *Newsweek* featured Reagan on its cover with the heading: "Ronald Reagan: A Rising Star in the West?"

On July 11, the statewide California Field Poll gave Governor Reagan a 74 percent approval rating.

On July 24, *U.S. News and World Report* headlined the story: "A Look at the Reagan Boom."

On August 11, *TIME* magazine reported, "When the California legislature ended its 1967 session last week ... even such powerful critics as Democrat Assembly Speaker Jesse Unruh conceded, 'I think, all in all, that Reagan did very well.'"

During that same week, on August 13, the *San Diego Union* put it more concisely. "Legislative Honeymoon is Over, But Marriage Lasts."

§§§

During June '67, I returned to San Francisco to open a political office in the same decrepit building that once housed our '66 campaign offices. I then resumed management of Reagan's presidential campaign.

Clif White and I had arranged for a major Reagan visit to Nebraska, one of our primary-election state targets. Reagan, Nofziger, Van Court, and I flew to Omaha via chartered jet on Friday, June 23, for his address to the National Young Republican (YR) Convention. While not an all-encompassing Republican group, those YRs assembled in Omaha were the activists who knew how to work conventions. RR got wildly positive responses, repeated applause during his delivery, and a standing ovation at its close.

One tangible benefit: A successful Kansas businessman, Henry Bubb,[62] watched with awe as Reagan wowed the YR crowd. He returned to his home in Topeka to open a serious, well-funded, and well-staffed Draft Reagan national headquarters. That entity became a pillar of the National Reagan for President Committee, operating far beyond the ken of Reagan's financial backers in Los Angeles.

The next morning, RR breakfasted with 200 of Nebraska's Republican leaders from the eastern part of the state. We then flew west, to Scott's Bluff, for a Reagan talk to the students at Hiram Scott College. Unlike their peers in Berkeley, they were euphoric in their enthusiasm for the ideas Reagan expressed.

At the end of June '67, Reagan attended a meeting of the Western Governors in Montana, followed by a meeting of Republican Governors at Yellowstone. Reagan used these governors' forums and their attendant press opportunities to tell the nation about his first-term achievements in Sacramento.

"Fewer state employees, more closed offices," were Reagan's oft-repeated metrics.

These conferences were convenient venues for me to bring White and Spencer into one room with RR. We met at length on Thursday afternoon, June 29, for a discussion of the '68 campaign. White reviewed delegate counts. We then reviewed our planned fall travels, intended to target the barons of the Republican Party. A smiling and happy Reagan was fully aboard.

---

62   CEO of Capital Federal Savings Bank and a member of the Kansas State Board of Regents

These visits to Yellowstone also offered up some of the greatest photo ops of the year: the real Reagan out West, on horseback, in his own well-worn cowboy gear.

This media attention came as a mixed blessing. Reagan used one press conference to identify me as his "political advance man," code words for "campaign director." Those remarks confirmed that a campaign was underway, thus bringing a flood of hopeful Republican state chairmen to my doorstep. They all sought a Reagan visit.

Back in Los Angeles, the press coverage emerging from the Rockies produced a different response. Reagan's peers and neighbors, the Los Angeles Elders, made up one annoyed group. Over the Independence Day weekend, a highly agitated Holmes Tuttle and Taft Schreiber travelled to Reagan's house to assail him on the subject of these press reports.

"What the hell are you doing out there, Ron?"

In response, our angst-averse governor made a full disclosure of campaign plans and accomplishments. His revelations to Tuttle and Schreiber included delegate counts, the involvement of White and Spencer, and my responsibilities for managing his national political affairs.

Reagan's visitors were outraged—not at the idea of a campaign, but that they had been left out. They summoned me to a meeting in Los Angeles on July 13, at which time both men berated me harshly for not keeping them informed.

"Everything must be stopped," they demanded. "We need time to review all this."

"Sorry," I responded. "Travel arrangements are too complex."

That was a hedge. My real concern was confidentiality. While Tuttle was fully committed to Reagan's political success, I feared Schreiber 's disclosure of too much information to others in the Nixon and Rockefeller camps. He and his boss at MCA, Lew Wasserman, had multiple irons in too many fires.

Four days later, on July 17, White, Spencer, Battaglia, Nofziger, and I met with Ron and Nancy Reagan at their house in Sacramento. After dinner, we reviewed the status of the campaign, our fall plans, and the Tuttle-Schreiber grievances that had thoroughly upset the Reagans. As noted before, RR did not like angst; he was a placater. Over coffee, he began to waffle.

§§§

Another observer disturbed by these reports from the Rockies was Richard Nixon. While not yet an announced presidential candidate, Nixon felt it was time to deal with the Reagan threat via the back channels he worked so well. As a first step, I believe he prodded Taft Schreiber into the Independence Day confrontation with the

Above: Nixon, Murphy & Reagan at the Bohemian Grove, July, 1967

governor described above. Two weeks later, on July 23, Nixon tried to close off the Reagan campaign with a private conversation at the Bohemian Grove.

Senator George Murphy, a longtime Reagan friend and another former president of the Screen Actors Guild, but also a Nixon ally, had arranged for Nixon and Reagan to join him for lunch at his Lost Angels camp in the redwoods.

After a light meal, the three men moved to a small circle of canvas-backed chairs. As Reagan nursed his Vodka and orange juice, Nixon hunched forward to put Reagan on formal notice. He, the former vice president, was going to seek the Republican nomination. He did not plan to announce until the end of the year, but he wanted Reagan to know. From Schreiber, Nixon had learned that his ambitions were not consistent with Reagan's plans.

While hospitality was in the air, threats hung in the branches overhead. Nixon and Murphy sought Reagan's endorsement and cooperation, but those prizes were not forthcoming. Reagan delivered his usual cheerfully ambiguous responses.

"Gee, fellas..."

I did not get a full debrief on this conversation, since Reagan was about to enter his local hospital for minor prostate surgery, but on August 8, I met with him at his home in the Palisades to check on recovery.   There was no mention of Nixon. When I tried to review autumn travel plans, RR turned to the Elders' grievances. A three-dimensional collision lay just over the horizon.

Ch. 11 A Coup in the Governor's Office

B ill Clark was a good Catholic; Reagan was an upbeat Irishman. So, it was most fitting that Bill Clark play the role of St. Patrick in cleaning out the snake pit in Sacramento. That was a reasonable characterization of Reagan's gubernatorial staff operation during the first half of '67.

The Villain

During the final stages of the '66 gubernatorial campaign, I had developed an antipathy toward Phil Battaglia. The problem was not that he was imposed on me as a state chairman in June of '66. We needed some statewide leadership, and I had been proposing various names to Reagan and Roberts all spring. Perhaps it was Battaglia's lack of a philosophic framework that bothered me. I could find no guiding principles in his mindset, only an ego and a lust for power. But there was something else wrong, a furtiveness that struck me as odd.

On November 10, 1966, two days after Reagan's election, RR announced that Battaglia was to serve as his executive secretary, the formal title for the governor's chief of staff. From the opening bell, Battaglia used that mantle to full advantage. During the transition, he gloried in the spotlight. With Reagan's inauguration, egomania bloomed. Battaglia exploited the new governor's disinterest in management to accrue power and adulation until Battaglia's conduct became an embarrassment to the staff and a joke to the press.

"Battaglia set up ... a curtain around Reagan," one biographer wrote.

Upon Reagan's taking office, Battaglia used his newfound powers to pursue strategies not consistent with the governor's priorities and beliefs. By the summer of '67, Battaglia was behaving as if he were the real governor, implying as much to the outside world. The press corps, among them Bill Boyarsky writing for the Associated Press, confirmed this view, referring to Battaglia as "the Acting Governor." Lou Cannon reports other journalists' derisive use of the expression "Deputy Governor" in referring to Battaglia.

Those scribes had it just about right. The well-dressed young executive officer was treating our newly elected governor as irrelevant.

Early in the administration, Battaglia gave us one of his many grandiose assurances:

"I can handle Unruh." Battaglia was referring to the veteran speaker of the State Assembly, Jess Unruh, a political sumo champion who carried the nickname "Big Daddy." Unruh was not easily "handled" by anyone.

During the early days in Sacramento, and as a token of this new "friendship," Battaglia elevated four of Unruh's allies to the judicial bench without involving the merit appointment system we were so carefully building.

To the Battaglia shooting star, Reagan was simply the tail of the comet, a man to be told of any decisions after the fact and then only if Battaglia decided the governor had a real need to know.

A good example was Battaglia's '66 naming of Bill King to the job of appointments secretary without the governor's knowledge or approval, as recounted earlier. Another was Battaglia's premature and highly controversial '67 announcement of personnel layoffs in the state's mental hospitals, done prior to any RR involvement in the decision.

Cabinet Secretary Clark was dismayed by the growing disintegration of the governor's office along with Battaglia's complete disregard for Reagan's role in its operation. Clark was working 20 hours a day to establish a system for managing the state's business, but certain members of the senior staff were seldom in the office, nor were they reachable by telephone. While Battaglia was always front and center with the media, he attended only six of 24 cabinet meetings during the late spring of '67. When a hurried and distracted Battaglia could be found, he would accept whatever state actions Clark was proposing with as little discussion of the details as possible.

Legal Affairs Secretary Ed Meese had little contact with Battaglia in the office itself, but he was offended by Battaglia's wasteful ways. Executive Officer Battaglia had urged state employees to "volunteer" for work on the President's Day holidays, while at the same time he was travelling about the country in a private jet funded by the taxpayers of California. When visiting Washington, Battaglia went first class, holding court at the lobbyists' favorite haunt, the Madison Hotel. No Holiday Inns on Battaglia's itinerary.

Press man Nofziger was appalled by Battaglia's imperial attitude toward the media. He was 50 minutes late for a one-hour appearance on the Jim Dunbar TV show, an important interview program originating in San Francisco.[63] The on-air host noted Battaglia's tardiness every few minutes.

Cabinet member Ike Livermore, the natural resources secretary who had become a mythically respected figure to environmentalists, timber interests, and the new governor, was dismayed by Battaglia's distance from pending decisions. A proposal to create a Redwood National Park was wending its way through both Congress and the Johnson Interior Department. If adopted, this park would impact thousands of timbering jobs, from Bodega Bay to Crescent City. Other constituencies were concerned about the survival of endangered species. The planned Redwood Park was highly controversial. Battaglia could allocate only the time available during a cab ride from office to airport to hear Livermore's briefing on this subject.

I saw Battaglia as a self-promoting autocrat, uncommitted to Reagan's conservative agenda or to any other values other than his own personal prestige.

---

63   KGO-TV, the CBS affiliate.

In all of this profligacy, Battaglia was abetted by his principal deputy, Richard M. "Sandy" Quinn, along with a few other staffers, all of whom appeared to have a special relationship with Battaglia. The lavish Battaglia-Quinn lifestyle was paid for either by the State of California or from a governor's office slush fund established by Quinn in March '67. The latter cache, opened as "The Governor's Office Account" at the First Western Bank in Sacramento, was initially funded by leftover and minimally audited campaign monies from Southern California. The new account required only a single signature, Battaglia's or Quinn's, to withdraw funds. Bank statements were sent to Quinn's personal post office box in San Francisco.

Two months after opening this Governor's Office Account, Battaglia withdrew $5,000[64] from that kitty. The check stub entry, made by Battaglia's secretary, reads: "Cash, given to PMB," followed by a question mark. (See documentation on the following page.) There were no supporting records, receipts, or justifications.

While Battaglia was supposed to be the governor's executive officer, quietly running the store, his speaking schedule was more prolific than the governor's. During the two months preceding the August showdown described below, Battaglia made more than two-dozen appearances at service clubs, trade groups, unions, and public policy forums, along with radio interviews, up and down the state. Such appearances averaged well over two a week.

---

64      $35,000 in 2014 dollars

FIRST WESTERN BANK
AND TRUST COMPANY

Sacramento Main Office • 800 J Street • Sacramento, California 95804 • 444-3150

March 20, 1967

Letter from First Western Bank, Sacramento, opening the "Governor's Office Account" on March 20, 1967, with statements to be sent to P.O. Box 285 in San Francisco.

Check stub below, with notations by Lee Holt (Battaglia's secretary), withdrawing $5,000 in cash on May 31, 1967, with the notation, "Cash given to PMB." No documentation.

Balance remaining after that withdrawal, $22,050. (About $150 K in 2014 dollars.)

PERIOD ENDING 09-29-67
PAGE 1

GOV REAGANS OFF ACCT
ATTN RICHARD QUINN
P O BOX 285
SAN FRANCISCO, CA. 94101

PLEASE ADVISE US OF ANY CHANGE OF ADDRESS

STATEMENT OF ACCOUNT WITH
SACRAMENTO MAIN OFFICE
SACRAMENTO, CALIF. 95804
First western Bank

Messrs. Philip Battaglia
and Richard Quinn
Governor's Office
State Capitol
Sacramento, California

Gentlemen:

Your confidence in our Bank as expressed by your recently opening Governor Reagan's Office Account with us is greatly appreciated and we are very happy to welcome you.

We are enclosing your temporary supply of checks together with your receipt for the initial deposit.

Again our sincere thanks for this new account and if we can be of further service, please contact us.

Sincerely,

J. G. Dunn
Assistant Manager

ms
Encls.

№ 104
$5000.00
Date 5-31 1967
To CASH
For (Given to PMB)
?

Amount brought Forward	27,049	95
Amount deposited		
Total		
Amount of this Check	5000	00
Balance Forward	22,049	95

The Alert

At noon on Friday, August 11, 1967, Bill Clark called me to share reports he had received from Ed Gillenwaters, the State of California's man in Washington.

"There's a homosexual ring in the governor's office," Clark announced.

Battaglia's principal deputy, Sandy Quinn, a man who had earlier served as a US Senate aide, had a reputation in DC for homosexual activity.[65] In the 1960s, in contrast to today's standards, homosexual conduct was not acceptable. Even 20 years later, in the mid-eighties, such conduct remained a criminal offense in 16 states, from Michigan to Texas. The Supreme Court upheld Georgia's anti-sodomy law as late as 1986.[66] Gillenwaters' disclosure could not be taken lightly.

One tip came from California's Senator George Murphy. After that first warning in July, Gillenwaters passed the information along to Quinn's boss in Sacramento, Phil Battaglia. Gillenwaters received no response, no suggestion that some corrective action might be called for.

A few weeks later, Battaglia made a trip to Washington with Quinn. Their recreational conduct left no doubt in Gillenwaters' mind that both were participating in activities unacceptable to the general public or media pundits of that time. Word was spreading rapidly in Washington.

As one writer put it in a draft column shared with Gillenwaters during the summer of '67: "The governor's office in Sacramento is a den of homosexual activity, dominated by a secret cabal with an agenda of its own." The columnist was asking for confirmation, which Gillenwaters would not provide.

The details of these men's lives are unimportant now, a half century later, but back then, when viewed from the outside, it was clear that certain members of Governor Reagan's senior staff were engaged in off-duty activity that, if unearthed by the press, would surely become political poison. Only three years before, the arrest

---

65   *Nofziger*, Lyn Nofziger, 1992, Regnery Gateway, pp 76-78
66   Bowers vs. Hardwick

of LBJ aide Walter Jenkins [67] in the YMCA men's room had rocked LBJ's election campaign.

To the insiders, to the governor's office staff, and to our political allies, Battaglia and Quinn were covertly, if not intentionally, destroying Ronald Reagan's future. Their self dealing, their extravagant lifestyles while demeaning civil servants, their dismissal of RR's intellect, their inattention to critical state issues, and their leaking of inside political information to their DC friends, all combined to lead the rest of us to a simple conclusion. Battaglia had to go.

When Clark called me, it was as though a flashbulb had gone off. Of course! That's why there seemed to be a network of which we were not a part. That's why a few members of the staff seemed to have the script in advance of every meeting. And that was why groups from the office disappeared for days at a time. It explained Battaglia's rise in the campaign. He had been nominated to serve as Southern California Chairman by Asa Call and a few others of the L.A. Elders, but he had been accepted and promoted by the unmarried and later confirmed homosexual campaign manager, Bill Roberts.

On August 11, Clark outlined his concerns to me. He said he wanted to talk at once, in person. We did, meeting in the American Airlines Admiral's Lounge at the San Francisco Airport two hours later. As we compared notes, it all began to make sense.

Clark called Ed Meese on that same August day. The governor's legal affairs secretary and future attorney general of the United States was at Ft. Sill, Oklahoma, putting in his two weeks of US Army reserve duty. Clark and Meese connected on Sunday, August 13. Meese's reaction was the same as mine: "Of course. That explains it all."

The Committee

Others in the Reagan Administration already knew about Battaglia's conduct. Gillenwaters' close friend from San Diego,

---

[67]   Jenkins had engaged in homosexual conduct with a stranger, but he was only charged with disorderly conduct. White House Counsel Clark Clifford asked the Washington papers not to run the Jenkins story, but they did. Jenkins resigned from the White House staff a week later.

cabinet member Gordon Luce, was aware of the Washington rumors as well as the leaks from Sacramento into Quinn's DC network.

Art Van Court, the governor's security man, found the explanation for Battaglia's strange behavior to be compatible with his own observations. He had become alarmed by the verbal abuse Battaglia heaped on the second-tier employees in the governor's office.

Curtis Patrick, the man who ran the governor's communications systems, declared Battaglia and Quinn's frequent travels together to resorts irrelevant to state business. They shared a room at each stop.[68] Patrick was horrified by the costs. During their August holidays, Battaglia and Quinn rented expensive convertibles at every stop—at state expense. They hired a Jet Commander aircraft to ferry them from Bakersfield to San Diego at a cost to the taxpayers of $440 per hour[69] even though there was commercial service available.

By then, I was long gone from the governor's office. I had not been comfortable there. My political interests lay in the national scene, as described earlier. I had a business to tend to, and my mother had just died, leaving my 67-year-old father alone. Perhaps the Battaglia matter was not my problem.

On the other hand, with no action by Clark and me, Reagan surely would have no political future at all. His governorship was in danger of disintegration from within; Battaglia's politically poisonous lifestyle would be disastrous when exposed from the outside.

Clark and I decided to assemble a working group composed of others aware of the problems and as concerned as we. Our intent was to pool information and then plan some sort of action. This self-appointed committee was to include Clark and me along with Gillenwaters, Luce, Meese, Nofziger, Patrick, and Van Court, with the addition of Paul Haerle, my successor as the governor's appointments secretary and a very careful lawyer. We all foresaw the need for a defensible written brief.

---

68   During the campaign, Battaglia always *demanded* a private room.
69   About $3,000 per hour in 2014 dollars.

In our telephonic discussions, this group confirmed its original conclusion. "Battaglia is a disaster; he must go." But office malpractice would be hard to prove. More to the point, we knew "mismanagement" would not drive Reagan to action. His relaxed "who's next in line" personnel policy, and his reliance on staff to work out internal conflicts had *caused* our problem.

Reagan's detachment resurfaced 15 years later during his first term as president. By 1982, RR had delegated presidential authority to a quadriad[70] of staffers. Some malevolently pursued perks and power at the expense of others, using press leaks to discredit their peers. These episodes reflected badly on the president. Mike Deaver tried to confront his boss, urging Reagan to take action, to stop the infighting.[71]

"Mr. President, this is just awful. I don't think you understand what is going on around here."

"Well, Mike," RR responded, "I think you're exaggerating. I think this is just the media."

"Well, if you think that, we're in even bigger trouble," Deaver countered. "I'm telling you, it's guerrilla warfare out there [in the West Wing hallways]. I can't take it anymore."

Deaver knew that one of the contestants for White House power was covertly cultivating criminal indictments of his peers.

"What do you want me to do?" the president asked his assistant.

"I want you to bang some heads together," Deaver responded. "We can't operate this way anymore."

RR brought Baker, Clark, Meese, and Deaver into the Oval Office, but nobody engaged. RR rambled, then escaped via delegation: "You fellows work this out, will you?"

The quartet nodded, but none of them meant it.

To me, then working at the National Security Council, Reagan's senior staff looked like four scorpions in a bottle. While they agreed there was a problem, they never converged. Within a

---

70   Chief of Staff James Baker, Deputy Chief of Staff Michael Deaver, Counselor Edwin Meese, National Security Advisor William Clark
71   From Michael Deaver's Oral History, Miller Center, 2002, pg 45.

year, Clark left for Interior, Baker to Treasury, Meese to Justice, Deaver to seek medical help. Iran Contra soon followed.

In the summer of '67, all of this lay well into the future, but even then we understood that RR would never take strong action in the face of office warfare. With Battaglia controlling the levers of power, a "bad management" memo would lead to only an autumn of internal strife, politically and professionally fatal to all, including the governor.

Thus, we decided to make Battaglia's *personal* behavior the primary and only stated reason for seeking his immediate removal. This posed a serious intellectual challenge to all, since each of us held conservative, if not libertarian, beliefs about personal privacy: "Leave people alone. Let them live their personal lives as they see fit."

Reagan shared this view. Many of his movie-industry associates were gay.

One of Nancy's unauthorized biographers[72] noted that, "While living in New York and Hollywood during the early forties, most of Nancy's closest relationships were with homosexual men."

But public life in the sixties was different. Once you start spending the people's money and controlling their lives, the standards change. Any exposure of Battaglia's lifestyle would have been highly damaging to Reagan, to his administration, and to his career.

The reader must bear in mind America's media-driven moral standards at that time. In 1960, Allen Drury's Pulitzer prize-winning book, *Advise and Consent*, was a best seller. Otto Preminger turned it into a hit movie two years later.

In Drury's story, Brigham Anderson, a fictional senator from Utah, is driven to suicide when threatened with the disclosure of a wartime homosexual encounter in Hawaii 20 years before. This sad story line had its basis in reality. In 1954, Senator Lester Hunt (D - WY) committed gunshot suicide in his Senate office when Senators Styles Bridges (R - NH) and Herman Welker (R - ID) threatened the disclosure of a homosexual member of the Hunt family unless that man resigned from the Senate.

---

72   Kitty Kelley, *op cit*

Journalists, writing in the late sixties, reported "a scandal in Reagan's office," but the executive secretary's sexual preferences were not the real issue. Battaglia's lifestyle, so unacceptable at that time, would simply be the lever used to pry him out. From our perspective, he was destroying Reagan's future, along with the hopes of millions of the governor's followers. There was no "scandal" in the governor's office. There was just a good old-fashioned struggle for power.

Bill Clark and I talked again on Monday, August 14 to review our conversations with others in the group and to settle on a plan of action. All had agreed, "Keep it simple." We needed to document our case, to provide an ironclad basis for decision. We wanted to spell out the procedures for RR to affect a prompt firing, an instant "OK RR" on some piece of paper. His indecisive approach to personnel matters could be professionally fatal to all of us if Battaglia had time to counterattack.

Documentation

Our opening lead came from a young Washington secretary who had unexpectedly intruded on her boyfriend at his apartment, a man then engaged in homosexual acts with his roommate, Sandy Quinn. The boyfriend, whom we code-named Zebra, disclosed the identities of seven other partners, many in the Reagan gubernatorial office or campaign staff, as a means of justifying his activity.

"Everybody's doing it," Zebra said to the astonished woman.

She relayed the conversation along with a warning to Gillenwaters and Luce. "I work for Larry O'Brien,"[73] she warned. "I'm not going to tell him, but he'll find out."

With those eight names as leads, the committee started the process of documenting the inappropriate personal behavior of Battaglia and Quinn. That was not easy, given our resolve to stay within the law. On the other hand, the prime targets, Battaglia and his deputy Quinn, made the job rather straightforward. Once August came to Sacramento, the legislature went home, Reagan

---

73   Larry O'Brien managed John Kennedy's senate and presidential campaigns. In 1964, he became a key LBJ advisor.

went to the beach, and the staff was left to handle the state's business. In the case of the two primary suspects, August was their month to travel and frolic around the state at the expense of others. They made little effort to hide their ways.

During this whole process, we had not involved the Los Angeles Elders because of their casual approach to security and because they had selected and supported Battaglia in the first place. We were concerned they would gossip among themselves; that they would tell their wives what they had heard and that at least one of those women would then tip Nancy. The families of the offenders deserved better.

On the other hand, we had learned that when bringing unpleasant news to Reagan, especially on personnel matters, it worked best to have all constituencies onboard. We decided to involve Holmes Tuttle and William French Smith immediately before we met with RR, giving those two enough time to read and digest our memorandum, but not enough time to alert Battaglia. I would call Tuttle and Smith on Friday morning, August 25, to apprise them of the crisis at hand.

The Showdown

In August '67, the governor and Nancy were spending a few weeks at the Hotel del Coronado in San Diego. RR had undergone prostate surgery on July 31; by then the legislature had gone home. On August 8, I met with Reagan at his home in Los Angeles to keep him current on political matters and to see how he was doing. He was recovering well, so by late August Reagan was hardly an invalid.

The Coronado Peninsula lies to the west of San Diego, forming the bay to its east and fronting on the Pacific Ocean to the west. The hotel itself is a massive piece of Victorian gingerbread, hosting clusters of cottages and cabanas along the shore. And what a beach! Miles of white sand facing the ocean, with warm, calm waters lapping the bay side of the peninsula. Art Van Court was there to handle the Reagans' security, schedule, and access.

The committee, plus Tuttle and Smith, converged on the hotel in the late afternoon. California's First Couple wore beach robes, chatting in their small cottage, when Van Court gave them a few minutes' notice that a delegation from Sacramento, plus Tuttle and Smith, needed to see the two of them at once. Curtis Patrick tapped on the door, and Nancy let the group in as an air of apprehension filled the room. Then Reagan's unfailing good humor took hold.

"Golly, are you all quitting at once?" he joked.

He displayed the same wit 14 years later after being shot by John Hinkley. While being rolled into the emergency room at the George Washington Hospital, RR looked for a laugh.

"Hope you are all Republicans," he chuckled at the assembled medics dressed in scrubs.

The Reagans moved into their sunny sitting room, settled into a pair of rattan-upholstered seats, and waited as the 11 of us assembled on chairs in a large circle. I handed copies of the memorandum to Ron and Nancy. We then waited as they read it.

August 25, 1967

Dear Governor:

During the spring of this year there occurred several leaks of highly sensitive and closely guarded information that have never been adequately explained.

In May, the executive secretary was advised of serious security risks on which no action was taken.

Since that time facts have come to light which indicate conduct which has, and could continue to have, a serious impact on the governor's office. This appears to involve Phillip M. Battaglia, the executive secretary, and his assistant, Richard M. Quinn.

The following is a report concerning the facts now available to us.[74]

---

74   A fuller, though still sanitized, text at Appendix B

The Reagans' faces turned white, and tears welled in Nancy's eyes. There were a few questions along the lines of, "Are you sure?"

As the conversation circumnavigated the room, each participant reaffirmed the evidence of personal behavior so inappropriate to the sixties. There was no wiggle room. No one mentioned the governor's office mismanagement.

Both Reagans were products of Hollywood; neither was personally offended by homosexual behavior, but for once, Nancy's obsession with appearances rather than substance was of great help. She called for immediate action. "This is terrible!" she announced.

"Yes, we must act," Reagan responded decisively. "Phil must go."

Several of us were surprised with the alacrity of the decision, but Reagan was a decisive man. Having all constituencies present in that room certainly helped.

The group made it clear that this was not something we could chat about next week. Battaglia had to be fired now. He had an appointment to see Smith and others of the L.A. Elders over the coming weekend at Taft Schreiber's home in Los Angeles. It was agreed that Smith would deliver the termination notice to Battaglia at that time, while he was away from Sacramento.

We also received Reagan's approval to move Battaglia out of his office. We did not explain what that meant: Patrick and Van Court had individuals in place, ready to change the locks and clean out the desks of the now-terminated employees. A former convicted safecracker, now crossed over into the legitimate world, was to do the job. By '67 he was a trusted employee of the Los Angeles Police Department. No locals for this delicate job.

The Aftermath

An hour after our arrival at the Del Coronado, the committee left. Smith and Tuttle stayed behind with the Reagans. Some returned to their homes locally. Bill Clark and one or two others rushed back to Sacramento, since the complete evacuation of the governor's office on a business day, even if it was a Friday, would seem unusual.

The rest of us drove to the airport on a more leisurely basis. Once there, led by Nofziger, we headed to the bar to rejoice in the fact that we few, a band of brothers, at great personal risk, had saved Reaganism from certain disaster.

In Nofziger's oral history, bequeathed to the Miller Center at the University of Virginia, the press secretary identifies "only three true villains in Ronald Reagan's political career: Phil Battaglia, John Sears,[75] and Jim Baker.[76]"

When Clark returned to his office in Sacramento, he found a call from the governor awaiting him. *Oh no*, Bill thought. *He's changed his mind.*

Not so. Reagan was calling to ask Clark to take over the duties of executive secretary.

On Sunday, all 11 of us, including Tuttle and Smith, reassembled at the Reagan home in Pacific Palisades for lunch. RR confirmed that William French Smith, the Designated Terminator, had delivered a firing notice to Battaglia during a meeting at Taft Schreiber's residence at 10:00 that morning. Reagan then confirmed his selection of Bill Clark to serve as his new executive secretary.

Reagan also wanted to talk about the national presidential drive, since over the weekend the Elders' telephone network had been in overload. The Battaglia crisis allowed them to disparage all the younger staff members, from Sacramento to my political office in San Francisco, as being inexperienced and untrustworthy.

This was a serious affront to the committee. It was those men, the L.A. Elders, who had created and empowered Battaglia in the first place; we had just saved Reagan from their folly. But reality got lost in the shuffle. RR was more comfortable with his

---

75   The Nixon-connected manager of Reagan's losing 1976 presidential campaign, continuing as a mis-manager in 1980 until the Reagans fired him in March of that year.

76   James Baker III, a Bush crony from Houston, chosen at the end of the '80 campaign to be Reagan's chief of staff. Baker is described by Nofziger as "an arrogant man of overweening ambition and self-importance who thought he knew better than the president. Not an honorable man. Another Battaglia."

When Nofziger departed the White House, he "went into the conference room where an autographed picture of Baker was hanging. I took it down, dropped it on the floor, and stomped on it. Then I headed home."

contemporaries and peers. Neither he nor Nancy wanted to hear any more complaints about the "kids."

As the following week unfolded, some of us undertook conciliatory conversations with a few of the secondary players mentioned in the Reagan charge sheet. One gentleman, a close friend, confirmed to me every name, every aspect of our findings, but he was also deep into depression. This being the sixties, he feared for his economic survival. On the spot, I asked him to come work for me, to help with real estate due-diligence work that involved political zoning and permitting efforts. We worked together for almost a year until he moved into similar real estate work in the Southland.

It would take a month for Reagan to sort through all he had heard. August had brought him a full load of angst, a shipment of narratives he did not want to hear.

When I talked all of this over with Homes Tuttle a decade later,[77] he confided his belief that the events of August 25, 1967, had been a defining moment for Reagan.

"If he had waffled," Tuttle recalled, "the stories would have flooded the press, and the governor's office would have been torn apart. Ron would not have known how to recover from either." Tuttle felt that with one misstep at the beach, "It all would have been over, even the prospect of a second term. It was Reagan's first major crisis and he handled it decisively and well."

Clark felt the same way. After two weeks of preparation, as he walked into the Reagan cabana on August 25, he trained his eyes directly on the governor's countenance.

Did Ron have the "right stuff"? Clark wondered.

He did.

By Labor Day, the snake pit in Sacramento had been cleaned out. Bill Clark, who enjoyed the full confidence of the committee, was now the executive secretary. We were sure he would treat the seat at Reagan's right hand with fiduciary responsibility. It was time for all of us to return to the beaches and our own homes. Surely, there would be nothing but good times ahead.

---

77   At his residence in Montecito on June 21, 1982

Ch. 12   The Brass Ring Slips Away

In the aftermath of the coup, the Los Angeles Elders seemed distracted by the 1968 Republican Convention, now less than a year away.

"Who is to be a delegate?" some asked.

Others wanted to settle old scores. "Who is *not* to be a delegate?"

The lesser players were more interested in the creature comforts. "Where is the California delegation going to stay? Who gets the suites?"

But with the approach of Labor Day, the more vocal members of that group returned to hounding the governor's staff. The rhetorical question repeatedly posed to the Reagans over dinners in Los Angeles: "Who caused the Battaglia problem?"

Their proffered answer was: "Those kids." Looking in the mirror was not an acceptable alternative.

In time, the Elders returned to an older refrain: "Why is Ronnie getting all this presidential attention? What's going on?"

I foolishly ignored all of these queries as those gentlemen clouded Nancy's mind, in time disturbing the governor's tranquility.

The Texans Make a House Call

On Monday, September 11, Peter O'Donnell of Texas called me at my office. Senator Tower called Reagan. Both expressed a desire to meet—soon. Their agenda was obvious: they wanted to discuss the Republican nomination.

Half a year earlier, on March 27, I travelled to Dallas to meet with O'Donnell in an attempt to recruit him into my Reagan '68 organization. O'Donnell had become my friend in the aftermath of 1964, but he had not been as easy to recruit as Clif White. By December '66, O'Donnell had already joined the Nixon organizing committee.

In the spring of 1967, however, O'Donnell dropped out of that network, disillusioned by Nixon's bizarre management schemes. That is probably why O'Donnell was willing to receive me in his Dallas office in March of that year. He was looking for a thoughtfully organized winner.

Senator Tower once harbored presidential ambitions of his own, but by the late summer of '67, he had grown realistic. He found little support for his candidacy.

Both Texans were seeking a new candidate for '68. I made arrangements for a meeting. They arrived a week later. I met their plane, hosted them for an early supper at my home, then brought them to the Reagan residence in Sacramento. O'Donnell and Tower were accompanied by Anne Armstrong, the Republican National Committeewoman from Texas, and her rancher husband, Tobin.

Ron and Nancy Reagan greeted their guests warmly. Nofziger, Clark, and Gordon Luce, a member of the governor's cabinet, waited inside. Once settled on sofa and chairs, a surreal exchange began.

The Armstrongs, fully prepared to support Reagan, opened unequivocally.

"Are you going to run?" Anne Armstrong asked.

"Well..." Reagan began as Senator Tower interrupted to broaden the question.

"If we commit ourselves, will you become an active candidate, Ron? I don't mean now, but come January?"

Peter O'Donnell remained quiet. He was weighing his options. As Texans, they knew of Lyndon Johnson's vulnerabilities better than most others. All four were looking for a winner, but they did not want to be left hanging if Reagan decided not to run.

When O'Donnell spoke, his query was functional. "Who's going to run your campaign, Governor?"

Nofziger and I were Reagan's political operators in the room. As our visitors tried to focus on the business of '68, Reagan began the amiable sidestep we had seen so often before.

"Johnson's on thin ice..." he started, as though speaking to Tuttle and Schreiber, trying to keep his interrogators happy while avoiding the questions. "I think there's a Republican opportunity out there..."

Nofziger and I exchanged resigned glances.

We hoped RR would articulate a crisp answer, such as, "I have to establish my credibility as a governor this autumn, but next year, with the coming of '68, I'll be responsive to a draft. If the support is there, I will run."

Alternately, he might have said, "Tom and Lyn here are the fellows who will run that campaign. Clif White is developing a field organization. Stu Spencer is my strategist."

But that was not the message Reagan delivered. He dissembled while the two other California staffers in the room, ill-informed on campaign strategy, muddied the water by arguing their perspectives.

"Fate takes a hand in these things," Reagan concluded. "The office often seeks the man."

It was a disastrous non-conversation.

The Texans left perplexed and unconvinced.

My Return to the Back Bench

During the week following the Texas meeting in Sacramento, the Elders resumed their steady drumbeat. The Del Coronado confrontation of August 25 had shaken Reagan's confidence in his younger staff, even though we were the ones who had saved him from disaster.

With the coming of September, the political season was warming up. Stories appeared about Reagan's presidential ambitions, and details of the Texas meeting leaked to the press. To the Elders, there seemed to be a black hole in Reagan's political life. It was sucking in people and money while emitting no light. RR's peers were eager to illuminate that void.

The now-familiar benching came on Tuesday, September 19, '67 two days after the Texans had left town. Bill Clark called the day before to warn me.

"Tuttle and Smith are planning a takeover," he said.

I met with Reagan in San Francisco on that Tuesday. His agenda was the Elders' unhappiness.

"I want Bill Smith to serve as chairman of the presidential nomination effort," he began, with no final phrase in mind. "I'd like you to meet with Holmes and Bill to work out the details." That meant, *Please get those two, along with the other fellows, off my back.*

Reagan did not ask me to go away. On the contrary, he just wanted "all the boys" to be happy.

On Friday, September 22, I drove to Tuttle's office on La Brea Avenue to be told of his group's deliberations earlier in the day.

"We're in charge here," Tuttle announced. "That's the way it's going to be."

We glared at each other across Tuttle's functionally littered desk. I had not been invited to a debate; rebuttal was pointless. We shook hands and I left.

Tuttle's words were unsettling, but over my evening margarita I concluded I deserved them. I had unwisely excluded Tuttle and the Elders from my earlier delegate search plans. It was now payback time.

The day after, on Saturday, September 23, I had the usual end-game meeting with Reagan and William French Smith in Reagan's Pacific Palisades den. I say "the usual" because I had seen this process before: all the pieces correctly arranged on the chess board; only the "checkmate" call to come in the governor's voice, backed up by the presence of the Designated Terminator.

I had my settlement claim in mind. In closing out my campaign responsibilities with RR, I wished to become the next Republican National Committeeman from California. This is an arcane political post, but it was one that would give me a voice in the direction of the national party. It would also entail a serious convention role, from platform debates to the allocation of tickets. Several of the Elders wanted the job, but in our Saturday discussion, I secured

Reagan's pledge of support. In exchange, I agreed to continue with the management of his out-of-state travels during the autumn and winter to come.

Two weeks later, I tendered a formal separation letter to Reagan:

I want to make clear that I am no longer in the business of collecting delegates on your behalf. I can no longer direct or fund Clif White's activities. I will be glad to help with your travels, but I cannot meet further with Holmes or Bill Smith to discuss the nomination process.

As we discussed when meeting in your den, I would appreciate your support in my election to the Republican National Committee.[78]

Spencer-Roberts redirected its efforts to focus on California legislative races.

"Lean back and enjoy life; watch the show," Spencer advised.[79]

Clif White was left in limbo. His inability to get organized perfectly matched Smith's inability to lead.

While I remained on duty, executing Reagan's fall and winter travels, William French Smith had neither the time nor the inclination to accompany his candidate on those tours.

Blowing off the Barons

A week after my return to the sidelines, and consistent with my pledge to RR, I joined the governor aboard a chartered jet for what was to have been our campaign kickoff. Nofziger and security man Art Van Court accompanied us.

The first stop, on Thursday, September 28, was Peoria, Illinois, and Reagan's alma mater, Eureka College. The fall colors were spectacular. Everett Dirksen, one of our targeted Republican Barons, greeted our plane and escorted us to the steps of the campus library where RR delivered a touching evening speech. The crowd was huge, the students loved Reagan's talk, and when it was over,

---

78   This letter was drafted during late September, delivered on October 10, 1967 after the Illinois, South Carolina, and Wisconsin tour described later, but rejected by RR in telephone conversations on October 12.
79   On September 25, 1967

we all adjourned to a serious Republican reception being held in one of the ivy-covered campus halls. Both Dirksen and the junior senator from Illinois, Chuck Percy, were there, but when Reagan huddled with Dirksen, the talk was of football.

"Are you in this thing?" the Senate minority leader growled to the visiting distinguished alumnus.

"Well, I think the office seeks the man," was Reagan's rote response.

Both moved on to cookies and punch. That was it. No deal.

The next day we flew on to Columbia, South Carolina, to a large and enthusiastic greeting at the airport. Our advance men had arranged for a speaker's stand and sound system. Reagan put them to remarkable use. After that performance, we headed downtown for a press conference, a Republican finance reception, and then a fundraising banquet, the most successful such event in South Carolina's history.[80]   Reagan delivered a sensational performance with one man in mind: Senator Strom Thurmond.

After the cheering was over, it was time for serious business. Reagan, Nofziger, and I met with Senator Thurmond and his sidekick Harry Dent in a small but functional side-chamber at the banquet-hosting hotel. By then I knew Dent quite well. His boss, the senator, was most cordial in recalling our first meeting in New Orleans three years earlier.

"Good to see you again, Mr. Reed," was his gracious opener.

"One helluva night in New Orleans," I responded. "You put on a great show, Senator. Lots of courage."

"Thanks," he said as he turned to query his primary target.

History hung in the balance. Thurmond asked specifically and repeatedly about Reagan's plans. The governor's response was vague, interjecting the dreaded "office seeks the man" line— only that and nothing more. Neither Nofziger nor I dared expand with a "What he means is..." This was the key moment, and opportunity was fleeing before our eyes.

Thurmond gave up. He closed out the conversation with a perceptive forecast. "You'll be president someday, young man, but not this year," he predicted.

---

80   The event raised $350,000, about 2.5 million in 2014 dollars.

Reagan was not being coy, nor was he playing poker. He simply wanted tranquility at home, freedom from grumbling by the Elders.

We went to our separate rooms to watch LBJ tell us more about Vietnam.

On Saturday, we moved on to Wisconsin, one of our three primary-state targets, where Reagan spoke at a Republican finance lunch in downtown Milwaukee. He then met with several grassroots groups that hoped for some encouragement. RR gave them none. An evening rally at the Milwaukee arena was a great success for the local party: 2,800 people on the ground floor at $100[81] each plus another 3,000 in the balcony for free. Republican Governor Knowles accompanied us, but again, there was no closure with anyone.

The last stop, on Sunday, October 1, was a propitiously selected refueling in Grand Island, Nebraska, another of the opt-out primary states we planned to contest. Clif White's group had assembled most of the volunteers that were to organize the local Draft Reagan committee. The result was a mini rally in the general aviation facility, but Reagan gave no encouragement to the would-be campaign workers. Then we flew home.

The next day, on Monday, October 2, John Tower gave me a call. He had been offered a position of leadership in the Nixon campaign. He was in San Francisco and wanted to talk. We connected at 10:00 p.m. on his preferred turf, the lobby bar in the St. Francis Hotel. Our conversation was brief. The senator outlined the importuning laid upon him recently by Richard Nixon. He declared his support for Ronald Reagan before articulating his quandary.

"What am I to do, Tom?"

My only response: "Go ask William French Smith."

I paid the bar bill, we shook hands under the crystal chandeliers, and he headed for the door.

Reagan left the impression with every party factotum he met during that last week of September that his campaign was a vague and headless monster, and that he was going to improvise as the

---

81   About $700 today, grossing over two million in 2014 dollars.

convention approached. That is not what these old pros needed to hear. They did not want to get caught on the losing side of a struggle for the nomination. By early October, all were reluctantly joining what they felt to be Richard Nixon's inexorable ride to nomination, the only realistic alternative to a Rockefeller recapture of the party.

Robert Finch, the Republican lieutenant governor of California, a man who went on to join the Nixon cabinet, put it this way in a post-election interview with Lou Cannon. "As long as Nixon had Tower, Thurmond, and Goldwater, there was no way Reagan could take any massive amount of Southern delegates." We agreed.

It Gets Worse

Reagan's disordered political world imploded once he boarded the *SS Independence* during the third week of October.

Lou Cannon, at the time a reporter for the *San Jose Mercury News*, had just run an opinion piece discussing Phil Battaglia's mysterious disappearance from the governor's office. Our party line was that Battaglia had resigned to become a Sacramento lobbyist. That made no sense to the perceptive Cannon, who said as much in his October 13th column. Weeks before, Karl Fleming wrote in *Newsweek's* "Periscope" section about a "top GOP presidential candidate having a sordid scandal" in his office.

On October 16, the governors of all 50 states boarded the *SS Independence* in New York City. A limo delivered the Reagan entourage into a cavernous dockside building on the Lower West Side, a structure that could have housed a Zeppelin. Every cubic inch was needed to accommodate the egos and impedimenta of 50 political executives, many who lusted for even higher office. Governor and Mrs. Reagan were accompanied by Executive Secretary Clark; Communications Director Nofziger; Mrs. Reagan's press aide, Nancy Clark Reynolds; and me.

Clif White did not join the cruise as part of the California delegation, but he was there, credentialed by another friendly governor. We, along with several hundred of our new best friends, were headed off for a governors' conference at sea. The *Independence* would put in at the US Virgin Islands three days later. Clark and I found it ironic that we had been assigned to the quite upscale suite originally reserved for Battaglia and Quinn.

Reporters who boarded the *Independence* gave it a nickname. This three-day compression of governors of both parties, their ambitious staffs, a scandal-hungry press corps, and a surfeit of alcohol, all aboard a cruise ship with no telephones or exits, came to be known as "The Ship of Fools."[82]

During the days, the conference held sessions on federal-state relations, the role of the National Guard, labor relations, constitutional revisions, etc. Clark and I did our best to represent our governor at the meetings he could not attend, but when the sun passed over the yardarm, the press corps turned their attention to Reagan's often-imbibing press secretary, Lyn Nofziger. They wanted an explanation of Lou Cannon's mystery, Karl Fleming's hint of scandal.

"What's going on?" they asked. "Why did Battaglia *really* leave?"

Nofziger was willing to oblige. Chatting through an alcoholic haze, Nofziger briefed many of his longtime press colleagues "on deep background." He was trying to defuse the Battaglia story before it blew open, but in so doing he only fed the Fourth Estate's craving for scandal.

On October 19, the *Independence* made landfall in St. Thomas, and the previously cloistered reporters could now access telephones. Ten days later, fittingly on Halloween, columnist Drew Pearson ran with the story, spelling out the details of "two homosexuals on the governor's staff." A press firestorm ensued. A day later, on November 1, the *San Francisco Examiner's* Jack McDowell wrote a more detailed account.

Two weeks after that, when Reagan held his first post-cruise press conference, he was queried about these stories.

Q: "Governor, is there any truth to a published report that a homosexual ring has been uncovered in your administration?"

---

82   After the 1965 movie of that name, about an ocean liner headed from Mexico to Germany in 1933.

A: "No, there is no truth to that report," Reagan lied.

He then went on to attack Pearson. "Three presidents of both parties have, publically, called Drew Pearson a liar," Reagan spat out. It was one of the rare occasions when, in trying to protect innocent families, I saw RR lose his temper.

After issuing further denials of the homosexual ring story, Reagan turned to his communications director. "Want to confirm it, Lyn?"

Nofziger: "Confirmed."

Everyone in the room knew better. Several reporters had been aboard the *Independence* and had heard the story firsthand from Nofziger. With those words, the relationship between governor, Nofziger, and reporters disintegrated into a swamp of distrust. That is not a good arrangement when dealing with a sophisticated press corps.

Carl Greenberg, the *Los Angeles Times'* veteran political reporter, later commented to Nofziger, "I wondered how long it would take you guys to find out about Battaglia." Greenberg had known for more than a year.

Nancy Reagan was furious about Nofziger's leaks aboard the *Independence*, and then by his denials in Sacramento. She demanded his resignation. He offered to accommodate, but Reagan, ever sympathetic to the unemployed, would not accept until his press secretary found new work. That turned out to be a year away.

§§§

With year's end, the Reagan presidential quest ground to a halt. Nofziger's bad judgment, the Elders' caterwauling, and the governor's vacillation all combined to end the post-coup euphoria of summer.

Happily, I missed much of this imbroglio. When the *Independence* docked in New York, I turned my attention to family. My recently widowed father was about to remarry in Connecticut, and my oldest son was to enter kindergarten back in California. A business project I had started in 1965 was blossoming nicely and it needed my attention.

I spun away from Sacramento. Henry Salvatori picked up Clif White's contract. Spencer-Roberts shifted its attention to state work. I saw the Reagan train as stalled on a siding. The show appeared to be over.

Ch. 13   Hemingway Redux

During the late summer of '67, while still in charge of Reagan's quasi campaign, I solicited two landmark speaking engagements for the governor. I sought venues that would call for serious comment on national problems, not Republican cheerleading.

The first was to be a November 11 Veterans Day speech in Albany, Oregon, our top primary-election target state. Albany lies in the center of the Willamette Valley, 20 miles south of the state capitol in Salem where we hoped to cement the support of Governor McCall and Speaker Montgomery. I saw this as the time and place for a thoughtful Reagan speech on Vietnam.

The second target was the Economic Club of New York. I had seen JFK perform there, four years earlier. It was the heart of America's financial establishment. During the summer of '67, I connected with the club's executive director, Dwight Eckerman. He was delighted with the prospect of a Reagan appearance. We set the date: Wednesday, January 17, '68. I envisioned this as our campaign's kickoff, a chance to both brag about what Reagan had done in California, and to expose the folly of Lyndon Johnson's guns-and-butter approach to the war in Vietnam.

Mindful of the Gridiron Club fiasco earlier in '67, I wanted to find a serious speechwriter for these events. I was seeking true literary talent, a writer who could add resonating structure to Reagan's oratory. A good political speechwriter must ascertain his candidate's goals; hopefully, they match his own. He/she should then conjure ideas, seek out and double-check facts, and then propose policies or critiques in support of those goals. Along the way, the speechwriter must coordinate his ideas with campaign staff in a hunt for hidden land mines. Once focused, the wordsmith must then concisely compose a few pages for his candidate's adaptation and use. His writing must deliver maximum impact with a minimal word count.

"Getting the most from the least," as Ernest Hemingway put it.

Those were the clinical qualifications. But writers who are to play in the major leagues, those who compose for would-be presidents, must produce more than accurate essays. They must produce lyrics. Listeners must feel they have *smelled* the detritus in the South China Sea, and that they have *seen* the jungle rains darken the body bags at Ton Son Nhut. Hemingway became my template in this search.

My opening candidate was Charles J.V. Murphy, a compelling national security reporter at *Fortune* magazine. His February '62 nuclear testing piece in *LIFE* magazine[83] was well researched, compellingly written, and concise. It provided accurate insight into the policy choices then facing our president. Murphy knew what he was writing about, and he said it well.

Never hurts to ask, I thought.

On the evening of October 15, prior to our boarding the *Independence* in New York, I connected with Murphy. We met for dinner at New York's 21 Club. The ceiling of this once-speakeasy bar was festooned with airplane models, donated over the years by generations of fighter pilots. Drinks were delivered with jet-like speed to the red-checked tablecloths below. During that same evening, the Reagans dined with the Bill Buckleys on New York's more austere Upper East Side. I'm sure I had the better time.

Murphy was an effervescent riot. He was of Reagan's age, though carrying a less-disciplined physique. Murphy dressed well enough to gain entrance to 21, even though a spot of hollandaise embellished the lapel of his rumpled brown jacket. Once settled in place, he attracted martinis as bees are drawn to honey. He was an aging Ernest Hemingway.

---

83   "Now the President Will Decide on His Own," *LIFE*, February 16, 1962.

Murphy appreciated my adulation for his 1962 nuclear testing article. He feared he had gotten in over his head with the physics, though he knew he had gotten the geopolitics just right. By '67, Murphy was semi-retired. With the coming of the Johnson years, his sources had dried up, but his scorn for the rising Bobby Kennedy knew no bounds.

When the curried chicken and Pimm's Cups arrived, I got to the point.

"Charlie, how about doing some speech writing for Ronald Reagan?"

His response was explosive with laughter. "Wow! Jesus, yes! I'll drink to that! He's the man we need! When can I meet him? When do we start?"

"Right now, Charlie. A Veterans Day talk on Vietnam comes first. After that, a January performance at the New York Economic Club," I explained.

"You got Reagan the New York Economics Club gig?" Murphy was impressed. "To kick off the New Year? Wow!"

We agreed Murphy would start work in his Washington office. He was to put together a thousand words on Vietnam for insertion by RR into the Veterans Day talk, now only four weeks away. We would coordinate by phone. With e-mail not yet invented, we would exchange drafts by snail mail or telex for delivery of product to the governor by November 1.

§§§

That was not an auspicious time for RR. The Drew Pearson article appeared the day before, but even so, RR was receptive to new, solid ideas for Veterans Day. On November 2, I drove to Sacramento to meet with the governor and deliver Murphy's four pages. Reagan was appreciative. He knew he could not spout his usual California-booster talk when he got to Oregon, not on Veterans Day.

On Friday I joined the governor and security man Van Court at the Sacramento airport for our charter jet flight north. First stop, Seattle, for a Republican luncheon, followed by a drive to Portland for a Republican dinner. My journal notes a "quiet response" to both of those "standard Republican fare" talks. The Drew Pearson story was at the core of most questions.

On Saturday we continued south, from Portland to Oregon's capitol. RR rode with Governor McCall, another former broadcaster. We attended the Oregon-USC football game, where RR enjoyed the changed environment. Then we went on to Albany, the Veterans Hall, and the Murphy-augmented lecture.

The response was stunning. The crowd was attentive during delivery; it exploded into applause at the end. There were no questions about Drew Pearson and "the scandal," only queries about the bloodshed in Vietnam.

Over breakfast the next morning, when scanning the papers, we were pleased to find the words "intelligent" and "thoughtful" high up in many appraisals of Reagan's performance. It had not been a California-cheerleading speech; it had substance. Reagan was willing to accept Murphy's observations on how we were drawn into the morass of Vietnam along with the harsh actions needed to get back out. They matched Reagan's prior conversations with Eisenhower earlier in '66.

"I'd like to meet Murphy," Reagan said while sipping our Oregon coffee.

That request made my day.

I called ghostwriter Murphy to tell him of our success in Oregon, of RR's desire to meet, and to caution him about the challenge that lay ahead.

"Please understand, Charlie. Nobody writes speeches for Ronald Reagan. He writes for political theater, for TV, better than any human on this earth," I explained. "What he appreciates is new information, easily digestible facts to nail his case shut, along with well-written phrases that capture the spirit of what he is trying to say. Want to give the New York Economic Club a try?"

I expected his response, and I got it: "Damn right!"

Murphy flew to San Francisco on Friday, December 1. He had been doing his homework, having met with Bill Buckley in New York to toss around ideas and to plumb the Reagan speaking style. I met Murphy's plane and brought him to my house, where we brainstormed ideas until the malt mellowed the evening to mirth. Slightly before midnight, I installed him in the local motel with the understanding that there would be no frivolity on the morrow, only coffee, until I saw some production.

On Saturday, I picked up Murphy for lunch. Sure enough, he had used California's economic statistics as props to create good theater. We talked about ideas the New York elite would welcome, then worked separately until proceeding to dinner with friends.

On Sunday morning, December 3, I collected Murphy from his hotel. We drove to the San Francisco airport to join RR and Nofziger along with security man Van Court on a commercial flight to New York. Reagan was headed to New Haven, invited to visit Yale as a Chubb Fellow.

Murphy and Reagan spent most of the trip seated together. This was their first meeting, and they spent the day chatting like long-lost Irish cousins. Both loved to tell stories and loved to laugh, but when they got serious, their minds ran on parallel tracks. They agreed that Johnson's Great Society ideas were unfeasible, his plans for Vietnam confused, and his SecDef's stewardship a disaster. Even the jealous and protective Nofziger was pleased that I had recruited such talent.

Reagan and Murphy exchanged ideas on what they wanted to articulate at the Economic Club. The merits of a free economy and the evils of state intervention topped the list. Reducing those ideas to compelling rhetoric would be a challenge. The two men parted at the JFK terminal with Murphy promising to return to California right after Christmas.

During the first week of January, Murphy delivered. Reagan revised those words into a masterpiece. We travelled to New York on Wednesday, January 17, checked into the Waldorf, and then proceeded to the ballroom where RR spoke for 20 minutes. His recitation of stunning facts surrounded by amiable humor captivated the crowd. Reagan then answered questions from that most perceptive audience for another quarter hour.

A flood of high-level fan mail followed us back to the governor's office.

George Champion, chairman of Rockefeller's Chase Manhattan Bank, wrote, "You did a superlative job last night ... Tough questions; you handled them well."

With the creation of that speech, RR had established a sound relationship with a first-class, but carefully creative, policy coordinator, a man supremely knowledgeable in national security matters. I had found my nonfiction Hemingway.

I nursed our relationship with a February invitation to Murphy to come meet Reagan's cabinet, to better understand the man and to brainstorm ideas, but beyond that, I was just the travel manager. The Reagan-Murphy link remained dormant until mid-March. Only then did events in Hue, South Vietnam, and Concord, New Hampshire, return our campaign to life.

§§§

Once relieved of campaign management responsibilities during the late summer of '67, after enjoying time with my family as the autumn colors flourished in New England, and when the Drew Pearson flap had blown past, I was able to rejoin the Reagan team as tour manager.

In mid-November, I accompanied RR on the Veterans Day trip to Oregon noted earlier. The real excitement came on the flight home. Travelling in a small, gas-guzzling jet, we needed to refuel halfway between Salem, Oregon and Santa Monica, California. Our pilot selected Redding Municipal Airport for the job. Redding is a farm town at the north end of California's Central Valley. It boasts clear skies, a 7,000-foot runway and attentive refueling service by the FBO.

Unfortunately, there is another 1,800-foot runway nearby. Tews Field's gravel strip is used by glider pilots and private aircraft. It lies a few miles to the west of Redding Muni. Those two runways are parallel. On final approach to Redding, our pilots lined up on the wrong runway. This happens more often than we passengers care to know.

The error only became apparent when our wheels hit the gravel and, apparently, the far end of the runway became all too visible all too soon. Thrust reversers went into overdrive, brakes began to screech, and small rocks hit the side of the cabin. There was no comment from the cockpit; they were busy. But it was obvious to the four passengers that this was not a standard landing.

RR hated flying, perhaps a leftover from his wartime days on the edge of a casualty-stricken Air Corps. He had a "trains only" provision written into his earlier contract with General Electric. Only Reagan's conversion to a political career forced changes in those rules. This unfolding drama in our aircraft's cabin confirmed Nancy's every warning, but RR kept his cool. There were no worried looks, no shouts of alarm, just a studied gaze out the window as the dust and grit rose to obscure the sun. The din seemed endless, but none of us held our breath for very long. We used up our 1,800 feet of runway in less than 15 seconds. At the end of that interlude, the aircraft spun slightly to the left and then came to a stop with one wing hanging over a small gully at the end of the runway.

As the turbines wound down, and as we passengers relaxed our grips on the armrests, a sheepish pilot emerged from the cockpit. He began his apologies as a dust-trailing pickup truck approached our cabin door. The locals had never before seen a jet land at Tews Field. A half-dozen sunburned men and Levi-clad women were quite curious.

"Who are these nuts?" their eyes seemed to ask.

Ronald Reagan rose to the occasion. As the pilot lowered the door, RR stood, straightened his jacket, and smiled to the gawking audience: "Afternoon, folks. I'm your governor. You probably wonder why I called you all here."

None on the ground could believe their eyes, but after some nervous laughter, they offered other, more downscale transportation. The governor went first class, riding in the mud-encrusted right front seat of the pickup after his host moved wrenches and rope aside. The rest of us climbed into the truck bed, welcomed by the owner's dusty sheep dog, a couple of girlfriends, and a bale of hay. We drove to the real Redding Municipal Airport and from there got a proper commercial flight home.

§§§

During the winter that followed, I tended to personal business, but on Sunday, February 11, '68, I travelled to Los Angeles for what my notes describe as a "sham meeting." Bill Clark had asked for a conference with the politicos[84] at RR's residence to discuss press leaks. But once there, Stu Spencer and I, along with Clif White, delivered a more realistic message. We wanted to make clear to RR that we were not actively working on his behalf.

"The votes are not there, Governor."

Helping with travels and conferences? Of course, but soliciting delegates was out of the question.

We adjourned for other chores; I took the family on a long President's Day vacation to Hawaii. My eight-year-old daughter and I rode horses every day along the breathtaking vistas of the Big Island. As the Wisconsin primary filing deadline passed, as George Romney withdrew, and as Nelson Rockefeller entered the presidential race, I was focused on healthy living and birthday parties. But on Sunday, March 3, Bill Clark asked for another meeting at the governor's residence in Sacramento.

Ron and Nancy were there, along with Clark, Nofziger, Clif White, and William French Smith. Clark continued to fuss about information security: who was briefing whom about convention matters? That led White to review Nixon's delegate strength, along with unfolding events in Wisconsin. We reminded RR that since he had *not* signed a withdrawal affidavit, his name *would* be on the Wisconsin ballot.

Reagan was not shocked by this reminder. With further discussion, it became clear he wanted some understanding of the political landscape in the Badger State.

"Some survey work would help," he noted.

Reagan continued to articulate his thoughts in the passive voice. He closed with, "A poll ought to be done." Implicitly, "...by somebody else."

Smith said he would discuss this matter with the Elders.

---

84   Spencer, White, Nofziger, Smith, and me.

CH. 14   A GLOVE THROWN DOWN

March 10, 1968 dawned as just another perfect Sunday in Southern California. By noon the temperature had risen to the low seventies with a soft breeze blowing in from the Pacific. Wisteria entwined the trellis surrounding Ronald Reagan's pool. Bright yellow jonquils smiled through the large windows on the south side of his living room. As the governor sat watching the morning interview shows, he spied the first limo pulling into his constricted driveway. Many more were to follow.

The Los Angeles Elders, Reagan's coterie of contemporaries and financial supporters, had requested a meeting. They wanted to discuss seating, perhaps on the UC Board of Regents, perhaps at the upcoming Republican Convention, or perhaps just at the Coconut Grove. But few came to talk about standing—about RR's standing in the presidential race. Reagan's peers wanted assurance of control. They viewed the governor as an appreciating political asset; few saw him as a near-term presidential candidate; none saw him as a pal.

Some of these men had enduring ties to other presidential contenders, e.g., Richard Nixon or Nelson Rockefeller. Others simply wanted to be "in." They gathered at Ronald Reagan's house on that balmy Sunday to savor Nancy's coffee, to confirm the status quo, and to enjoy the fellowship of their peers.

At LAX, a less complacent Clif White, the Che Guevara of mid-sixties American politics, was emerging from a long aluminum tube.

White had flown in at my request. The New Hampshire primary was two days away. I wanted us to be there, with Reagan, as that state's results rolled in. Reporters would surely raise the subject of New Hampshire with the governor on Wednesday morning.

After our Monday morning coffee, White courageously taxied downtown by himself to face the Elders meeting at the California Club. Bill Smith was there, along with Schreiber, Salvatori, Hume, Dart, and Tuttle's alter ego, Ed Mills. They subjected White to a harangue about RR's continuing presidential publicity, followed by a similarly fruitless tirade aimed at Lyn Nofziger.

"Why is he still there?" Schreiber demanded.

"I don't work in the governor's office," White tried to explain. "I'm a political consultant from New York." White then turned the discussion to his mission. "Ron would like some polling done in Wisconsin."

"Forget it," was the shouted response.

"No more raising political money for Ron," Schreiber added, driving home the message. "Wisconsin is for Cheeseheads; New Hampshire is irrelevant."

Anticipating the Elders' disinterest, White and I had already arranged for our expanding National Reagan Committee to finance RR's requested Wisconsin surveys. When White's California Club interrogation ended, he returned to LAX. We reconnected there for a flight to Fresno. The governor was staying in the heart of the San Joaquin Valley for a planned speaking engagement that evening.

Reagan's name was not on the ballot in New Hampshire, but the tremors within the Democratic Party were rocking the furniture in Washington.

First Lightning

Six weeks earlier, at the end of January, the Viet Cong and the North Vietnamese Army unleashed their Tet Offensive all across South Vietnam. They suffered enormous casualties[85] in the streets of Saigon, the temples of Hue, and a hundred cities and smaller towns all across the country. Despite those losses, the North Vietnamese won a brilliant political victory on America's

---

85   Over a hundred thousand Viet Cong killed, wounded, or missing

TV screens. When the last death squad fled, Lyndon Johnson could no longer belittle Viet Cong military power. His secretary of defense, Robert McNamara, had already left the Pentagon.[86] To most American voters, the war in Vietnam had no guiding strategy, no apparent end.

In November of the previous year, Senator Eugene McCarthy (D - MN) had entered the presidential sweepstakes as a staunch opponent of the war in Vietnam. Few observers credited him with much of a chance—until Tet. But in its aftermath, and with the McNamara resignation an accomplished fact, most pundits suspected that Lyndon Johnson might not be able to hang on.

After RR's speech in Fresno, White and I met with the governor in his farm town motel room. Reagan munched on an apple while I sipped coffee as the first New Hampshire results came in.

"Nixon wins hands down on the Republican side," a young woman reported from a noisy motel ballroom in Concord. An hour later, she gave us the details.

"With all the precincts in, Nixon won 78 percent of his party's vote. Rockefeller got 11 percent." With a smirk she added, "Local enthusiasts wrote in Reagan's name on 362 ballots."

None of this came as a surprise to the three of us in Fresno. It was the Democrat balloting that delivered a bombshell.

An older man, reporting from a subdued newsroom, sounded the tocsin. "Johnson's in real trouble here."

LBJ won only 49 percent of the Democratic vote in New Hampshire. He carried only half of New Hampshire's counties. Peace candidate Eugene McCarthy won 42 percent while carrying the other half of the Granite State's provinces.

With that, McCarthy had become a credible challenger and Johnson was en route to a one-term presidency.

Before heading off to bed, White offered some opinions to our leader.

"Johnson's presidential days are numbered, Ron. We expect a lot of surprises in the weeks ahead. Bobby Kennedy is making

---

86   On February 29, 1968

noises. You better give serious thought to your own presidential prospects."

Reagan's crinkly eyes smiled.

We urged caution in any conversations with the press.

§§§

White left California to return to New York; I travelled to Sacramento where I met with Bill Clark. Reagan's fellow cowboy was quite good at getting inside the governor's head.

"What were you guys smoking down in Fresno?" Clark asked. "Ron came home a different man, Tom. He's got attitude."

We went in to see the governor. I reviewed the details of the voting in New Hampshire along with the explosive, multi-candidate response then underway within the Democratic Party. Our conversation closed with my mention of Reagan's meeting with the Elders on the previous Sunday. Noting their demand for full political control, I reminded RR that I had my hands full with his travel logistics as well as my own business career. I again offered to separate myself completely from his political world and the Elders.

Reagan smiled.

"No," he responded. "Let's withstand the pressure. Why don't you two [Reed and Clark] put together a more practical organization chart?"

What?

"To what purpose?" I asked incredulously.

"Oh, we can discuss that with Bill on Friday. Come on down to L.A. That's the Nebraska filing deadline, isn't it?"

What?

Reagan was calling a council of war. Clark and I were stunned. RR was reasserting control over his own political fate.

On that Friday morning, even before we assembled, Clark called with a "heads up."

"You won!" he blurted out. "Ron is serious."

"Ron said he wants to run," the chief of staff went on, "at least in California, to lead a favorite-son delegation to the convention.

You are to serve as the Republican National Committeeman from California. He wants Smith to tend to delegation logistics, to keep the boys happy, but he wants you and Clif to manage his travels and operate the trailer, the command post in Miami, in pursuit of delegates."

The trailer? The command post? In pursuit of delegates? I thought. *You gotta be kidding.*

"Furthermore," Clark's voice turned solemn, "Ron knows that today is the filing deadline for the Nebraska primary. He was quite explicit about that, Tom."

Clark's speech slowed as he repeated Reagan's words carefully.

"His exact words, Tom: 'I'm in.'"

I'm in? an inner voice shouted out in disbelief. *HOLY MACKEREL!*

Clark was not overjoyed. He viewed all campaigning as a distraction from his management duties in Sacramento, but he welcomed the clarification of roles and missions.

Smith, Clark, and I met with Reagan at his Pacific Palisades home later in the morning. The governor laid it all out, just as Clark knew he would.

"Tom, you run the campaign," Reagan directed before turning to Smith. "Bill, get the boys to the convention, keep 'em happy. Mr. Clark, you run the store. You're doing a great job."

Reagan understood the need to broadcast a decision once made. On that Friday evening in March, Reagan gave his press secretary the "go" order.

"Announce my plans to form a California favorite-son delegation to run on the June primary ballot," Reagan directed. "Announce Reed as my choice for election to the Republican National Committee."

The Ides of March

On a chilly but windless St. Patrick's Day[87] in Washington, a week after the New Hampshire primary, 42-year-old Senator

---

[87]   Sunday, March 17, 1968, five days after the NH primary

Robert F. Kennedy, (D - NY) strode into the US Senate Caucus Room where his brother, John, had announced his presidential ambitions eight years before.

"I am today announcing my candidacy for the presidency of the United States," RFK intoned.

The scribes of Washington were not surprised. They had already written their opening ledes for the evening news and Monday papers.

Reagan watched every broadcast, read each statement, with intense interest.

On Monday morning, Holmes Tuttle called me. In a calm and friendly voice, he extended an invitation. "Tom, can you come down to the desert for dinner tomorrow night?"

The leader of the Elders had talked with Reagan. Both had heard from concerned Republican heavies across the country. Lyndon Johnson's political disintegration and Bobby Kennedy's entry had focused a lot of minds. Visions of another Kennedy-Nixon TV debate haunted the party's leaders. Many felt it was time for a new face.

On Tuesday, March 19, I flew to Palm Springs for a lengthy one-on-one dinner with Tuttle at his winter home. He wanted to establish a solid working relationship.

"Ron has changed," Tuttle noted. "He's got a new outlook."

Reagan spent that third week in March attentive to Robert Kennedy's every word. I know, from later conversations with Clark, that the Kennedy '62 grand jury summons, RFK's apparent closedown of "The General Electric Theater," the embarrassment at the Gridiron Club, and the glorious recovery on *Telstar* were all resonating within Reagan's cavernous mind. He must have imagined Lady Justice standing in the wings, beckoning with her empty scales.

Reagan saw '68 as the final round, a chance for retribution on the grandest stage of all, playing to the biggest audience in the world.

I did not understand these Reagan-Kennedy relationships in mid-March '68. Only now, with the benefit of the Reagan children's recollections, a reading of Eisenhower's concerns, and

Dan Moldea's documentation of the Kennedy investigation into the MCA-SAG link,[88] does Reagan's '68 turnaround make sense.

Six years after Bobby Kennedy's assault on his career, Reagan became fully engaged. On Monday, March 25, the newly aligned Reagan team met with Ron and Nancy at their home in Sacramento. The governor had requested the meeting. Those in attendance: Bill Clark, Clif White, William French Smith, Lyn Nofziger, and I, along with Paul Haerle, the former appointments secretary now returned to the practice of law. He had been assigned the additional duty of managing hotel and command post logistics for the California delegation at the upcoming Miami convention.

When we gathered, there was no earth-shattering announcement from the governor. He simply chatted from his armchair next to the fireplace, speaking about the California primary, now less than three months away, and about the 86 delegates at stake.

"Of course, there needs to be an effort to win those delegates," he said. "Perhaps a few more campaigns elsewhere," he hinted.

It all seemed quite logical.

White responded by reviewing the options now on the table. "If you like, Ron, you can be the fall-back candidate," White explained. "With California's 86 delegates, you'll have 12 percent of the votes needed for nomination. The mountain states surely will give you another three or four dozen. Taken together you might have a quarter of the votes you'd need. You can hold on to those, wait to see what happens, what the other governors do."

"They'll hang loose," Reagan opined. "I know those guys. Besides that, Fate takes funny turns."

"That's true," White responded. "On the other hand, we can begin to move the ball forward. That will produce a lot of squawks from your pal George Murphy, and from your lieutenant governor."

"Taft won't like it, either," Reagan laughed.

White closed with a warning. "Dick Nixon has a lot of friends all over this town, Ron, and he doesn't play nice."

I then took the floor to make sure the governor and his wife understood how their lives might change if he chose to proceed with a serious campaign.

---

88   Sunday, March 17, 1968, five days after the NH primary

Reagan's response to our admonishments was prompt and unequivocal: "Forward, Clif. Forward."

Forward? I thought. *That's a pretty clear Reagan order. That's a decision.*

Turning to the others present, the governor continued, "I want Tom Reed and Clif White to take charge."

The words rolled out quietly, but in articulating them, Reagan was sending word to the Elders, via Smith, that there had been a change of command.

In the face of a possible Kennedy restoration, Reagan was now fully attentive to his campaign. We had blown our chances with the Republican leaders of Illinois, Texas, and South Carolina, but the prospect of a Kennedy-Nixon rerun gave us access to the party rank and file; the hundreds of delegates whose names, as down-ticket candidates, would also be on the November ballot with the Republican nominee. Those men and women remembered the disasters of the early sixties, and they wanted to win in '68.

Ron and Nancy agreed to an escalated travel schedule, to the showing of our TV biopic in the target states, and to the re-enlistment of Charlie Murphy to the speech-writing team.

§§§

On Sunday, March 31, at the end of a lengthy presidential television address discussing the war in Vietnam, Lyndon Johnson seized the nation's attention. "I shall not seek, and I will not accept, the nomination of my party for another term as your president," he said.

Within minutes, the students in Berkeley poured out of their dorms and apartments, cheering and honking horns as if it were New Year's Eve. Many of us in the Reagan camp felt the same euphoric joy.

In reality, Johnson had little choice. According to our surveys, LBJ was headed for a 2:1 loss to Senator McCarthy in the upcoming Wisconsin primary, now two days away. The presidential contest in America had changed overnight. Ronald Reagan knew that, and he was fully engaged.

Ch. 15   A Campaign Returns to Life

Monday, April 1, 1968 started as a cold and foggy morning in San Francisco. I sat sipping coffee in my airline club, peering out at my delayed and rain-washed 707, when an odd perspective began to unfold.

Today is April Fool's Day! Who is kidding whom here?

My thoughts meandered from one would-be president to another.

Does Richard Nixon, that surly and sweating loser, think he can stand up to the TV power of the Great Communicator? If Nixon wins the Republican nomination, does he truly believe he can outshine a Kennedy in another debate? I don't think so.

My ruminations then turned to our own campaign.

Does Ronald Reagan really believe he can outwit Tricky Dick? Can we, Ron's quite inexperienced supporters, out-solicit Richard Nixon in the retail marketplace for delegates?

I was coming to better appreciate Nixon's web of relationships.

If nominated, is RR ready to play in the major leagues? And if Ron wins the presidency, what are we, a bunch of total neophytes, going to do about Vietnam?

With that sobering prospect, my mind turned to the other side of the street.

Maybe Bobby Kennedy is the best candidate for April Fool. Does he truly believe he can dance away from his family's complicity in the murder of South Vietnam's president? Does he think he can distance himself from their subsequent plunge into Vietnam's civil war? In the near term, does Bobby Kennedy really think he can steal the anti-war banner from Eugene McCarthy's hands? If he wins the presidency, what is Kennedy's agenda? He is not a soft and cuddly politician.

As the fog continued to roll across the airport, clouds also spanned my own mind.

Why am I here?

My agenda had been to see the end of Lyndon Johnson's and Robert McNamara's political careers.

Hasn't that been done? I asked myself.

McNamara had already left the Pentagon, sequestered at the World Bank where he could do little further damage. Johnson had removed himself from the world stage during the evening just passed. Or had he?

The papers on the club's reading table offered a discomforting headline.

"Nixon is Shaded Two Points by LBJ." The story reported on a Harris Survey just completed giving Johnson a 41 percent to 39 percent national lead over Nixon. A month before, at the beginning of March, those numbers showed the two contenders in a 39 percent dead heat.

Nixon can't even out-poll a war-bungling, now-withdrawn incumbent, my inner voice warned.

During the week that followed, a Los Angeles Times headline read: "LBJ Has a Chance." Their columnist, Bill Henry, went on to write, "Those who thought [LBJ] had been relegated to the shelf, to be just a lame-duck onlooker for the rest of the year ... have found that, instead, he is the Man of the Hour." Henry suggested that a Paris settlement of the Vietnam conflict could spin Johnson's fortunes on a dime.

With a year to go, LBJ can still do great harm, I thought. Like Frankenstein's monster, a jolt of lightning running from Hanoi to Paris could restore Johnson's political life.

I had grown tired of all the Reagan ambiguity, the on-again, off-again and now on-again campaign. I had taken too much browbeating from the Elders, men who had created, then hidden from, the Battaglia problem. I had spent too few days at home preparing for a new addition to the family.

But as my thoughts wandered, LBJ's face appeared on the club's TV screen. He was offering more explanations about Vietnam.

Don't let Johnson change his mind, I had to conclude. *This is not the time to quit.*

My flight to Atlanta was called. I gathered my belongings and exited the club.

§§§

As I settled into my welcoming airline seat, I jotted down the week's to-do list. First of all, exploit whatever comes out of the Wisconsin primary tomorrow. Then pay attention to Nebraska. But how?

Next, line up the spokesmen needed for some good TV spots. That was one of the reasons for my travel to Florida. We had to win the Oregon primary, now only eight weeks away, and I doubted Reagan would campaign there. We would have to win that one over the airwaves. We needed some good testimonials telling viewers what a great job RR has done, how he is an overpowering winner.

With the glories of the Yosemite Valley clearly visible out the window of our climbing aircraft, I turned my thoughts to the non-primary states. As a starter, we needed to connect with the Republican governors in the industrial northeast, such as Ohio, Michigan, and Pennsylvania.

Just like Ron in California, I thought, those governors will want to keep control of their delegations. They'll all be favorite-son candidates. Those men are not driven by ideology; they seek leverage, the prerequisite to power. Those governors are not likely to cede their delegates to Nixon if they can help it. We've got to connect with them.

As our plane leveled off, my mind returned to the Republican Barons.

We have to keep Barry Goldwater neutral. We gotta reassemble the fragments left behind in Texas and the Thurmond South.

My mind wandered as I considered these perhaps insoluble challenges. A welcome sleep ensued.

Florida

Upon arriving in the Sunshine State, my first item of business was meeting with Ralph Cordiner. That widely respected former head of the General Electric Company had retired to Florida in 1963. He had been RR's mentor within that company, and I wanted him to do a one-minute TV cameo for a Reagan biography show now in the works. I hoped Cordiner would attest to RR's understanding of real-world economics.

Cordiner remembered our earlier hunting lodge conversations, and he was most willing to help. We taped his endorsement later in the week. It added great authenticity to the Reagan biopic.

The next item of Florida business was to negotiate with Bill Murfin, chairman of that state's Republican Party. He wanted Reagan to do some fundraisers in Florida.

My question, "Who gets Florida's votes when we get to Miami?"

We targeted mid-May for a Reagan speech in New Orleans, to be followed by a meeting with the Southern Republican chairmen in that city. I hoped to skim off a few of their delegates, those with emotional ties to RR and those focused on winning, despite Thurmond-apparent support for Nixon. We agreed to close the May tour with the fundraising appearances in Florida that Murfin wanted.

Those Southern chairmen were a diverse and wily lot. Mississippi's leader, Clarke Reed, wanted to meet with RR, but he was a walking catfish. In the months and years to come, evasion and duplicity would become his stock in trade. He delivered his delegates, and thus the nomination, to Nixon in '68 and Ford in '76.

Alabama's chairman, Alfred Goldthwaite, was made of sturdier stuff. I had connected with Goldthwaite when in Louisville during October of '67. At that early date, he unequivocally pledged his and much of his delegation's support to RR. In later conversations, he offered to yield Alabama's alphabetical priority to California when the roll call started in Miami. That would let us place Reagan's name in nomination first. When followed by the voting of California's 86 delegates, that would give us early momentum. Such tactics were important at conventions in those days.

When the roll call actually came, Nixon did not win the nomination until the convention clerk called out "Wisconsin." Goldthwaite remained a reliable ally through the final count, even though Nixon pried away 14 of his 26 delegates. Al Goldthwaite was a remarkable friend in that fluid world of presidential politics.

Harry Dent was the South Carolina chairman. He and I were in regular contact. His attendance at a May meeting in New Orleans was assured, though he was Thurmond's man. It would be hard to peel away any South Carolina delegates. We never did, but Dent remained a close friend.

I returned to California that evening.

Wisconsin

Tuesday, April 2, was primary day in Wisconsin. Reagan's name would be on the ballot, but Nixon was sure to win. Our focus was on the Democratic results.

Reagan and I watched the election returns from our respective homes, but at an early hour, California time, we were on the phone with each other in a celebratory mode.

"You got 11 percent in Wisconsin, Ron, with absolutely no campaign. Yes, Nixon got 80 percent," I continued, "but you just replaced Rockefeller as Number Two."

Reagan laughed. "That's progress?"

My rejoinder: "Wisconsin is only the first step."

In conversations with White and Spencer the following day, we settled on a set of objectives: double the vote with every succeeding opt-out primary. Get 22 percent in Nebraska and at least 44 percent in Oregon. We might even win up there in California's neighboring state to the north. That would blow the game wide open. We did not understand Oregon's provincial mindset.

On the Democratic side, April 2 was a downer. The already-withdrawn Johnson got only 35 percent of his party's vote in Wisconsin, but it was even worse for Bobby Kennedy. He collected only 6 percent. The big winner, with 56 percent, was peace candidate Eugene McCarthy. He was a Wisconsin neighbor, the US senator from Minnesota with a constituency similar to Wisconsin's, but his success was due to a broader surge. McCarthy was connecting with the anti-war base across the country. His win made it clear that RFK would not have a free ride to the nomination.

Washington, DC

Two days later, on Thursday, April 4, the Reagans and I met with members of the governor's staff at SFO for a commercial flight to Washington. The purpose of our trip was to meet with Republican leaders in the House of Representatives, to deliver a major address to the Women's National Press Club, and then to recruit speechwriter Charles J.V. Murphy back onto the campaign team. We planned to return to California on Saturday, but we had chosen an ill-fated day to begin our tour.

A grim-faced Ed Gillenwaters met us as we deplaned. "Martin Luther King, Jr. was just shot, Governor. He's dead," announced Gillenwaters.

"Where? How?" Reagan demanded.

"In Memphis, about an hour ago. Nobody knows the identity of the shooter. DC is a restless place."

The angry crowds we saw through our car windows en route back into town confirmed that view. We shared those people's grief, if not their turn to violence. As we settled into our hotel rooms, we spoke at length about how far the country had come in some respects, but also that the road ahead appeared cloudy.

On the morning of April 5, with the city of Washington disintegrating outside our hotel windows, I turned my attention to hosting Charlie Murphy at a working breakfast in the privacy of my room.

RR could no longer deliver one-liners with a rerun of the California story. The would-be president from Hollywood needed to articulate his views on the evils now gripping and ripping the entire country: Vietnam, inflation, civil disturbances, national economic priorities, and neglected defense planning. These were

Kennedy-Johnson chickens coming home to roost. Bobby Kennedy would surely recover from Wisconsin. He must not be allowed to run as an outsider.

Reagan already had well-thought-through views on the problems facing his country. The challenge in the spring of '68 was to articulate his solutions in a credible fashion. Charlie Murphy had done well in preparing RR for the Veterans Day speech in Oregon and then the Economic Club performance in New York. To me, he was the man for this now-bigger job. I made the re-enlistment pitch over a somber room-service meal at the Madison.

"Time to get back to work," I started off. "Johnson may be gone, but Bobby Kennedy is moving front and center. He'd be even worse."

Murphy's jaw tightened around his toast when I mentioned the words "Bobby Kennedy." He was horrified by the prospect of RFK moving into the presidency. Murphy was eager to rejoin the Reagan team.

After I summarized RR's planned performances during May, we settled on topics for each. Murphy agreed to work on drafts in his Washington office during the coming month. He would then come to California in early May to finish up. Our opening presentation was set for a governors' conference in Honolulu on May 11. That would be the right place for RR to spell out his views on Vietnam, since that war was nominally being run from the Pacific Command Headquarters at Pearl Harbor. We intended to tie that unfolding tragedy to Bobby Kennedy's coattails.

"Here's my address, Charlie. Here's my telex number. Let's see some production every week." I rolled out those words in my most imperious, youthful voice, followed by, "See you in a month."

The door to my room opened. Art Van Court had readied our transportation to Capitol Hill amidst the fires spreading throughout the city.

We met with a concerned Congressman Glenn Lipscomb (R - CA), who pledged his support for whatever course of action RR wished to pursue with the California delegation. We then moved on to the Women's Press Club. The governor did his usual good job in speaking about his fiscal achievements in Sacramento, but it was still a California-boosting lecture, an updated version of his talk to the Economic Club in New York two months before. As there were few links to national issues, the audience's thoughts lay elsewhere.

By late in the afternoon of April 5, vandalism and rioting were being layered onto the glowing embers of downtown Washington. All agreed that the governor's place was at his desk in Sacramento and in the streets of Los Angeles, assuaging the grief sweeping California's cities. We drove to Washington National, inching through "surging looters," as my journal noted. Van Court had found us seats on a one-stop 8:00 p.m. flight to Los Angeles.

En route home we talked about Martin Luther King, Jr.'s contributions to history, about events unfolding in DC, and about Lyndon Johnson's withdrawal from the presidential race. With an unsmiling countenance, RR was sadly clinical as he analyzed the forces now running wild within the country.

A Return to the West

I next met with Reagan in Los Angeles in mid-April upon his return from Easter week with family in Phoenix. While there, the Reagans had dined with the Goldwaters. RR filled me in.

"*Unity now* was the theme, Tom. Barry wants me to stop campaigning, to second Nixon's nomination as the roll call begins in Miami, and then to throw California's 86 delegates to Dick at the first opportunity. Reagan's face was drawn as he reported on his discouraging conversation with America's conservative pioneer. "I didn't commit us to anything, Tom," he said finally.

No chance of getting Goldwater to remain neutral, I thought.

At a press conference a few days later, RR responded to questions about his candidacy with an upbeat, "I wouldn't turn my back on a draft."

Later in the week, RR gave an informal talk at Oakland's Jack London Square. We arranged that venue to tape the eight minutes needed for our final Nebraska and Oregon TV spots. On April 24, I shipped a set of those commercials, along with five copies of our full half-hour Reagan documentary, to our people in Omaha and Portland.[89]

In Nixon's *Memoirs*, the '68 candidate describes that Reagan biopic as, "a very effective half-hour documentary." Unfortunately, for us, it also inspired Nixon to expand his campaign in Oregon.

"Unlike Reagan and Rockefeller, I went there to campaign," Nixon later wrote.

That decision may have been reinforced by Nixon's understanding of our Oregon-focused campaign strategy, accessed via his plant in Clif White's entourage.

At the end of April we flew to Boulder, Colorado, to overnight with beermeister Joe Coors, by then a primary member of my national Draft Reagan finance team. Coors was also a popularly elected Regent of the University of Colorado.

Reagan spoke to a standing-room-only crowd in the university's student auditorium. The young folks on hand welcomed RR's remarks about the unfocused war in Vietnam and the profligacy of big government. There were repeated applause interruptions followed by a standing ovation at the conclusion of his talk. At the time, Boulder was Berkeley's political antipode.

That evening we flew home in our chartered mini-jet to prepare for a full month of policy-oriented speeches that would spell out Reagan's vision for a transition from the war-torn sixties to a sunnier seventies to come. Those talks, coupled with our quiet campaign activity designed to avoid political stresses within California, were intended to reach fruition in the Oregon primary on May 28.

Three days after our return to California, on Tuesday, April 30, the voters of Massachusetts headed to their respective party polling places. Governor John Volpe's name was the only one on the Republican ballot, but surprisingly, Nelson Rockefeller had organized a well-orchestrated coup. He won that primary with 32,000 write-in votes, thus pocketing all 34 Massachusetts delegates. That was an extraordinary achievement. It also alerted the political world that the race was still on.

---

89   To view the Reagan Biopic, see Appendix A or go to <reagan68.com>.

On the following weekend, Charlie Murphy arrived in San Francisco to begin a week of serious writing. As Murphy's editor, one of my jobs was to keep him connected to Reagan. That was easy. Those men were contemporaries. They loved to have a drink and tell stories, perhaps a harbinger of RR's relationship with House Speaker Tip O'Neill a dozen years later. My challenge was to focus Murphy's work on the topics set for each appearance, then to enforce the deadlines.

The Murphy-Reed drafts provided the structure and the accurate recitations of history needed for our planned appearances. Reagan's writing and performance skills provided the polish. Our resulting May presentations met with repeated media acclaim.

The Visions Emerge

Reagan delivered the first of these papers at the opening of the Western Governors Conference in Honolulu on May 11. Entitled "The History and Significance of the US Role in the Pacific," the talk included a discussion of the war in Vietnam, of Johnson's mismanagement of that war, and of the Kennedy clan's role in establishing the policies that had drawn us into Vietnam.

Not stated, but evident to practiced observers, was the source of Reagan's "strike hard if negotiations fail" policy. It originated in his conversations with Dwight Eisenhower during the year past.

The key sentence in the Honolulu talk: "Nearly all the so-called Johnson policies, so violently attacked by some Democrats today, stem directly from the very policies which were developed by the late President Kennedy when some of these same critics [meaning RFK] were close to his side."

The response by the governors, their families, and their attending staffs, was impressive, but that was not the target audience. We wanted to speak to the nation, to Republican candidates and delegates across the country, and specifically to Republican voters in Nebraska and Oregon. We hoped the wire services would serve as our pipeline. They did so most effectively.

The Associated Press produced a 16-column-inch report under the headline, "Reagan Calls for Full Effort if [Paris] Talks Fail."

The opening paragraph: "Gov. Reagan called on the United States to use whatever power and technology we have at our command to end the Vietnam War if negotiations fail." The AP then went on to quote John Kennedy's inaugural pledge to "pay any price, bear any burden to make sure what we stand for will endure," followed by Reagan's scorn for "those who inherited the power, but who no longer hear that trumpet, nor recognize its grand notes."

United Press International covered the speech a little differently, with a headline directly referring to the negotiations in Paris: "Don't Bargain Margin Away, Reagan Warns."

UPI reported, "[Reagan] hit hard on a theme that the Democratic Administration had failed miserably in its conduct of the Vietnam War—and that Sen. Robert F. Kennedy (D - NY) was part of the administration which drafted the policies."

We were pleased by the specificity of that article.

Reports on the Honolulu talk spread across the nation as we had hoped. Subsequent editorials in the California papers noted "something new in the air."

The Nebraska primary followed, three days later, on May 14.

Two months before, Reagan had received 362 write-in votes in New Hampshire's primary, an election he had not entered and did not contest. In Wisconsin, where RR's name was on the ballot, he had garnered an unexpected 11 percent of the vote. Our goal was to double that in Nebraska, and we did. Reagan seldom visited the Cornhusker State, but during his Des Moines sportscaster days, he had connected with those people. On May 14, he collected 22 percent of the Nebraska Republican vote. At least we were on track.

But so was Robert Kennedy. He won the Nebraska Democratic primary with 52 percent of his party's vote to Eugene McCarthy's 31 percent. With Kennedy taking his party's lead, RR savored the prospect of an autumn encounter. He no longer had to be coaxed to his waiting campaign limos.

Reagan delivered his second Murphy-Reed talk to a luncheon meeting of the National Newspaper Association, gathered in San Francisco on May 18. This one was entitled "Rising Expectations and the Tinderbox." It opened with a favorable accolade to the print media.

"Newspaper publishers deal in the printed word, and that word gave men hope. Where before there was darkness, the words that issued from Gutenberg's printing press lit up the renaissance and illuminated the aspirations of men. Print allowed thought to be separated from action, and it gave birth to rationality and logic. It allowed men to inspire—but also to conspire."

Reagan then proceeded to his theme: "Civilization cannot afford demagogues in this era of rising expectations."

The *Los Angeles Times* gave political editor Carl Greenberg 20 column inches to tell this story in their Sunday edition. The headline: "Reagan Says Nation is Totally Out of Control; Sharply Attacks Johnson, Kennedy in Speech to Newspaper Group."

Greenberg went on to quote the governor: "[Civil society] cannot afford prophets who shout that the road to the Promised Land lies over the shards of burned and looted cities."

The reference was to an RFK statement, "There is no need to tell the Negroes to obey the law."

We viewed the National Newspaper Association as the ideal conduit to the breakfast tables of every convention delegate, and it was. The Greenberg article was syndicated nationwide.

Murphy's colleague at *Fortune*, Max Ways, picked up the theme with an article entitled, "The Dynamite in Rising Expectations."

On Sunday, May 19, our travels took on all the trappings of a full campaign. RR, his communications director, security aide, tour managers, and policy staff joined 40 members of the press corps aboard a chartered 727 jet. There could be no doubt we were seriously pursuing the presidency.

This entourage flew to New Orleans, where RR delivered his third Murphy-Reed paper to a gymnasium full of enthusiastic Tulane students. The talk was entitled "National Priorities and the Negotiations in Paris." RR discussed the need for hard choices between guns and butter, since trying to have both was fueling a growing inflation. "No one in the federal government seems to be in charge of these national priorities," he pointed out.

Carl Greenberg of the *Los Angeles Times*, now travelling with us aboard our 727, was given a full page in the Monday edition of the *Times* to report, "the governor received a tumultuous ovation from 3,000 persons at Tulane University."

Greenberg quoted Reagan's comments on "storm trooper tactics" being used by "students and radical faculty members who are employing college and university campuses as staging areas for revolt and rebellion." The crowd at Tulane seemed to agree with that view.

In reporting on that same appearance, *The Washington Post* turned to scare tactics. "Reagan invoked Dwight Eisenhower's name to justify a threat to invade North Vietnam if peace talks fail," they accurately wrote. Reagan had discussed Vietnam with Eisenhower when visiting the former president in Gettysburg and Palm Desert. Speechwriter Murphy was a longer-term acquaintance of the retired general.

That evening, we moved on to Antoine's Restaurant in New Orleans for dinner with the Southern states' Republican chairmen.[90] The Big Easy knows how to entertain; Antoine's has been welcoming guests for more than a century. RR was escorted into that landmark via a side door. Once inside, he was warmly welcomed and well fed, surrounded by enthusiastic fans, if not committed allies. Pointedly, no one ordered the Oysters Rockefeller. The assembled Southerners were pleased to read from the menu that Antoine Alciatore, a refugee from New York City seeking a better life down south, had founded the restaurant 125 years before.

It was a late evening with a lot of conversation, though not much hard bargaining. These men were Reagan fans, but they also wanted to win in November, and they dreaded a Rockefeller recapture of the party. Many had long been entangled in the Nixon web of favors and promises.

---

90   Mel Owen was the advance man for this event and thus the source for these dinnertime observations.

On Monday, May 21, we flew to Charlotte to help Congressman Jim Gardner raise money for his gubernatorial race. He hoped to become North Carolina's first Republican governor since Reconstruction, and he had been RR's most prominent supporter in our search for delegates. We had asked Gardner to place Reagan's name in nomination at the Miami convention.

We then flew to Tampa, where Reagan delivered a Murphy-Reed talk on "Atlantic and Caribbean Foreign Policy." He tracked John Kennedy's actions from the Bay of Pigs (April '61) to Vienna (June '61) to the Soviet violation of the nuclear testing moratorium (September '61) on through the Berlin crises and a return to Cuba in '62.

Reagan's point about the island nation was that there had been adequate warning of the Soviet missile build-up during the summer of '62. His speech spelled out the CIA informant's name,[91] his Paris connection, and the details of his report to CIA Director John McCone during the summer of 1962.[92] Reagan then decried the fact that only when U-2s brought home photographic proof, a few weeks before the mid-term elections, did the Kennedys act.

Greenberg of the *L.A. Times*, by now the tour's syndicated scribe, wrote "Reagan scoffed at those in Washington who made a fetish of complexity. His barbs were aimed in large measure at the New Frontier's 'technipols' ... saving some of his sharpest barbs for Sen. Robert F. Kennedy now contending for the Democratic presidential nomination."

Surprise?

The closing policy speech, "Defense Preparedness," Reagan delivered in Cleveland on May 22 in the aftermath of a governors' conference in Columbus where we assiduously courted Ohio's Governor Jim Rhodes. This was a critical time, with the Oregon primary less than a week away.

Reagan's "Defense Preparedness" speech drew heavily on my experience in the US ballistic missile program and on Murphy's close ties to the postwar Air Force chiefs of staff. It criticized the phoniness of John Kennedy's 1960 "Missile Gap" claim, the US

---

91   Phillipe Thyraud de Vosjoli, a friend of Charlie Murphy's
92   Confirming correspondence available in the Kennedy Library archives

incompetence reflected in North Korea's January '68 seizure of the *USS Pueblo*,[93] and the mismanagement of the war in Vietnam. Reagan then moved on to broader issues, comparing the military cancellations and cutbacks of the Kennedy-Johnson years, all overseen by Robert McNamara, to the technological flowering of the Eisenhower era.

In lines that set the stage for Reagan's actual presidency a decade later, the talk closed with an ominous warning about the Soviets' imminent achievement of nuclear parity. RR foresaw such a "correlation of forces" as soon casting a threatening shadow across the US and Western Europe.

The Cleveland *Plain Dealer* headlined its coverage: "JFK's Missile Gap Now Exists—Reagan." The story that followed quoted from Reagan's speech. "The Kennedy-Johnson-Humphrey administration has increased defense spending at the rate of $75 billion a year, and all it has to show for it is the longest and first wholly inconclusive war in the history of the United States and a political airplane, the TFX, that won't fly."

§§§

With those pieces in place, I flew home to northern California—just in time. Two days later, on May 24, at 11:00 p.m., my second son, third child, was born at Marin General Hospital. Eleven pounds, nine ounces! Mother seemed unfazed; new son appeared happy and healthy. I set about entertaining (distracting) the older kids while Grandma prepared the house for its new occupant.

The Oregon primary was two days away. A Reagan victory there would discredit Nixon, reminding every delegate of the VP's losing track record. An Oregon success for RR in the wake of Wisconsin and Nebraska, followed by an impending victory in California, would give us the momentum we needed to take the lead. Reagan's fate was now in the hands of the Republican voters up north.

---

93   The *Pueblo* was a US Navy SIGINT collection ship cruising in international waters, but boarded and captured by North Korean forces on 23 January 1968, a week before the Tet Offensive began. In mid-May, when Reagan's talk was given, the *Pueblo* and her crew were still in captivity, being tortured. They were released 23 Dec '68.

Ch. 16   History's Furnace

O n Tuesday afternoon, I stopped only for party supplies. The Reagan '68 team was gathering in our San Francisco office, awaiting the returns from Oregon.

We settled onto shopworn wooden chairs inherited from other campaigns, popped our beers, and poured our coffee. Champagne waited in the fridge. Bags of chips replaced the dinners we had foregone while assembling for this key evening. Street sounds from seven floors below coursed in through an open and soot-encrusted window frame. Those distractions, along with friendly chatter, filled our space until, a little after seven in the evening, we clicked on the network news.

"This just in. Exit polls from Oregon indicate an easy win for Richard Nixon in that state's Republican primary ... Now leading with two-thirds of the Republican vote."

Wham!

"Not so good for Bobby Kennedy," the talking head went on. "Peace candidate Gene McCarthy seems set to win the Democratic balloting."

Wow!

A deathly silence filled the room. The faces of the youngsters and old pros gathered around me all turned to stone. They resembled the façades on Easter Island.

A young advance man broke the hush. "Maybe Bobby and Ron are *both* finished," he started. "Maybe the voters just want some peace and quiet. Maybe they want a muted contest between tired old vice presidents."

We sighed.

Could be, I thought. *That kid may be right.*

I began calling our people up north. They were as distressed as we, but they were less surprised.

The paid staffer making coffee in our eerily quiet Salem headquarters delivered his verdict. "Oregon is a pretty liberal state, Mr. Reed. The other guys hung the ultra-conservative label on us. That tag outweighed our attempted 'winner' image."

Our state chairman picked up to add a different dimension. "Nixon out-organized us, Tom. His chairman, conservative icon Howell Appling,[94] was the key."

When I called our campus organizer in Eugene, she put the story more bluntly. "Nixon recruited all the heavy Republican hitters, Mr. Reed. Serious Republicans in Oregon were dismissing Reagan as a spoiler."

An older member of the finance committee, reached in Portland, gave us the historical perspective. "Reagan was a no-show," he said. "Rocky won this primary in '64 with the slogan, 'He cared enough to come.' Years ago, Oregonians adopted a 'must opt-out' primary law to get attention. Our folks were not going to support a candidate who didn't come here, who didn't ask for their votes." He closed with attempts at consolation. "Maybe with Kennedy losing to McCarthy, we got rid of Bobby for you, too."

Exhaling slowly, I expressed my thanks.

We don't need to call our governor, at least not tonight, I thought.

"He's got a TV set," one staffer confirmed.

Another staffer suggested caution. "Let's get the facts, wait for the hard numbers. Let's get a clearer picture of what happened to Bobby."

With that, we turned out the lights, headed for the elevators, and drove to our homes. The stale chips and champagne were left for the janitor.

---

94   Appling was Oregon's secretary of state in 1960. He did not seek reelection in '64, instead assuming leadership of the Goldwater campaign in Oregon. That was a hopeless cause, but it became a confirming conservative credential four years later. If Appling, Mr. Conservative, was supporting Richard Nixon, many concluded RR must be too extreme.

§§§

On Wednesday morning, I travelled to Sacramento to meet with the governor, along with Nofziger and Clark, to prepare for the press conference to come. As it unfolded, RR was suitably bland, reminding the press that he had not campaigned in Oregon.

"So what's the question?" he asked.

After that, the four of us met in the governor's office for a more wide-ranging discussion. Clark and I believed Reagan's campaign was dead in the water. Spencer and White, consulted earlier by phone, agreed.

"It's been a bad night for a lot of people," I said, reciting the obvious. "We didn't do any better up there than we did in Nebraska. Here's the good news, Governor. Rocky is dead, too. His vote was in the single digits. When I talked to Stu this morning, he called it, 'A Rocky horror show.'" I concluded with a verdict. "We think it's over, Ron."

The governor sat impassively. He provided no clues to his thoughts as he surveyed Capitol Park through the green-tinged windows.

Seeking some response, or perhaps trying to brighten his day, I turned my discourse to Bobby Kennedy. "Kennedy needed a win up there, Ron, but he didn't get one either. For the Dems, Oregon is a liberal, anti-war state," I pointed out. "That's where Bobby had to beat McCarthy if he was to take control of the Democrat 'peace faction,' but he couldn't cut it. He lost, 38-44 percent. You know that."

Our governor turned from the windows. An aggrieved scowl crossed his face. "Too bad" were his only words.

Reagan's chances of a grand shootout with RFK were slipping away.

"Bobby may be on the ropes," I continued. "If he's to stay alive, he's got to win big in California next week."

How ominous those words would turn out to be.

My mention of California's impending vote enlivened the governor's demeanor, so I turned to the details of our upcoming primary, now six days away. "Kennedy and McCarthy are going to have their definitive face-off right here, Ron," I said. "As you know, you'll be unopposed on the Republican ticket, but even so, you'd better pay attention."

I reminded RR of another incumbent Republican governor, his friend John Volpe of Massachusetts, who had run unopposed in his own primary a month before, only to be beaten by a Rockefeller write-in campaign.

"Not likely here, but you'd better pay attention, Governor. Get out there and campaign anyway," I warned.

"OK," was Reagan's laconic response.

§§§

At the end of the week, Bill Clark held a more thoughtful one-on-one conversation with Reagan at his home in Sacramento. Clark was the closest thing RR had to a true friend. They were fellow trail-riders, men with few out-of-bounds areas between them.

In reacting to the Oregon defeat and with a few nights' good sleep, Reagan displayed the same placid inner compass that the world saw after his shooting a decade later.

"Fate takes a hand in these things," the governor told Clark. "Maybe 1968 wasn't the year. Perhaps it'll be '72. Oregon was OK. The people there just weren't ready for me."[95]

RR then shifted gears. In one breath, Reagan reverted to his unyielding competitive side. "But let's stick with our Miami plans, Bill. No declaration of candidacy, but let's keep collecting delegates."

Clark was not surprised.

"You never know," the governor shrugged as Clark rose to leave.

Richard Nixon held a more productive discussion over that weekend. On May 31, armed with an unbroken string of primary victories, Nixon flew to Atlanta to meet with Senator Strom Thurmond. Those two veteran poker players put their cards on the

---

95   In 1976, Reagan lost the Oregon primary to Gerald Ford. Reagan carried the Oregon primary easily in '80 to defeat George H.W. Bush

table, one by one. They opened with national security concerns; they closed with textile tariffs. There was no bluffing. As Nixon put it succinctly in his memoir, "I emerged from this meeting with Thurmond's pledge of support."

The California Primary

I took the bus to Sacramento in the late afternoon of June 4. The polls closed at 8:00 p.m. Kennedy moved to an early, though not crushing lead in the Democratic primary. When all the votes were counted, Kennedy beat McCarthy, 46-42 percent. More than two million Republicans voted in their primary, but a quarter of them did not endorse Reagan's candidacy for president. Kennedy did better in South Dakota that same evening, winning 50 percent to McCarthy's 20 percent.[96] By late evening, RFK seemed to have recovered his momentum.

I returned to my usual overnight lodgings at the Senator Hotel. Once settled into the bar, I expected a pleasant evening of post-election chatter with lobbyists and legislators, but a little after midnight, party Vice Chairman Dennis Carpenter burst in.

"Kennedy's been shot!"

Wham!

In the early hours of Wednesday, June 5, the young senator from New York was rushed to Good Samaritan Hospital in Los Angeles. Reagan's security staff soon arrived to offer every assistance.

"Get out," the Kennedy people ordered. "We don't need Reagan's help."

June

Robert F. Kennedy was pronounced dead in the early morning hours of June 6. With that, and with the primary election over, the scales of political fortune in California again began to sway.

Nancy Reagan's fears of political violence blossomed; the Los Angeles Elders regained their voice. With the California vote

---

96   LBJ, still on the ballot in South Dakota, got 30 percent.

over, some of those men turned their attention to convention perks. Others were responding to demands from their clandestine patrons. Nixon, and to a lesser degree Rockefeller, wanted assurances from their men in California. Both were seeking first-ballot California votes on the convention floor if Reagan *really* pursued the nomination.

Nixon knew he *must* win on that first ballot. He had to close the deal before the Thurmond-controlled delegates began to vote their hearts rather than their pledges. If Nixon fell short, he would need a few dozen votes pirated from the California delegation to put him over the top.

At the same time, Rockefeller knew that a first-ballot Nixon victory would foreclose all hope for a brokered convention that *might* turn to him.

Reagan had already told Clark of his intentions. "Let's stick with our Miami plans," he said.

But Kennedy's death led to a Reagan decompression. His enthusiasm was waning.

Will Ron hang in there? I was not sure.

On June 9, the first Sunday after the primary, the Los Angeles Elders showed up at the Reagan residence for an outbreak of open civil war. They met with the governor and Bill Clark (but not me) for three and a half hours.[97]

William French Smith had requested a gathering to discuss his budget for upcoming convention activities, but the discussion soon flew out of control. Much of the afternoon was spent in a shouting match between Henry Salvatori, demanding Reagan's immediate announcement of candidacy, and Taft Schreiber, urging negotiations with Nelson Rockefeller. Nixon supporters on the sidelines added verbal fuel to the fire.

In the process, Schreiber attacked Henry Bubb's Draft Reagan Committee in Topeka and then Lyn Nofziger's continued presence in the governor's office. It was a true free-for-all, according to Clark.

---

97   My understanding of these June 9 discussions came from Clark, who called to give me a report soon after the meeting ended.

Salvatori and Schreiber were both world-class shouters; I was sorry to have missed the fireworks. Later in the afternoon, Justin Dart apparently joined in, saying he would not raise any money for convention activities until he knew if RR was in or out of the race. Others in the room shared that caveat.

The melee ended with Reagan's usual vague instructions to Smith. He was to call Clif White and ask him to "do something."

The good news: with my now-limited goals and extended financial network, covering our delegate-tracking expenses was not a problem. Our national Draft Reagan finance committee had matured into a major force, now ready and willing to pay for command post and communications costs in Miami. Only delegation perks remained for the Elders to fund.

By the middle of June '68, Ronald Reagan's political machine appeared to be in meltdown mode. Kennedy was gone; Reagan's personal fires were banked. Nixon had the momentum. Although we did not know it at the time, Nixon had acquired the allegiance of most Republican Barons. The Reagan machinery, still in place, was a headless juggernaut.

To me, this array of delegates, convention planners, and advance men resembled the European royalty of a half century before, mindlessly mobilizing their forces in anticipation of the Great War (World War I) to come. It's a story well told by Barbara Tuchman in her classic work, *The Guns of August*. Like Tuchman's characters, we were moving from Sarajevo to the trenches of Flanders Field, from the California Club to the Miami Convention Hall, without really understanding why.

§§§

On the other hand, polling clouds hovered over Richard Nixon's head. He did not appear to be a winner, and despite his unbroken string of primary victories, Nixon did not yet have the delegate strength needed to clinch the nomination.

Nixon needed 667 delegate votes. By mid-June he appeared to control fewer than 600. Many Republican governors were holding out. Nixon's pacts with the Southern leaders were strong, but the docility of the Southern rank and file sitting behind them was yet to be tested.

In the wake of the California primary, as I closed the door on our rubbish-strewn San Francisco headquarters, I thought about Reagan's reliance on fate. Elizabeth Bowen's characterization fit pretty well: "Fate is not an eagle; it creeps like a rat."

Exactly.

We had no idea how this summer was going to unfold.

The Governors

In mid-June, we flew to Tulsa to attend a meeting of the Republican governors. This was pivotal work, since most of the large, industrial, and delegate-rich Northeast and Midwest states had Republican chief executives. Reagan needed to court them, since many, in their own states, were running as favorite sons. Other governors were, at the very least, important local warlords.

Jim Rhodes was the governor of Ohio. He maintained control of all but three of his 58 delegates through the only ballot in Miami.

George Romney was the governor of Michigan. His presidential ambitions had disintegrated, but as Michigan's favorite son, he kept custody of all but four of his delegates.

Nelson Rockefeller was the governor of New York. Taft Schreiber had tried to promote a Rocky-Reagan ticket during the June 9 shouting match at the Reagan residence, but that was never going to happen. Rockefeller kept control of all but four of his New York delegates. With the support of others in the Northeast, Rocky collected 277 votes in Miami.

Bill Scranton had just left office as the governor of Pennsylvania. As a solid Rockefeller ally, he hoped to deliver his 63 votes to his mentor, but Scranton's successor in Harrisburg was not so sure. On Friday, July 14, we met with Pennsylvania's Governor Shafer. He agreed to remain uncommitted for as long as possible.

John Volpe was the governor of Massachusetts, an important bloc of votes, but he did not control them. Rockefeller had torn them away in that state's primary.

Warren Knowles was the governor of Wisconsin, Norbert Tiemann the governor of Nebraska, and Tom McCall the governor of Oregon. These three states had been our targets in the primary season. RR had not done well enough there, but we still wanted the support of those governors if convention voting took an unexpected turn.

We were pleased with our time spent in Tulsa. Most Republican governors remained comfortable with their favorite-son status. We saw no signs of a Nixon stampede.

With that, we headed home. Reagan turned his attention to the tug of war that accompanies the end of any state legislative session.

Counting the Votes, Choosing a Veep

At the end of the last week in June, I flew to New York to meet with Clif White and his regional directors. I wanted to eyeball each, to hear firsthand their perceptions of the vote count, both in terms of numbers and fluidity. My end-of-the-afternoon notes show Nixon with "possibly as many as 625 votes," depending on the impact of the Unit Rule on Southern delegations. This rule, when adopted by a state's political convention, directs the delegation chairman to deliver all of a state's votes to the candidate winning a majority of the delegates' support in caucus.

Nixon apparently needed another 50 votes to win. Our counts showed Reagan with about 250 votes. Rocky could count on "no more than 300." Half a dozen favorite-son governors held the balance.

A week later, Clif White and I connected in Los Angeles, and then drove to the Reagan residence to discuss our final preconvention countdown. We debated options, from folding and endorsing Nixon to a full-blown Reagan candidacy. The governor chose the middle road, "standing firm while not splitting the party."

We also reviewed the vice presidential possibilities and confirmed Ohio's Governor Rhodes as our choice. Ohio had the delegates in Miami, it would be pivotal in the fall, and the two governors had become close friends. They trusted each other.

White and I were authorized to extend the offer and negotiate for delegates.

Miami

On July 24, White and I, along with an army of vote-counters and logisticians, all poured into the Deauville Hotel on Miami Beach. This was California's assigned headquarters. I was blinded by the shiny steel and overwhelmed by the mildew and disinfectant.

Across Biscayne Bay, at the convention center, our more-pristine

Clif White (standing) and Tom Van Sickle (seated) in one of the Reagan trailers in Miami.

trailers were connected to the convention floor via radio-telephones. Other handsets were hardwired to the outside world. TV screens adorned the walls. There were, of course, no laptops.

On Monday, July 29, I presided at the first on-site staff meeting in Miami. Our count showed Nixon with only 570 firm votes, but with a hundred more under negotiation. Our problem lay with the Florida and Mississippi delegations. Both confirmed their intent to stick with their winner-take-all Unit Rules. That was going to cost us dearly.

On Wednesday, I breakfasted with Ron and Nancy Reagan at the Deauville. We shared a two-bedroom suite with a spacious two-story living room between us. After I outlined the week's objectives, RR headed over to the convention hall for an appearance before the Platform Committee. He later met with the Florida delegation and then talked with reporters.

By Thursday evening, CBS was awarding Nixon 644 delegates, still 23 short of victory. That count seemed about right to us. We continued to negotiate; success lay in the hands of a few delegates in the Unit Rule states.

On Friday, August 2, the L.A. Elders began to arrive. In the evening, I joined the Reagans and their well-dressed friends for dinner at Leonard Firestone's palm-shrouded palace along the waterway.

On Saturday evening, the California delegation, along with a substantial press entourage, landed at the Miami-Dade County Airport. They arrived aboard chartered jets flying in from Los Angeles and San Francisco.

On Sunday, we hosted a buffet brunch for the California delegation in the towering Reagan suite. It seemed to be a sunny event, but in a side conversation, conducted in the governor's bedroom, former Senator Bill Knowland (R - CA) proposed that RR formally announce his candidacy in response to a delegation "draft" that Knowland would engineer the next morning. This was not a display of Knowland altruism; he was just settling old scores with Nixon.

Reagan agreed. There was no consultation with others, not even Nancy.

On Monday, August 5, the Republican Convention opened amidst large anti-war demonstrations in the streets and causeways leading in from Miami Beach. There were clouds of tear gas and some police actions, though none were as vicious as the rioting that accompanied the Democratic gathering in Chicago two weeks later.

After the morning formalities, the California delegation stayed behind to caucus. Knowland rose to move the adoption of his Draft Reagan resolution. It passed with a thundering voice vote from the majority, and sullen stares from the Nixon-favoring minority. Reagan accepted with his usual smile. He was now an announced presidential candidate.

Nixon's allies on the delegation were outraged. They knew the former veep did not yet have the votes needed to win. Even worse, they knew Nixon's support was contract-based, one ballot deep; it did not enjoy the emotional backing of the Republican rank and file. Nixon's fate lay in the hands of the chairmen in the Unit Rule states.

Mississippi's 20 votes sat in the Nixon column based on a 12-8 vote in caucus. Florida was similarly marginal. A mind-change by three delegates in either state could reorder the scoreboard. Bob Finch, Reagan's lieutenant governor (but also a close Nixon ally), found himself in a tight squeeze. His orders were to break apart the California delegation if a first-ballot Nixon victory was not assured. That might achieve a Nixon nomination, but it would destroy Finch's political dreams in California.

On the Tuesday morning after Reagan's acceptance of candidacy, a booze-toting Bob Finch sought a private audience with his governor. "This is craziness," he muttered to the aides escorting him into the governor's suite.

Nothing was resolved; suspense escalated.

At midday Tuesday, with the nomination hanging in the balance, we invited the chairmen of the Alabama, Florida, Mississippi, and South Carolina delegations to join Reagan and me for lunch in our hotel suite. Those four men were to lead 102 delegates onto the convention floor. If allowed to vote with their hearts, half of those men and women would choose Reagan. They had told us as much when polled. With such defections, Nixon would get only 630 votes. The convention would go to a second ballot, our fondest dream.

Most observers then, and most historians now, agree that such a second ballot would have been a melee. On the third round, Reagan would have won it. But we were not dealing with unencumbered men and women. Strom Thurmond was an icon. Unit Rules could gag free-spirited delegates. With such rules enforced by a delegation's chairman, we would be fortunate to garner a dozen votes from these four states. Nixon would then win on the first ballot.

Those were the chips on the table as our club sandwiches and coffees were served.

Reagan greeted the group with a smile and good humor, but once seated, he turned deadly serious. It was a classic Reagan performance. He spelled out the dangers facing the US, and the stakes in November along with the consequences of a loss to a Lyndon Johnson heir. Reagan then turned to his track record as a winner, his million-vote margin in California.

Not a word or a cough from our guests; not a bite was eaten.

As Reagan wound up, Alabama's Chairman Goldthwaite was the first to respond. He pledged no Unit Rule in Alabama. Half of his delegates were planning to vote for RR; they were free to do so.

Our other guests dropped their eyes to their plates.

Florida's Murfin broke the silence by expressing appreciation for all Reagan had done for the party in Florida. At the same time, Murfin defended the Unit Rule as convention tradition and sound politics. He advised that his delegation had again just voted. Nixon won a slim majority, but we knew that a handful of switches could turn the tide. The Unit Rule was, after all, a two-edged sword.

South Carolina's Dent was gracious, but he was Thurmond's man. Ol' Strom had made his deal with Nixon. Thurmond's conversion to the Republican Party in the dark days of '64, had earned him the right to lead. Dent concluded, "We gotta follow Strom, Governor." But then he repeated the senator's admonition to Reagan 10 months earlier. "Not this year, Ron, but sometime."

I cannot recall Clarke Reed's exact words. He rambled through a discussion of Mississippi traditions and loyalties, but he ended by supporting the Unit Rule. No doubt in my mind that Nixon had offered the best deal.

A dispirited and embarrassed group of men departed our suite, headed for their dates with destiny.

The Vote

The Reagan team expected to get a dozen votes from Alabama and perhaps a quarter of the votes from the other Southern states not represented at lunch: Georgia, Louisiana, and Texas. But that would not be enough.

We knew the game was over. Our afternoon count put Nixon over the top with about 680 votes. But even so, Reagan hung in there. He returned to our trailer adjacent to the convention hall. He spent that afternoon and the next morning in a windowless conference room only large enough for a small, sticky-topped table attended by a trio of castoff office chairs. This was not a smoke-filled room, since Reagan was not a smoker, but the air was close. Light came only from a fluorescent strip in the ceiling. The room resembled a police interrogation cell—a claustrophobe's worst nightmare.

Though unconcerned, and in fact, entertained by the perks of power, Reagan was a fierce competitor. Once the battle was joined, once the race was underway, or once the goal was clear, a second prize was absolutely unacceptable to him. From his first political race (slow to enter but overpowering at the end) to the climax of the Cold War ("Somebody is going to win and somebody is going to lose"), he was unstoppable. Confusing Reagan's perceived lack of ambition and short workday with a willingness to finish second was a lethal mistake for candidates and empires throughout the second half of the twentieth century. The possibility of not winning in Miami was unacceptable to our candidate.

One by one, a trickle of delegates met with the governor. All were torn; some were in tears. Reagan offered them comfort and a route to relief, but we knew better. These men and women were bound by enforceable oaths.

A handful of those visitors could have flipped Mississippi and Florida's 50 Unit Rule votes out of Nixon's column, thereby leaving him a dozen votes short on the first ballot. Nixon had no Plan B. Without a clincher on that first ballot, his game would have been over. But his contracts held.

Formal convention balloting took place on Wednesday afternoon, August 7. Reagan knew what to expect, but he did not like losing. As vice chairman of our delegation, I sat with him on the convention floor. Reagan's piercing blue eyes focused on his luncheon guests of the day before as they cast their unified delegation votes.

Nixon collected 692 votes on the first ballot, a dozen higher than our expectations, since most politicians dread being caught on the losing side of any vote. The Thurmond-controlled South provided 38 percent of Nixon's votes.

The favorite-son governors of Ohio, Michigan, Kansas, Arkansas, and of course, California, held on to most of their delegates. The Nixon machine was only able to fracture the favorite-son hopes of New Jersey Senator Clifford Case, making off with half of his delegates.

The '68 Republican Convention votes by region are shown below. They are tabulated by state in Appendix C.

Northwest 107 votes	At Left: Nixon-voting delegates, by region	CA (Reagan)	86
		OH (Rhodes)	55
		MI (Romney)	44
Mountains and West 158 votes		NJ (Case)	22
		KS (Carlson)	20
	At Right:	AR (W. Rock'r)	18
Midwest 161 votes	First-ballot votes held back by favorite-sons		
South 266 votes			

Oregon's Republican Chairman Don Hodel was on the convention floor in '68, seated directly in back of the South Carolina delegation. The Palmetto State envoys, in an exchange with Hodel on the floor, confirmed Nixon's need to win on the first ballot. They apologized for Senator Thurmond's lock-up.

"We really want Reagan," one young South Carolinian cried. "We'll vote for *him* once we get past this first-ballot pledge." But the second round never came.

Fourteen years later, cabinet member Hodel[98] met with President Reagan in the Oval Office to discuss federal business, but in opening their conversation, Hodel mentioned the '68 convention.

The president responded, "Miami was really close, Don. If South Carolina..." He remembered it all quite well.

---

98   Reagan's Energy Secretary, 1982-84, then Interior Secretary, 1985-89. This conversation took place in the Oval Office in 1982.

But it was over, and Nixon had won. After the roll call, Reagan worked his way to the podium to move for a unanimous vote in support of Richard Nixon. That was a generous gesture, warmly received and fully endorsed by all the delegates present.

RR had lost, but along the way he had undergone a transition. The TV personality performing for millions learned to be a nitty-gritty politician, operating at coffee-stained tables for two. He traded his air-conditioned studio for a hot and muggy trailer, facing delegates who would not budge, chairmen whose evasions were artistic, fighting a web he could not see.

While Reagan learned some lessons in '68, he ignored others. But he never gave up. Not in '68, not in '76, and certainly not in '80 when the payoff finally came.

Autumn Leaves

Ronald Reagan retired to the warm and healing sun of his favorite beach in San Diego while Richard Nixon held his campaign-planning sessions nearby. The two men met, their relationship always warm, and Reagan assumed serious responsibilities for the Nixon campaign in California. He also paid attention to his state legislative races.

Democrats controlled the Assembly 41-39, and the State Senate 21-19. Republicans dreamed of reversing those numbers in November, to control the legislative agenda for the remainder of Reagan's first term.

The governor also agreed to travel elsewhere in the US to assist other Republican candidates in their races for statehouses and congressional seats. He helped with close races across the board, but he focused on those individuals who had stuck their necks out for him in Miami. That downward loyalty established a useful record for the future.

In the fall, the Reagan apparatus took full charge of California's legislative campaigns. We won control of the Assembly, 41-39, with a 20-20 tie in the Senate to be broken by the Republican lieutenant governor.

Biographer Lou Cannon put the results of '68 this way:

"The men who had wanted to make Reagan the President of the United States instead provided him with the working legislative majority he needed to govern California."

As a consequence, we also disabled Jess Unruh, California's second most powerful politician. He had become Speaker of the Assembly after the reapportionment of 1961, accumulating ever more power until the votes were counted in November '68. With those Republican victories, Bob Monagan became speaker, and Unruh's power base disappeared. He remained in the state legislature, but his ability to raise money dwindled. His 1970 bid for the governorship, running against Ronald Reagan, was a hollow echo of what it might have been.

Electing Nixon

The 32 million of you who thought you elected Richard Nixon are mistaken. I actually voted for him in '68; you only voted for me or other Electors pledged to the candidacy of Nixon and Agnew.

The Founding Fathers expected these Electors to be the brightest and best, to use their judgment in selecting the next president, but two centuries later only reliability counted. On November 5, 1968, after a late-night conclusion of the vote count, the people of California elected Ronald Reagan and me, plus 38 of our associates, to serve as their Electors.

On Monday, December 16, we met in Sacramento for a ceremonial luncheon and then adjourned to the ornate and historic chambers of the State Senate to cast our votes. At the appointed time, California's secretary of state distributed six copies of the presidential ballots to each of us. We duly checked off one box marked "Richard Nixon" and another marked "Spiro Agnew" on each ballot and then signed our names. The clerk collected these cards and announced the results. A photographer snapped our picture; then we were out of there and into the history books.

Later in the week, California's secretary of state distributed those ballots. Two copies went to his own archives, two copies to the Archivist of the US, one to the Chief Judge of the 9th Circuit District Court, and one to the presiding officer of the Senate in

Washington. The latter gentleman delivered those ballots to a joint session of Congress where they were opened and counted. With 301 electoral votes, Nixon and Agnew were declared the winners. A few weeks later, they were sworn in as the President and Vice President of the United States of America.

Messrs. Nixon and Agnew did not realize it, but they were only the opening players, akin to Hamlet's Rosencrantz and Guildenstern. They set the stage for the conservative revolution to come, but they did not survive long enough to participate in its climactic scenes.

In counterpoint, Reagan added to his knowledge of the presidential machinery. He noted that there was an electoral college, that those people really did meet and vote, and that a third-party candidate could be disastrously disruptive.

During his December visit to California's Senate chamber, Reagan also learned about "Faithless Electors." Twenty years before, Strom Thurmond won 39 Electors from otherwise Democrat states.[99] In 1960, 15 unpledged Electors voted for Harry Byrd of Virginia, a US senator who had not sought the presidency. Over the history of the Republic, more than 150 Electors have voted contrary to their pledges. Reagan noted the need to select one's Elector candidates with great care.

Ironically, eight years later, Reagan was the beneficiary of one such electoral defection. In 1976, Ford won Washington State's nine Electors although he did not carry enough states to win the presidency. Carter and Mondale triumphed with 297 electoral votes.

When Washington State's nine Electors met in Olympia, one became a "faithless elector" by casting his presidential vote for Reagan, then his veep vote for nominated candidate Dole. Thus, the final vote in 1976 was Carter 297, Ford 240, Reagan 1.

It was a beginning. Reagan would do better next time out.

The Winter Solstice

With the elections of '68 over, and as the holidays approached, Reagan's departing chief of staff passed along a fateful message to

---

99   This defection did not cost Truman his 1948 election.

me. "The governor intends that you run his re-election campaign in 1970," he said.

Those words, uttered by Bill Clark on December 20, 1968, were not an invitation; they were intended as a palliative.   Clark had made his career deal with the governor.[100] He wanted me to know there was something in Santa's stocking for everyone. To me, however, "the campaign in 1970" sounded like the proverbial lump of coal. I did not wish to be involved in any re-election campaign.

Two weeks after Clark's comment, the governor asked that I come have lunch in his office. On January 6, '69, over a healthy crab salad, Reagan put the question directly.

"Tom, I would like you to run the 1970 re-election campaign."

I demurred, citing "certain past problems," a reference to my recurring conflicts with the Elders. These discussions with Reagan continued, both in Sacramento and Los Angeles, for much of the following winter and spring. I tried to be helpful, but on May 23, in a meeting with Tuttle, Roberts, Meese, and Smith, I advised, "I've been asked to help with recruiting at the Nixon White House. I'll be moving to DC for a while. Sorry."

With that, I felt my responsibilities to Ronald Reagan were over.

Ronald Reagan returned from the '68 Miami convention with honor. He had preached unity, avoided harsh language, and moved the unanimous endorsement of his opponent. After the fall legislative election victories in California, Reagan was seen as a winner and a leader. His candidates, from top to bottom, had prevailed. He could look forward to significant achievements in the state capitol.

The holidays brought Reagan a season of peace and quiet. Elsewhere, politicians were planning inaugurals or cleaning out their desks, but to him, Sacramento was a place for reflection. He had made his first run at the presidency. It did not work because there was no consistent execution, no focus to that effort. Perhaps

---

100   Moving to the Superior Court bench in San Luis Obispo County in January '69, a beginning that led to his appointment to the California Supreme Court in 1973, late in Reagan's second gubernatorial term.

it was too soon, like John Kennedy's run for the vice presidential nomination in 1956. Even so, Reagan had come much closer to the nomination than most people realized.

He came to understand the machinery of political conventions where deceit can be common currency among delegates, where political barons fear being left behind, and where long-standing political IOUs, written by other candidates in different times, become bankable commodities. Reagan began to understand that delegates, like legislators back home, are mere mortals, their loyalty a negotiable commodity. A dose of skepticism crept into Reagan's sunny personality, and his naiveté factor was adjusted downward.

In '68, Reagan also learned that he could and must connect. Television was but one tool. The machinery of retail politics requires the use of many different hammers and wrenches if it is to grind out the desired sausage. Reagan abandoned his studio to bond with real people sitting across from him in steamy cafés and trailers. Reagan discovered, but did not remember, that a run for the presidency requires substance. A winning candidate's proposals must be carefully thought through and his opponent's errors noted. Articulating the candidate's vision requires the help of careful researchers and talented speechwriters. He also built a national network of financial supporters. When called upon, they would stand him in good stead.

Lou Cannon later said that Reagan came out of Miami a loser, but defeat laid the groundwork for victory. The missing piece was 1968. Cannon noted that the preparation and motivation that blossomed in 1976 came to fruition in 1980.

Reagan came to view the American presidency as an attainable personal goal, not just a revered-but-distant provision of the American Constitution. The year 1968 served as the fiery furnace; Miami was the crucible that reshaped Reagan's perspectives, and that hardened the steel in his spine. By the end of '68, Reagan could envision the White House from his casa in the Palisades.

In later years, Reagan denied any run for the 1968 nomination. In his 1990 memoirs[101] he wrote, "Running for president [in 1968]

---

101   *Ronald Reagan: An American Life*, Ronald Reagan, 1990, Pocket Books, pp 176-177

was the last thing on my mind ... I wasn't interested." Nancy Reagan took a similar position in her 1980 autobiography.[102] "Ronnie never sought the nomination in 1968."

When I first read those words, I was stunned.

Whose campaign had I been running?

I had met with Reagan over one hundred times in the company of others, often his wife, to discuss this project. We also consulted privately on another 21 occasions for one-on-one talks about the most sensitive aspects of our drive. I accompanied Reagan on dozens of politically funded flights on a chartered Jet Commander to meet with backers in our intended primary states, to talk with governors whom we might select as a running mate, or to solicit support from delegation members in swing-state Texas and the Thurmond-dominated South. When Lyndon Johnson withdrew from, and Bobby Kennedy entered the Democratic contest in March 1968, we moved up to a chartered 727 jet to accommodate over 40 members of the travelling press.

How—or perhaps more accurately, why—did all of this campaigning slip the future president's recall? That is a significant question, since Reagan's proclivity to erase bad news from his memory remains an enigma to this day.

---

102 *Nancy*, Nancy Reagan with Bill Libby, 1980, Morrow, pg. 165

CH. 17   CONFIRMATION

During the mid-sixties, Ronald Reagan appeared over America's western skies as the political marvel of the year. But was he a passing comet, an interesting light show, or was he an approaching supernova? If Reagan was to validate his place in the political galaxy as a new star, if he was ever to be elected to the presidency of the US, the next order of business must be his re-election to the governorship of California in 1970.

I did not want to run Reagan's re-election campaign. He had relegated me to the back bench twice before, not for bumbling, but because of my brittle demands for results. The discipline I imposed on staff, peers, and contractors clashed with RR's tolerant and inclusive nature. In the process, I had fallen out of favor with his wife, his brother, and the Los Angeles Elders.

I spent the summer of '69 in seemingly idle pursuits: helping with the White House talent search during the week, and explaining the fine points of kite flying to my children over the weekends. The New Jersey shore was a great place to unwind.

In mid-August I was ending those White House duties. I had been living at the historic Metropolitan Club, a one-block walk through the muggy summer heat from the Old Executive Office Building. On the evening of August 19, as I was packing, Lyn Nofziger called. He was also helping organize the new administration, and we had stayed in touch during the summer. I settled into the comfortable armchair in my club apartment to listen.

Nofziger's opening words did not bode well. "Tom, we've got a problem."

"How's that?" I asked.

"Ron is surrounded by amateurs."

Nofziger had been reflecting on Reagan's political future, about the governor's potential in the post-Nixon years, and about his ability to communicate ideas from the hinterlands without benefit of the bully pulpit. But Nofziger was concerned. He had heard of my refusal to run the Reagan re-election campaign. He knew from firsthand experience of Reagan's inability to organize his own campaigns or even his own office.

After several minutes, Nofziger got to the point. "Look, Tom, Ron has a rendezvous with destiny. Sooner or later, he'll have to fix this Washington mess. We all know that. Those of us who risked everything to save him in the summer of '67 are the trustees."

"Probably true," I acknowledged.

"Go run that campaign," Nofziger went on. "Neither those trolls in Sacramento nor the money people in Los Angeles have a clue."

"You're right with that one as well," I confirmed.

"Without good management, Ron will lose. You know that. It would be a disaster for history."

No response from me.

Nofziger then turned to the bigger picture. "Vietnam is going to eat Nixon alive, Tom. He might not even make it through '72. In any case, his lease runs out in '76. Then what?"

We argued only briefly. While reaching no conclusions, I thanked Nofziger for his call, but when I put down the phone, I had to acknowledge reality.

Lyn is right, I sighed to myself. Without good management, RR will lose. Yes, he does have a rendezvous with destiny. Yes, we are the trustees. Dammit. Well, let's see what happens next.

I headed off to the Jersey Shore. A day later, my wife, children, and I returned to California.

Structuring the Campaign

Reagan's call came on Thursday, August 28, as I enjoyed an end-of-summer swim with the kids. As noted earlier, such calls were unusual, but these were unusual times. The governor wanted to reopen our year-end discussions about the '70 election.

"I think it would be best if I talked with some of my associates first," I responded. "Then I need to hear from your friends in Los Angeles, the guys who shoved me to the back bench at every opportunity. After that, I'll come chat."

"OK," was the governor's concise response to my polite rebuff.

Reagan did not like calling people, and he avoided staff-management issues whenever possible. Something or somebody must have moved 1970 to the top of his "serious problem" list. Nofziger's call to me at the end of summer drove me to respond.

I started my consultations over the Labor Day weekend. On October 2, I returned to Sacramento for a working lunch in the governor's office. I was there to accept the challenge and to lay out a campaign-management plan. Three days later, on a Sunday afternoon in early October, Reagan called his entire political family to his Pacific Palisades home. He spoke while sitting on the stone bench in front of his fireplace. We assembled on the sofa and armchairs across the room. Spencer and Roberts joined us, along with two or three staffers from Sacramento, several of the finance heavies, and the volunteer leadership.

Reagan articulated my campaign management plans quite accurately. Tuttle and I were anointed co-chairmen, with me as campaign director, and Tuttle as the über-finance chairman and shepherd of the Elders. Bill Roberts was to manage the campaign. Justin Dart accepted the formal finance responsibility. Others were given their assignments. We agreed that Assembly Speaker Jess Unruh would be a manageable opponent. Only the role of the McCann-Erickson advertising agency lingered.

"We need to select the best agency we can find for this campaign," I pleaded. "The technology is changing. The Boomers, the campus protesters, are now old enough to vote. We need an independent firm if we are to win this thing."

"No, Tom," was Reagan's crisp response. "He's the only brother I have."

Neil had been part of the group that gathered in the Reagan home in September '65. He was a fixture in his brother's political life. That was not going to change.

Our October '69 solution was to leave the purchase of airtime, the printing of materials, the placement of billboards, etc., with Neil's agency. That's what earns the commissions and thus would keep the family happy. Russ Walton, the talented director of many a conservative TV show and political ad, would control content. Later in the year, this arrangement saved Reagan's political life.

In preparing for this campaign, I turned to Richard Wirthlin, an Arizona-based pollster first recommended to me by Barry Goldwater when I visited his home in April '68. Two years before that, during Reagan's first gubernatorial campaign, we operated with no survey data at all, only published polls. Those provided little insight into issues or demographics.

According to Wirthlin's early 1970 surveys, Reagan enjoyed a comfortable lead over Jess Unruh (51-31 percent) and his 49 percent job approval rating was OK, but the issues were in flux.

At the end of '68, Californians saw campus disturbances as the most serious problem facing the state. By more than a 4:1 ratio, they thought the instigators of such demonstrations should be expelled from their university at once. Even Reagan was seen as "not being tough enough" on this issue. Yet as 1970 began to unfold, as opposition to the war in Vietnam grew, that resentment of unruly students was evaporating. Other topics rose and fell in counterpoint. Richard Nixon had replaced Lyndon Johnson as the war-supporting demon-in-charge; Reagan and Nixon were seen as indistinguishable peas in a pod.

To make it clear that Reagan, his administration, and his campaign were open to new ideas, we adopted a campaign logo more suitable to a Beatles album cover than a conservative political campaign (at right).

On March 10, Reagan formally announced his candidacy, but with the coming of spring, all hell broke loose.

The Parrot's Beak

On April 30, President Nixon announced his intention to "go to the heart of the trouble" in Vietnam. He planned to send US troops into, and US aircraft over, the Parrot's Beak, a Viet Cong logistics enclave protected by four enemy divisions, all located only 33 miles west of Saigon. Unfortunately, those bases sat in the sovereign nation of Cambodia.

Nixon's invasion of Cambodian territory uncovered a vast Viet Cong arms depot, but it also triggered violent demonstrations all across the US. At Kent State University in Ohio, students began a campaign of arson and assault that was met with gunfire from the National Guard.[103] The shooting killed four students and wounded nine others.

Nixon's incursions into Cambodia and the ensuing deaths at Kent State demolished Americans' support for their president. His toxic coattails were dragging down Republican candidates all across the board. We in the Reagan campaign began to reflect on the viability of the "campus unrest" issue.

At the same time, Reagan, Tuttle, and I were beginning to lose confidence in Bill Roberts. He seemed inattentive to Reagan's re-election effort.

The whole campaign did not feel right. We looked forward to California's primary voting on June 2. There would follow a pause, a chance to reconsider our whole game plan. We needed to do that.

The General Election

For two days after the primary, Reagan, Tuttle, Roberts, Meese, and I met with our newly nominated slate of candidates at

---

103   Their actions authorized by Reagan's ally, friend, and prospective VP, Ohio's Governor Jim Rhodes who described the campus protesters as "worse than the brown shirts, communists, or night riders."

Reagan's home in Pacific Palisades. We laid out our plan to run as a "Team for the Seventies." But after that, Bill Roberts disappeared. While he had been hired to run the Reagan-70 campaign, he was nowhere to be found.

Tuttle and I were concerned. Campaign controller Colleen McAndrews extracted an explanation from her Los Angeles political network. "Roberts is not here," McAndrews noted, "because he's also running the governor's race in Hawaii. When not doing that, he's probably on the beach. That's where he's been for two weeks. He needs to be back here by June 18 to speak at a party gathering in L.A."

On the expected date, a well-tanned and lei-bedecked Roberts rolled off a United Airlines flight from Honolulu. His gait slackened and his face froze when he saw me at the gate. I ended his association with our campaign on the spot.

I proceeded to Tuttle's house alone. My co-chairman appreciated the actions I had just taken. The two of us then contacted Reagan to review this chain of events. The governor had long since shared our Roberts-oriented concerns. We next called Stu Spencer, Roberts' business partner, to ask for his comments.

"We want to keep the Reagan account," Spencer advised an hour later, "but I need time to think things through. I'll get back to you gents in a day or two."

The next day, Friday, June 19, allowed time for reflection. As Tuttle and I awaited Spencer's views, I took to strolling on the beach at Trancas, a few hundred yards from the Reagan summer cottage. For the first time, I could smell a whiff of defeat in the salty ocean air.

On Saturday, Stu Spencer called us back. After apologizing for his company's inattention,[104] he advised that Roberts was moving on to George Murphy's Senate re-election effort. Spencer proposed that I direct and manage the Reagan campaign myself with an operations chief to administer it.[105] He (Spencer) would move to the role of strategic consultant, rendering advice on key decisions and the campaign plan, but not acting as the implementer.

---

104   "Poor time management," as Spencer put it later.
105   Norman "Skip" Watts was given the assignment.

I'm afraid that's it, I thought. *Better follow Stu's advice. If we don't, Ron will lose, sure thing.*

On Monday, I telephoned Reagan to review these decisions. Tuttle had already done so in person on Sunday. RR approved, expressed his thanks, and gave me full authority to proceed as director of his re-election campaign.

In the summer of 1970, as Stu Spencer and I assembled our plans for the fall campaign, Dick Wirthlin's surveys were giving us good insight into the electorate's thinking. Reagan still seemed to enjoy an adequate 51-43 percent lead over Unruh, but such margins can disappear fast. Later studies showed that a third of the voters did not make up their minds until the last two weeks of this campaign. We sensed those floating allegiances.

To keep the Republicans unified, Spencer and I sought to recruit former Senator Tom Kuchel, a liberal Republican who had represented California in the US Senate for three terms. Spencer had run Kuchel's re-election effort in 1962.

Six years later, in '68, as Kuchel sought election to a fourth term, the Republican right wing demanded his ouster. They succeeded with an unfair, gutter-level primary campaign that was focused only on the removal of Kuchel, not victory for anyone else. Kuchel was understandably bitter about his loss, especially the personal innuendo involved—but every coin has two sides.

Any acceptance of those insults by Kuchel, a willingness to let bygones be bygones, would make the former senator a poster boy for Republican unity. Kuchel and Reagan always had been friends. If we could induce Kuchel not only to endorse Reagan, but to play a significant role in his campaign, it would send an unmistakable signal to all Republicans: "Reagan is a good man; Republicans should close ranks behind him."

The Kuchels, husband and wife, came to the Reagans' beach house in Trancas for a light supper on August 26th. We wanted a Kuchel endorsement as part of our Labor Day kickoff. The Reagans' guests departed well before sundown. Upon hearing of their exit, I strolled off the beach and into the Reagan summer home for a debriefing.

"We had a nice time," RR reported. "I think he'll endorse. He expects to see you in his office tomorrow, Tom. He wants your help in working out a statement."

I couldn't help grinning.

"We've always been friends," Nancy added.

I appreciated the euphoric airs, but politics is a continuing surprise party. I like to buy insurance, to have a Plan B. "Who's Kuchel's finance guy?" I asked. "Who does he listen to besides Spencer?"

"That could be Leonard," Nancy responded, referring to Leonard Firestone, the tire heir who had been Nelson Rockefeller's California finance chairman in 1964.

The Firestones were not Nancy's favorite people. He was an alcoholic, and his third wife was a disagreeable presence in Palm Springs.

"OK. I'll give Leonard a call," I said. "I'll do it in the morning, before it's too late."

During Nancy's offerings, RR had grown quiet. Then, from out of nowhere, Reagan added his thoughts. "The dark demon in a bottle can do a lot of harm, Tom." That was a pensive Reagan observation, followed by a striking disclosure. "My father was an alcoholic, you know."

"No, Sir, I did not know."

"My mother was a saint." Reagan almost whispered the words. "All our neighbors agreed. She pulled us through it all, but we never had a home. We lived as itinerants in downstate Illinois. We'd have been called 'homeless people' in today's jargon."

"What was your father's line of work?" I asked.

"He was a shoe salesman," Reagan responded quietly. "He chased rainbows. He was a kindly man, but he couldn't keep a job. Alcohol helped him cope with our ever-present financial struggles. I remember as if it were yesterday, Tom. I pulled Father off the porch. He was passed out, the snow frozen in his hair. I dragged him off to his bed."

I posed a softening query. "How old were you at the time?"

"I was 11 years old," the governor announced with a dialog-ending air.

Nancy redirected the conversation to farewells. The sun was sinking over the Pacific.

The following day Senator Kuchel welcomed me into his law office. I got the statement we wanted. It produced headlines and the desired editorials over the otherwise slow Labor Day weekend. We could hear the Republicans closing ranks.

Dark Clouds

A sinking spell overtook us on the third weekend in October. Reagan had been campaigning vigorously in blue-collar towns, on TV shows, and at rallies all over California. By mid-October we were charting his progress with tracking surveys. Pollster Wirthlin's research crew conducted several hundred telephone interviews every evening.

We felt confident with our campaign's progress, but on Friday, October 23, the warning bells went off. Unruh had been closing the gap over the past week. By that Friday he had cut our lead in half, to only five points. Democrats were returning to their party in droves. Only 10 percent of them remained in Reagan's column. While our margin was still satisfactory, the trend gave us cause for concern. We had 10 days to go before Election Day, time enough for the Democrats to consolidate for victory.

Wirthlin's surveys were timely and accurate. They were cross-indexed well enough to illuminate the problem: The voters' focus had shifted away from student unrest. Campus riots had disappeared as a campaign issue. The shootings at Kent State must have changed a lot of minds. Parents did not want to hear any more about "getting tough with those kids."

Other Nixon-supported campaigns did not get the message. The president's pursuit of the law-and-order theme had grown shrill, poisonously so for Republican candidates down-ticket. Pocketbook issues and the environment had seized the California voters' attention. Spencer and I reviewed these mid-October survey results with pollster Wirthlin and advertising content man Walton. As a result, we pulled our law-and-order ads overnight, substituting positive plugs for the governor's achievements on smog control, welfare reform, and property taxes. Spencer's acumen and decisive advice over that weekend fully redeemed the Spencer-Roberts name in my opinion. Wirthlin's insights earned him a place on Reagan's A-Team for the decade to come.

Election Day

The show ended on Monday, November 2, as the entire Team for the Seventies flew around the state hitting the major media markets in preparation for the vote on Tuesday. I checked the previous night's tracking and felt confident that Reagan would enjoy a safe margin of victory. Others, such as Senator Murphy, would not do as well. When we landed in

Tom Reed and Ronald Reagan winding up the final state tour, November 2, 1970

Burbank at the end of our tour, I bade Reagan farewell. I had done my job. He would still be standing when the smoke cleared on Wednesday morning.

I soon picked up the family and headed off for a ski vacation in Colorado. I watched the election results in Joe Coors' living room. In the decade to come, Coors emerged as one of the big wheels on Reagan's presidential locomotive, but on November 3, 1970, once the networks declared Reagan the winner, I headed off to bed.

The Post-Mortem

Although Reagan's opponent was of the governor's age, Jess Unruh was an unglamorous machine politician, a hack with little appeal to idealistic youth. He had been unable to capitalize on the anti-war unrest rocking the nation. Our youth organization likened him to Chicago's Mayor Daley.

Election night was successful, though not a landslide. Unruh carried a dozen of California's 58 counties, some in the San Francisco Bay Area, but also a few in the Central Valley and far north. The networks took a little while to predict a Reagan win, but they did it early enough to allow for a relaxed evening. Reagan won 53 percent of the total vote, Unruh got 45 percent, and other minor candidates polled 2 percent.

Reagan's margin over Unruh was slightly more than half a million votes, down substantially from the million-vote blowout of '66. RR ran behind most other Republican statewide candidates,[106] Senator Murphy lost to Democratic Congressman John Tunney, and the Republican Party lost control of both State Assembly and Senate. As a harbinger of things to come, Reagan barely carried Los Angeles County (50.9 percent), although he did win 26 percent of the Democratic vote statewide.

We brought the campaign in slightly under budget, expending $2.287 million vs. $2.290 budgeted.[107]

All across the country, 1970 was a disappointing year for Republicans. The GOP lost a dozen seats in the House of Representatives. Eleven Republican candidates for governor went down as well; only a few endured, but Reagan was one of them.

Reagan's survival was a major accomplishment, but oddly enough, he devotes only one paragraph of 80 words to the election of 1970 in his memoirs. Perhaps that is because 1970 marked the beginning of a downward slide into a decade of missed opportunities. Years later, when recounting the history of that election to his ghostwriter,[108] Reagan probably viewed it as just another bad-news event, something to be forgotten or ignored.

---

106   Lt. Governor Reinecke, Treasurer Ivy Baker Priest, and Controller Houston Flournoy each garnered more votes than Reagan.
107   About $16 million in 2014 dollars.
108   Robert Lindsey

CH. 18   THE SUPERB HERMIT

Some journalists have used the words "Kitchen Cabinet" to describe the cluster of affluent Southern California men who bankrolled Ronald Reagan's post-'64 political career, who oversaw his personal life, and who catered to his wife's social needs, but Kitchen Cabinet is not an accurate sobriquet.

That expression originated in President Andrew Jackson's time. It referred to a small knot of ministers and journalists of substantial intellect who met in the White House kitchen at the invitation of the president to formulate foreign policy. It is not an appropriate term for the men I identify as the Los Angeles Elders because, to my knowledge, Reagan seldom sought their collective advice. During the first decade of his political career, RR never brought them together for anything other than formal events, such as inaugural dinners. They were not a Brain Trust; they were a Greek Chorus, a theatrical term from millennia past.

A Greek Chorus is often defined as "a homogenous group who comment on the dramatic action with a collective voice, but with no role in the outcome." The dozen high rollers I refer to throughout this book as the L.A. Elders fit that description. They commented and cajoled during Reagan's gubernatorial years, they supported his campaigns with money, and they maintained back-door contact with Nancy. Aside from providing campaign cash, however, this group had little positive effect on substantive matters.

Reagan's instructions to Bill Clark, to me, and to others, were simple: "Just keep the boys happy." He repeated those instructions often. He wanted us to defuse the free advice and complaints from the Elders as early as possible. Their grievances, if untended, would surely percolate into his quiet space via Nancy. Even worse, their bearers might barge through the front door of his home.

Some writers claim this cluster of men, by whatever name, tagged Reagan early on, that they promoted his advancement to political stardom, that they created the Reagan of the late sixties to meet their conservative needs.

Not hardly.

During California's booming mid-century years, the social hierarchy of Los Angeles was dominated by powerful families in the oil, water, real estate, insurance, and finance industries. Some retail kingpins were admitted to the group, but the movie industry was scorned. Actors and studio chiefs were viewed as phony untouchables not welcome in the halls of the California Club.

Ronald Reagan, a B-actor in a second marriage to a younger movie starlet, was one of "those people." He was invisible to the establishment until the Funding Fathers heard Reagan perform at a Goldwater rally, until they bought the airtime for a national broadcast that changed the world. Only when millions of Americans responded to Reagan's "Time for Choosing" speech did the Los Angeles establishment begin to pay attention, but then only to Reagan as an appreciating political asset, not as a friend.

Reagan had no friends. He had a host of compartmented allies. Bill Clark was a fellow horseman; Reagan was close to his pastors; he entrusted me with his political life; but there was no one with whom he would simply hang out. Some claim Nancy fulfilled the role of "friend." Not so. She was a close ally, his dearest love, and in his golden years, his protector. But she was not his friend.

During his youth, Reagan's anchor was his mother. Nelle Reagan was the saint who kept the family together throughout an itinerant lifestyle driven by an alcoholic father. A photograph of Nelle Reagan adorned RR's White House desk.

The still-living associates consulted for this book agree that while Nancy entered Reagan's life as lover and wife, by the late sixties she had become the surrogate for the protective mother Nelle. When addressing Nancy in private, RR always called her "Mommy."

Nancy provided the protective bubble, but on matters of

substance, she was ignored. When RR extended a helping hand to the down and out, "Don't tell Nancy" was the mantra.

First daughter Maureen Reagan spelled out this distancing in her memoir.[109] "Sorry Nancy, but [Reagan's black mare] was the real love of his life."

Mrs. Reagan confirmed this isolation in her memoir.[110] "He [RR] doesn't let anybody get too close. There's a wall around him ... I feel that barrier."

Maureen went on to attribute this barricade to his father's alcoholism. "A flaw that drove the Reagan family to a nomadic life of poverty through small-town Illinois," she wrote.

In Nancy's view, Jack Reagan's addiction to alcohol bequeathed an untrusting and isolated mindset to his two sons. The governor confirmed that observation in his conversations with biographer Paul Kengor: "This reluctance to get close to people never left me entirely."[111]

Reagan's isolation was further confirmed by second daughter, Patti. "He came in smoke, and disappeared in smoke," she wrote.

Like Nancy and me, the Elders were compartmented associates. Even so, they were an interesting bunch.

The Funding Fathers

The trio who started it all, the men who paid for the now-famous nationwide broadcast of Reagan's "Time for Choosing" speech in October '64, were Holmes Tuttle, Cy Rubel, and Henry Salvatori. They became the core of the Elders.

Oklahoma-born **Holmes Tuttle** was the central hero of the Reagan story, an early poster boy for "I built it." He was a self-made man who migrated to Los Angeles prior to World War II to open his own Ford dealership at war's end. Forty years later, Holmes Tuttle Ford was the largest such dealership in that auto-centric metropolis. I treasured Tuttle's friendship until his death in 1989.

---

109   *First Father, First Daughter*, Maureen Reagan, 1989, Little Brown, pg 93.
110   *My Turn*, Nancy Reagan, 1989, Random House
111   *God and Ronald Reagan*, Paul Kengor, 2004, HarperCollins

A.C. "Cy" Rubel was a World War I combat engineer war hero. By the mid-sixties, he had risen to the chairmanship of the Union Oil Company. From that desk, he helped organize the Friends of Reagan, but he passed on in '67.

Henry Salvatori was a model of the twentieth-century immigrant's success story: born in Italy and brought to the US by his parents in 1906. Determined and ambitious, he earned his B.S. from the University of Pennsylvania, followed by an M.S. in physics from Columbia University. In 1933, he founded the Western Geophysical Company, a pioneer in the underground mapping of oilfields. Salvatori sold Western Geophysical in 1960, turning his attention to philanthropy and anti-communist politics. He lived to see his biggest dream come true, the fall of the Evil Empire, in 1991. He died six years later.

The Others

Beyond the three Funding Fathers, **Asa V. Call** was the most prominent of the early Reagan supporters. *The Los Angeles Times* described him as "the last undisputed baron of the Los Angeles power structure." Call founded the Pacific Mutual Life Insurance Company and was one of a handful of men who first promoted Reagan's gubernatorial ambitions in '65. He fell ill after Reagan's first election, thus becoming inactive in politics until his death in 1978.

Edward "Ed" Mills made his mark going from stock boy to president of the Van de Kamp Bakeries, serving as president of Community Bank, and later rising to high executive positions at the G.I. Trucking Company. The successful but reserved Mills became the treasurer of every campaign that Tuttle chose to support. He tried to maintain a low profile until his death in 2000 at the age of 94.

Taft Schreiber sat at the other end of the visibility scale. As Reagan's agent at MCA, Schreiber salvaged RR's slumping film career in the early fifties by installing him as the well-paid host of the new MCA-produced TV anthology show "The General Electric Theater." This hiring occurred shortly after MCA received an unusual blanket waiver from the Reagan-led Screen Actors Guild. That authorization exempted MCA from SAG rules precluding agency-production company partnerships.

When the "General Electric Theater" gig ended in 1962, Schreiber found follow-on work for Reagan as the host of "Death Valley Days." He also lent a helping hand in maintaining the liquidity of RR's real estate portfolio.

Schreiber became an active Republican fundraiser with connections in every faction of the party, from Nixon to Rockefeller. His partner, MCA President Lew Wasserman, worked the Democratic side of the street. Schreiber did not like being left out of anything, but his life ended abruptly, the victim of an erroneous blood transfusion at Cedars-Sinai Hospital in 1976.

Justin Dart was the Rexall drugstore tycoon. Although he supported Rockefeller's presidential ambitions in 1964, Dart joined the Reagan campaign and was accredited to the L.A. Elders soon after the 1966 primary. Dart may have been the most effective fundraiser among the Elders; "brutal" according to some of his targets.

Dart and his wife, former actress Jane Bryan, were close social friends of Ron and Nancy Reagan. During RR's late-seventies out-of-office years, the Reagans usually stayed at the Darts' two-story penthouse when in New York. Dart died of heart failure in 1984; President Reagan awarded him the Presidential Medal of Freedom posthumously in 1987.

Leonard Firestone represented the liberal, inherited wealth end of the Elders' spectrum. He attended Princeton, where his chosen sports were golf and polo. During World War II, he served as a manufacturer of vital products (tires), continuing as a director of the family company until 1970.

In 1964, Firestone served as chairman of Nelson Rockefeller's primary campaign in California. After the '66 primary, he joined the Reagan team, to remain a member of the Elders until his death in Pebble Beach in 1996.

Alfred Bloomingdale was the most colorful of the Elders. He was born into the Bloomingdale department store family and attended Brown University, where he played football. Annoyed by the need to carry rolls of cash during his nights out in New York City, he launched a credit card business that eventually merged with Diner's Club.

Bloomingdale married Beverly Hills socialite Betsy Lee Newling during the fifties. As the Reagan star rose, Mrs. Bloomingdale connected with Nancy, in time earning the title "First Friend." She became Nancy's primary shopping companion.

Because Al Bloomingdale was such a prodigious political fundraiser, and because both Bloomingdales were so close to Nancy, Tuttle tolerated Al's lifestyle, then welcomed him into the Elders' inner circle.

During the sixties, Bloomingdale patronized a vast stable of call girls in Hollywood.[112]   Then, in 1970, at age 54, he took up with one Vickie Morgan, a highly visible, 18-year-old model whom he soon sequestered in a luxurious Los Angeles apartment. She stayed there until Bloomingdale's death in 1982, whereupon Ms. Morgan filed a palimony lawsuit against the Bloomingdale estate. Her complaint included intimate details of her sex life with Al, illustrating what she had to put up with and why she should now be paid off. The court dismissed the suit; Ms. Morgan was murdered a year later by her next boyfriend-roommate.

Jack Hume, founder of Basic Vegetable Products in King City, lived in San Francisco. As such, he became a non-resident member of Tuttle's Elders. He was often invited to the group's meetings at the California Club, but the L.A. members did not view him as a serious (six-figure minimum) contributor or fundraiser. His Northern California roots and his very proper suit-and-tie comportment contrasted with the auto-and-oilfield roughnecks down South. Hume served as Reagan's Northern California finance chairman in the '66 general election and again in '70. Hume, a close personal friend of mine, died in San Francisco in 1991.

William French Smith became the executive secretary and spokesman for the Elders in '66. He graduated from UCLA in 1939, Harvard Law in 1942. As a lieutenant in the US Naval Reserve, he performed legal work for the Navy during World War II.

---

112   These relationships confirmed by first-hand sources living in the same apartment complex.

After the war, Smith joined the prestigious law firm of Gibson, Dunn & Crutcher.[113] By the early sixties, as an expert in labor law, Smith progressed to senior partner status within the firm. His peers confirm that he was a serious "rainmaker" while there, but he did not do much actual fundraising for the Reagan campaigns.

These then were the principal members of the Los Angeles Elders, a coterie of wealthy, prominent, and vocal Reagan supporters who meant well, but who, operating without authority, and in pursuit of their own agendas, created turmoil within Reagan's staff and family.

There were dozens of others.[114] Nancy's social friends had to be included. Business partners of the core group became players as campaigns heated up and the Tuttle money machine reached across Los Angeles County. Even so, this core group did not "select" Reagan for high office any more than the Democratic machine in New York "selected" Franklin Roosevelt or the Communist Party in Russia "selected" Stalin. Those historic leaders understood their times, resonated with their constituents, and fought their way to power. Stalin used guns; Reagan used TV.

Before his "Time for Choosing" speech, Reagan was invisible. It was only after he burst onto the national stage that the Elders flocked to his side.

As Reagan left the California governor's office, as aging took its toll on all, the Elders became less attentive. Some opposed Reagan's '76 presidential run. Many were disturbed by his attacks on Gerald Ford. Only a few joined Reagan's mismanaged '76 campaign. None of these men were Reagan's friends. To repeat, he had none.

As Press Secretary Nofziger put it in his oral history,[115] "Reagan would have made a superb hermit."

---

113   Where MCA was a major client

114   A sixties governor's office social directory also lists the following as VIPs: Earl Adams, Charles Cook, Roy Crocker, and Charles Ducommon from the Southland. Ed Gauer, Marco Hellman, Lee Kaiser, and Arch Monson from Northern California.

115   Miller Center, University of Virginia, March 2003, pg 29

Ch. 19   A Second Try

I n the autumn of '74, Gerald Ford acquired a lot of problems. He had no time for tending to Ronald Reagan's ego. Ford succeeded to the Nixon presidency on August 9. Eleven days later, he nominated Nelson Rockefeller to fill the vacated vice presidency. Gordon Luce, the Republican Chairman in California, had organized his fellow Republicans across the country into a Reagan-for-veep network. RR was not interested in that job, but he was highly annoyed by Ford's failure to consider him, to consult on other names, or to pre-notify him regarding the Rockefeller decision.

A month after Ford's inauguration, the new president pardoned Richard Nixon. This was an emotional decision made to protect an ailing human being and to close a divisive national chapter. But the promulgation of the pardon was so inept, so devoid of bipartisanship, that it re-poisoned the nation's political climate.

In the congressional elections that followed, the president's party lost four Senate seats, a tally that gave the Democrats a 60-seat majority in that body. The Republicans also lost 49 House members. With the coming of the New Year, Ford would face the implacably partisan Watergate Congress. He was a president under siege.

Henry Kissinger had joined the Nixon Administration in January '69 as that president's assistant for national security affairs. In those days, Nixon called the shots; Kissinger was the messenger. But in July '73, with Vietnam disintegrating and the Watergate investigations hitting close to home, Nixon awarded Kissinger the State Department portfolio as well. This double-hatting arrangement was stable as long as foreign affairs expert Nixon remained at the helm. But when that president left office, Kissinger inherited full control of US foreign policy. Ford allowed him to keep both State and NSC portfolios for more than a year, until November of '75. Much to Reagan's horror, détente-dedicated Kissinger took that ball and ran with it, all the way to Vladivostok.

Ford and his SecState set off for a summit meeting in that far-eastern Soviet city three weeks after the November '74 elections. The Soviet general secretary, Leonid Brezhnev, had been in power for a decade. He was still coherent. In the autumn of '74, Brezhnev saw an opportunity to rope the inexperienced American president into arms control deals that would further strengthen the Soviet "correlation of forces." Only with great effort did the US Defense Department prevent a Kissinger give-away of cruise missiles. The blossoming of Kissinger's détente, embedded in the Vladivostok accords of November '74, infuriated Reagan.

§§§

A year before, in late '73, Reagan's political stature was diminished by the 54-46 percent defeat of his proposed tax-limiting initiative, Proposition 1.[116]   In late'74, Reagan's gubernatorial term ended with the inauguration of a Democrat, his predecessor's son,[117] a young man previously elected secretary of state as a result of Reagan's unwillingness to appoint a credible candidate to a death-caused vacancy.

Reagan's driveway no longer hosted a Highway Patrol car. RR was coming home for lunch. I believe, though I cannot prove, that Nancy was urging Ron to "Get a job."

The presidency would be nice, she may have thought.

During the 1970 campaign, in conversation with Nancy Clark Reynolds, Mrs. Reagan admitted to her envy of Jackie Kennedy's earlier lifestyle. "I would love that role," she admitted to her aide.

---

116   Conceived, written, and campaign-managed by Reagan's Sacramento staff.
117   Jerry Brown

Two members of Reagan's gubernatorial staff had restructured themselves into a Los Angeles public relations firm.[118] They would manage Reagan's schedule. Others, led by Lyn Nofziger, organized a Draft Reagan Committee in Washington. Both were self-appointed groups operating with Reagan's acquiescence, but no oversight.

I was no longer involved, having joined Jim Schlesinger's Pentagon staff in the summer of '73.

On January 2, '75, Reagan called me at my northern Virginia home. He had no obvious topics for discussion. He simply wanted to chat, to talk about his relationship with President Ford.

Ron's out of office and lonely, I thought. *Why else would he call?*

RR expressed annoyance at being left out of the Veep deliberations and disdain at being offered a second-tier cabinet post. Though not clearly articulated, RR was considering another presidential run.

"I don't want to be a spoiler," he hedged.

In winding up the conversation, I offered some advice: "Better decide who speaks for you back here in Washington."

And that's not me, I said to myself. *I'm happy where I am, here in the Pentagon.*

§§§

Later, in January '75, Reagan spoke to an adoring Conservative Political Action Conference (CPAC) gathered in Washington. He brushed aside those who would mimic liberal policies to gain votes. "Let them go their way," were his words.

The CPAC marked the opening salvo in Reagan's ideological war with the Ford-Kissinger White House. Reagan called for a sharp differentiation between political parties, those distinctions to be marked with "Bold colors, not pale pastels"—his first use of that expression. At the same time, Reagan displayed his pragmatic side by quashing conservative proposals to form a new political party. His longtime fan, Bill Rusher of the *National Review*, had

---

118   Deaver and Hannaford

issued such a call. Rusher had written a pamphlet that proposed a conjoining of Reagan enthusiasts in the West with George Wallace supporters in the South. Reagan viewed any such move as foolishness. In his remarks to the conference, Reagan made clear his intent to operate within the Republican Party. He urged his listeners to do likewise; to organize and win elections as Republicans.

Reagan stole the CPAC show with a barn-burning performance. The emotional response from his audience poured fuel onto Reagan's smoldering resentments of détente, presidential neglect, and electoral embarrassments at home.

During that visit to Washington, Reagan invited me to join him for supper in his suite at the Madison Hotel. If he had an agenda, it was lost in our discussion of defense matters. I do not think he had yet made the decision to pursue the presidency, but he was well on the way.

§§§

During the Nixon years, Reagan considered himself to be that president's heir—not necessarily a future candidate, simply the next in the line of succession. He had supported Nixon's presidential and gubernatorial campaigns. He was one of the last to abandon Nixon's Watergate-torpedoed ship of state. But when it sank, Reagan saw Ford as a usurper, an unelected heir to the throne. All of these feelings of resentment converged during the early months of 1975 in the wake of the CPAC gathering.

With the coming of spring, Reagan's staff in L.A. was assembling a campaign. On April 8, Deaver called me with an invitation to attend a planning session in L.A.[119]

"Wirthlin has some national survey results," he teased.

"Can't do that," I responded. "I work for Jerry Ford. I hold serious non-partisan responsibilities at the Pentagon."

Two weeks later, Holmes Tuttle called, irate about the poor treatment the Elders were suffering at the hands of the Ford White

---

119   Those who attended: Nofziger, Meese, Deaver, Hannaford, and Wirthlin, plus newcomers Stan Evans, Bill Rusher, and Bob Walker.

House. He may have been looking for sympathy, or perhaps an explanation.

Taken together, these calls confirm that serious campaign planning, fueled by ego damage all around, was underway.

As the cherry blossoms came to Washington, Reagan began his active pursuit of the Republican nomination. At the same time, he made little effort to recruit the talent needed to win the nomination or to prevail in the election to follow. As usual, RR allowed the self-appointed to deal with those problems.

Many of Reagan's past supporters, me included, were of a pragmatic view. At no time in American history had a political party deposed its sitting president and then won the ensuing national election. To many of us, it was Gerald Ford or a Democrat. On top of that, we liked Jerry. He was a friend doing the best he could in chaotic circumstances.

Thousands of miles to the west, Reagan was living in a different world. He made no effort to connect with the Republican Party in California, by then led by Reagan's former appointments secretary, Paul Haerle. There was no outreach to any volunteers or professionals who had worked the 1966 and 1970 gubernatorial victories. There was little effort to recruit those in our '68 network, from Clif White on down.   There were no calls to Charlie Murphy, no efforts to connect with any competent and experienced speechwriters.

A good senior policy coordinator might have kept RR out of the troubles that eventually took him down.

Worst of all, Reagan ignored the Spencer-Roberts team.

He did discuss his presidential plans with Holmes Tuttle and the Elders, but as several of them told me during June telephone calls, they were opposed to a Reagan run. Many of those men, led by Henry Salvatori, were actively supporting the Republican president already in office.

On Tuesday, July 1, while in L.A. on Defense Department business, I took time out to travel up to the Reagan home in Pacific Palisades. As we settled into RR's den, I tried to bring him up to speed on strategic arms treaty negotiations, but that only led to an anti-Kissinger monologue. Nancy joined us for lunch. She redirected the conversation to politics, the presidency, and all the people she did not like because they were supporting Ford. That list included Salvatori and Republican State Chairman Haerle.

When RR left the room for a moment, Nancy displayed a streak of pessimism. "I don't think Ronnie can even carry California," she said.

As the visit ended, neither Ron nor Nancy Reagan asked me to join their campaign, but then, I had tried to direct the conversation away from such matters.

"Satellite-based intelligence gathering is the wave of the future," I reported. "Remember what *Telstar* did for you and Bobby? We can play that card against Moscow."

Ron is going to run, I concluded as I drove south. *The only thing, the only person holding him back, is Holmes. Nancy will tend to that this summer.* I felt sure RR would decide in September and then announce at year-end.

Two weeks later, on a muggy summer afternoon in 1975,[120] the White House called to invite me to a one-on-one meeting with the president. We had crossed paths at the Pentagon earlier that day. Our secretaries settled on a 7:00 p.m. date for that evening.

I had seldom set foot in the West Wing, and though I had known Gerald Ford for years, it was the first time I was to meet with him as president. (See photo at right.)

Ford was most gracious. After a brief exchange about his days on the Defense Appropriations Committee, he got to the point.

"Tom, I want to talk about politics. I want you to take over as number two in my election campaign."

I knew the leadership of his drive was in trouble. By implication, I would be taking over full responsibility come autumn. The Ford White House had come to realize that Reagan really was seeking the Republican nomination, and that they had better pay attention.

The president went on to discuss the need for new blood, making the point that he would not be choosing either "Rocky or Ron" as his running mate in '76.

While complimented, I was also stunned by all this. I had no desire to return to the world of politics. I had successfully reentered my preferred domain of high-tech national security work, satellites, and cryptography.

After some conversation about the political challenges ahead, I made an observation. "Mr. President, you've already chosen one defense official, Army Secretary Callaway, to lead your campaign," I pointed out. "After all this country has been through, Sir, I don't think you should keep recruiting help from the Pentagon. Not a good idea. We need to keep the DOD out of this."

I reminded the president of Nixon's attempt to get my Pentagon telecommunications office to reproduce the famous tapes,[121] which I had declined to do.

After exploring his thoughts about campaign structure, I offered an alternative. "Mr. President, the man you really want is Stu Spencer."

The leader of the free world scribbled a note, agreed with my cautions, and then thanked me for my time. Our conversation ended 40 minutes after I had entered the Oval Office.

§§§

Two weeks after my visit to the Oval Office, a group of Elders, led by Holmes Tuttle and including Justin Dart, Jack Hume, and William French Smith, met with Reagan at his home.[122]   They

---

121   In 1971, Nixon installed an audio taping system in his White House. A year later, those recordings documented his complicity in Watergate. When the court demanded access, the White House advised that 18 ½ minutes of conversation was missing from Nixon's conversations of November 14, '73. Prior to turning over the tapes, Nixon asked his secretary of defense to have NSA copy them. We declined, fearing we would be blamed for any defects.
122   On Tuesday, July 29.

gathered to express their unanimous opposition to his rumored presidential plans.

"We told Ron he should *not* seek the presidency," Tuttle said.[123] "Ron was shocked," Tuttle went on. "He said he's going to let Nofziger's draft committee 'run its course.' Ron claimed that he was 'keeping Ford honest.' He believes his bargaining power is going up every day."

"That's ridiculous," was the Tuttle verdict. "I've told Ed Mills to return any checks already received."

Those present told Reagan they could not support his candidacy; they would not raise money for his intended campaign. He was annoyed, but gracious as they left.

§§§

By mid-September, Stu Spencer was under contract with the Ford campaign. On Monday, September 22, I welcomed Spencer to town with a dinner at Trader Vic's. We discussed his new duties; he sought my advice on campaign staffing. On Sunday, November 2, Ford readied his cabinet for the expected Reagan attacks. He transferred NSC responsibilities to Brent Scowcroft while leaving Kissinger as SecState. Ford also fired Secretary of Defense James Schlesinger, a longtime Kissinger adversary, replacing him with close ally, transition manager, and by then chief of staff, Don Rumsfeld. This latter move may have been intended to qualify Rumsfeld for the vice presidential slot on Ford's '76 ticket.

§§§

Earlier in the year, employees Deaver and Nofziger began creating the campaign Reagan wanted by recruiting John Sears to serve as its manager. Sears was a bright, but reclusive and alcohol-challenged[124] refugee from the Nixon White House. According to

---

123   Several of the Elders had called me earlier to disclose their opposition to a Reagan run. Tuttle phoned me on July 30 to report on their July 29 meeting with RR.
124   Presidential assistant Harry Dent confirmed alcohol as the reason for Sears' departure from the Nixon staff. As the Reagan campaign unfolded, many others noted this same problem.

three independent sources, Sears showed up drunk for Reagan's July pitch to the Southern Republican chairmen.

The Sears plan envisioned a Reagan victory in the early New Hampshire and Florida primaries, to be followed by a big win in Illinois, Reagan's home state. Stu Spencer, working for Ford, was arranging for things to turn out differently.

Given my regular August phone conversations with the Elders, all of them scoffing at a Reagan candidacy, I believe Reagan's decision to run was not made until early September. At that time, as a result of a steady Nancy drumbeat, some of the Elders came on board, while others did not. Reagan-76 would prove to be a mismanaged and cash-starved campaign.

On November 20,[125] Reagan made it official. At a press conference in Washington he blandly announced, "I am a candidate for the presidency, and I ask for the support of all Americans who share my belief that our nation needs to embark on a new, constructive course."

There was no mention of Gerald Ford in Reagan's announcement, although he did decry the possibility of "four more years of business-as-usual in Washington."

Soon after taking charge of the Ford campaign, Spencer's perceptive eyes noted that a young Reagan speechwriter[126] had given Spencer a golden opportunity. In response to conservative cries for new ideas, Reagan had proposed[127] "a systematic transfer of authority and resources to the states." But all across the board, the responsibilities to be so transferred downward far outweighed the revenues available to support them. The press soon entitled this mismatch "the Ninety Billion Dollar Blunder."

The federal government was paying 62 percent of New Hampshire's welfare costs in '76. The Granite State had neither an income nor a sales tax. Both would be needed to fill the Reagan-proposed shortfall. The voters of New Hampshire were not planning

---

125   While the decision was probably made in September, the announcement was held off to protect Reagan's ability to host his radio show and to accommodate the marriage of Reagan's son Michael on November 7.
126   Jeff Bell, a 33-year-old product of the conservative think tank world. Not a player in the Charles Murphy league.
127   In a Bell-written speech to the Executive Club of Chicago, September 26, 1975

to adopt any new taxes. In early February '76, Spencer used the Ninety Billion Dollar Blunder to narrowly win New Hampshire for Ford.[128] That win was contrary to the pollsters' expectations and a real jolt to the Reagan campaign.

The next opportunity came from a December '75 Reagan speech delivered to the Southern Republican Conference in Houston. It included a discussion of ways to make Social Security voluntary. Spencer's political partner, Bill Roberts, used that material to destroy RR in Florida, where retirement is a major industry. President Ford won the Sunshine State with 53 percent of the vote, 60 percent of the Republican seniors.

The final nail was a Reagan comment suggesting that the US might send troops into Rhodesia. That central African country was, at the time, locked into a white-vs.-black civil war. Spencer crafted a TV ad that, in today's lingo, went viral.

> Governor Reagan said he would send troops into Rhodesia. Remember Vietnam?
> Governor Reagan can't start a war, but President Reagan could.

With that commercial, and with Reagan's consequent loss of the Illinois primary, the last pillar in Sears' planned trifecta toppled to earth. The Reagan campaign was $2 million in debt. Jesse Helms briefly turned the tide for Reagan in North Carolina, but Ford and Spencer had a tenuous hold on the votes needed.

Spencer was nervous as the convention opened. As in '68, Reagan had an emotional hold on an overwhelming majority of the delegates, but in '76 Reagan did not dedicate himself to converting swing votes. There were no one-on-one meetings in a windowless trailer. Perhaps Reagan had grown too old for this game. In February, he celebrated his 65th birthday. Reagan now qualified for Social Security himself. He may have been offended by Ford's nods to Rockefeller and Kissinger, but at his age, did RR really belong on stage in a hot and noisy convention hall?

As Spencer and Ford huddled in Kansas City, they awaited the emotional bombshell that could shatter their hold on hundreds

---

128   By 1 percent of the votes cast

of "support our president" delegates. A play of the Panama Canal card might do it. As president, Ford had been negotiating a return of the Canal Zone to Panamanian control. Reagan's campaign rhetoric was diametrically opposed.

"We built it, we paid for it, it's ours!" Reagan exclaimed.

But the bombshells never came. There was no sense of strategy in the Reagan team. In fact, there was no "Reagan team" at all, only a passel of alcohol-fueled minor-leaguers sniping at each other. When the roll call came, Ford won by 117 votes, a 5 percent margin. Reagan's second try had failed.

Reagan had ignored some hard-earned lessons from '68. In time, it became clear that he did not absorb much from '76 either.

Fending off Jimmy Carter in the fall was a far more difficult challenge for Spencer. The Nixon pardon, accompanied by Ford's lack of mental agility when on stage, proved to be more freight than any campaign manager could carry.

Ch. 20   A Third Try

Two years later, in 1978, Spencer and I linked arms again. We accepted the challenge of managing Bill Clements' campaign for the governorship of Texas. The Lone Star State had not elected a Republican governor since Reconstruction; it was part of the Old Confederacy. The hot and muggy flatlands of East Texas had been cotton country.

In 1960, Texas awarded its electoral votes to Democrat Kennedy, aided by Lyndon Johnson, who then carried Texas for his own account in 1964. The state had been similarly supportive of Hubert Humphrey in '68, and Jimmy Carter in '76.

Bill Clements was the perfect candidate to break this pattern. He was a roughhewn drilling contractor, not an "oil man." He stood in sharp contrast to the Democratic candidate, a slick plaintiff's attorney from the big city of Houston.

I came to know Clements quite well during my Pentagon days. He had served as deputy secretary of defense, the COO of the Pentagon.

When Clements decided to seek the Texas governorship, he asked me to run that campaign. I was enticed by the opportunity to support a truly good man, to alter the political map, and to operate in an arena free of Reagan Elders and flacks. I saw a chance to inject some fresh Republican blood into the calcified Texas body politic, so I agreed to help. I recruited Spencer to provide the strategic guidance.

In thinking through our Texas campaign plan, Spencer and I saw two political bases calling for simultaneous coverage. In the dozen-plus Republican cities, from Dallas to Houston, we needed absolute party unity. We could not afford to lose a single GOP vote. There were too few. In the other 240 counties, we would seek the support of their local leaders over coffee, one by one.

To solidify the Republicans, Spencer and I hit upon the startling concept of a joint Reagan-Ford big city tour. Such united appearances, so soon after the '76 bitterness, could be Exhibit A in our campaign for party unity in Texas.

I took the plan to the Reagan home where the governor welcomed me with a gracious luncheon and pleasant conversation. We chatted as long-lost friends until coffee was served. That's when I made my pitch.

"How about a campaign visit to Texas, Ron? Bill Clements is hoping to break the Democrat stranglehold down there. You've met him. He's a great candidate. I think we can pull it off."

Reagan smiled approvingly.

"Oh, by the way, Governor, we want Jerry Ford to join you on this tour."

Reagan's eyes widened as if he had swallowed a pequiño pepper. "You gotta be kidding," he responded before bursting into laughter.

But RR remained calm. He listened as I discussed the importance of Texas.

"Carter carried Texas in '76," I explained. "He won it 51-48 percent. To head off a repeat, Stu and I are running Bill Clements' current campaign for governor."

Reagan's face lit up. "Bill's in good hands," he observed, but then his face darkened. "Is Ford in on this gag?"

"I believe he will be. Stu Spencer is having a similar talk with Jerry this very afternoon."

My mention of the Spencer name further furrowed Reagan's brow, but as always, he was the supreme pragmatist. With an eye on 1980, both its delegates and its electoral votes, Reagan agreed to make the appearance—much to my relief.

Gerald Ford was equally entertained when Spencer crossed the Palm Desert golf course to plant the tour idea in the former president's ear. Ford was pleased that Spencer and I were running the Clements campaign. Perhaps of greater importance, Ford also resented losing Texas' 26 electoral votes to Carter in '76. That was close to the deciding margin.

As happened in Pacific Palisades, Ford inquired about his co-star's participation. After some discussion, accompanied by assurances that Reagan's involvement was *sine qua non*, Ford agreed to participate.

In mid-October, the two Republican lions performed effectively as they swept across the Texas Hill Country. There was no animosity when they met; humor unfolded with every stop. Ford could not pronounce our candidate's name correctly. He urged a crowd in Dallas to support "Biff Klimicks" for governor. Reagan echoed that pronunciation at the next stop. Both men laughed. Their light touches made the day.

A month later, our man won the governorship by 17,000 votes out of 2.3 million cast.[129] Post-election surveys indicated minimal Republican defections.

§§§

During the summer of '79, Reagan again decided to seek the presidency. Several younger candidates were appearing on the horizon, but the aging conservative icon should have been able to breeze through to the nomination. Repeating the errors of the past, however, Reagan allowed the self-appointed, alcohol-fueled three stooges, Nofziger, Deaver, and Sears, to again take charge of his campaign.

Odd, I thought, *given Reagan's boyhood experience with alcohol in the family.*

By the end of pre-election year '79, fratricide was in the air. Sears was exiling the Old Sacramento Hands as fast as he could. He wanted total control.

Reagan paid no attention to the stresses in his campaign. There was no internal direction, nor did Reagan recruit talent from the outside world. He made no contact with anyone who had produced victories a decade before. Reagan also ignored the matter

---

129   Reagan carried Texas two years later, in the general election of 1980, 55-41 percent

of finance. The titans of Tuttle's money machine, so effective in the sixties, were an aging and ill constituency. Nofziger was serving as deputy finance director; the campaign was running out of cash.

On January 7 Nofziger called me.

"I'm appalled by Ron's detachment," Nofziger confided. "But who else is there?"

Nofziger was a serious patriot, a veteran of Omaha Beach. He was worried about his country's well-being and distressed by his disordered surroundings.

Three weeks later,[130] campaign pollster Dick Wirthlin called. I had recruited his firm a decade before. His research was key to Reagan's survival in '70, but his '80 polls were suggesting a different story. He saw Reagan's presidential campaign as stalled. Wirthlin was looking for future work when it collapsed.

When George H.W. Bush took the Iowa caucuses on January 21, chaos enveloped the Reagan camp as well as the nation's political cognoscenti. Published polls in Texas showed Carter leading Bush, Reagan, and former Texas Governor John Connolly in that order and by substantial margins. Texas appeared to be headed for a repeat of its 1976 support of Carter in the general election.

A week after Iowa, Henry Kissinger called. He knew I had run the Clements gubernatorial campaign, and we knew each other from Nixon Administration days.

"Carter's a lunatic," he observed. "He's making threats on which he cannot deliver.

Reagan is not up to facing the crises to come. Who are his supporters?"

This was Kissinger-speak for, "Who in the foreign policy establishment cares about Reagan?"

Henry answered his own question: "I haven't found any."

"George Bush is a lightweight, but I could work for him," Kissinger continued before dismissing John Connolly out of hand. "How about Bill Clements? It's a little late, but he's a strong character. I could support him."

---

130   On January 30, 1980

The former SecState was considering all the angles. He saw his adopted country at risk.

Two weeks after Iowa, Nancy Reagan called Bill Clark.[131] She described the anarchy within her husband's campaign and sought Clark's help. "Ronnie and I had a long talk with John Sears over the weekend," she explained. "The campaign is in chaos, and there's no central direction. Ronnie's mind is fuzzy. He can't think things through."

Mrs. Reagan followed this analysis with a question that took Clark by surprise.

"Could you leave the court, Bill? Could you take charge of this operation?"

It was the first Reagan attempt to reach outside the circle of wagons.

Within an hour Clark received the follow-up call from John Sears.

"Whatever happens in New Hampshire, Bill, things are going to unravel. RR is too distraught to function well," Sears said. "Nancy says she asked you to come help. I agree."

Sears did not understand that he was the core of the problem.

Once advised of the Clark-Reagan conversation, I called Stu Spencer for his take on the disturbances within that campaign.

His succinct verdict: "As of now, in January 1980, Ron is a loser."

Later that afternoon, Clark called to fill me in further on his conversations with Nancy and Sears. "A week ago, Ron came close to firing Sears," Clark reported. "He wanted to install Deaver as campaign manager."

Deaver? I thought. *Another unqualified minion, the next in line sitting outside the door. Seated because he's too drunk to stand. Nothing has changed.*

Clark continued with his story. "No real headquarters, Tom. Sears created an office in Northern Virginia with a 'field station' in L.A. But that's where Ron and Nancy live. That's where the action is. The campaign is bipolar if not incoherent. People wander in and out of Ron's life as they please."

---

131   On February 11, 1980

I could hear the anxiety in Clark's long-distance voice.

"My courtroom is a tranquil place, Tom. I'd only leave it if you, Cap [Weinberger], and Helene [Von Damm] come along. I'm headed up to Santa Barbara this evening to thrash this one out," Clark concluded.

"Okay, that's nice," I responded, offering no pledge of support. "Stay in touch, Bill."

A few days later, Clark called again to report on his five-and-a-half-hour discussion with Reagan.

"Longest conference I've ever had with Ron," Clark admitted. "Both of us are a lot older now. I think his campaign is pretty hopeless. I can't leave my judicial bench to join that maelstrom, but you and Ron ought to talk."

"Why?" I asked.

§§§

The next day, Bill's son Colin, working for the Reagan campaign as an advance man, tracked me down during my visit to family in Connecticut.

"Mr. Reagan wants to see you," he began.

"Really?" I responded. "I rather doubt that."

"Well, OK, he is willing to see you. Dad engineered the meeting," Colin admitted.

"That's more like it," I answered. "I'm in Connecticut right now. When and where?"

"How about tonight?"

Colin proposed an evening meeting at the New London Inn.

"Use the name 'John Martinez' when you arrive," Colin instructed. "Too much intrigue around here. Sears doesn't like the governor having outside visitors."

"OK," I sighed.

A scenic four-hour autumn drive led me to the New London Inn. With my password, I gained entrance to the Reagan suite where I awaited the candidate. RR arrived alone after a full day of retail campaigning in the coffee shops of New Hampshire. He was alert and welcoming, though in a formal way. Reagan was receiving a "visitor" as requested by Clark.

I opened by talking about our success in Texas, since that is where I last saw Reagan. I then turned to the campaign at hand. "I have some advice for winning and for losing," I started.

"Shoot," he responded.

"Two things are wrong with your campaign, Governor. Number one is management. You don't have any, but Nancy's call to Clark tells me you understand that," I said.

"Hmmm," was Reagan's only response.

"Number two, it's not you physically, Ron." I was trying for diplomacy. "It's your ideas that are old. From what I've read, you've been talking about the sixties. A decade has passed since then. Those campus protesters now have kids of their own. You need to address *their* future, the eighties, not the problems of the years past."

Reagan only nodded.

"If you win the nomination, the folks who worked for you in 1970 stand ready to help. If things do not work out, think through what you want from the Republican nominee. Be more than gracious; be objective."

I do not believe Reagan heard those closing words. Losing was never an acceptable outcome for him.

Our conversation, mostly my one-way monologue, ended an hour and a half later. We closed with a discussion of START treaties and the overhang of nuclear weapons.

RR did not ask me to join his campaign, and I did not offer to do so.

§§§

Two days later, pollster Wirthlin called Spencer. He was again looking for work once the Reagan campaign crashed. Wirthlin noted recent surveys taken by *Texas Monthly* that confirmed his own national findings. In Texas, Bush ran best against Carter, but no Republican beat the Georgian.

When I dined with Governor and Mrs. Clements that evening, they supported the *Texas Monthly* views.

"I don't think we can carry Texas in 1980," the governor warned.

During the last week of January, Reagan salvaged his campaign with a brilliant debate performance. He faced off against a frozen and stage-struck Bush. "I paid for this microphone ..." were his defining words.

But more than oratory was needed. The Reagan campaign was disorganized, demoralized, and broke. The Sears apparatus had burned through $12 million.[132] The campaign had only $5 million of expenditures allowable before the convention.

Three days later, as the New Hampshire primary results rolled in, Ron and Nancy, acting as a team, dismissed Sears and a few of his associates. With Clark's refusal to leave the California court, Nancy turned to Bill Casey, a 67-year-old former chairman of the Securities and Exchange Commission, to solve the financial crises and to take over as chairman of the '80 campaign. She did not know Casey well; they had only met at a Reagan fundraising dinner in New York earlier in the year.

That evening New Hampshire delivered a 2:1 Reagan landslide. He now had the momentum, but the professionals across the land had their doubts. Few thought the aging conservative from California could defeat Jimmy Carter in the fall. An ABC/Lou Harris Poll, conducted right after New Hampshire, confirmed that view. It showed Carter with a 58-40 percent lead over Reagan.

§§§

Two days after New Hampshire, on February 28, I lunched with Clark at a secluded club a few blocks uphill from the judge's office.

"Where did Casey come from?" I asked.

"I made that call, Tom. When in Santa Barbara, after I declined the Reagans' invitation to join the campaign, Nancy started talking about this fellow from New York. He sounded good to me. She

---

132   About $35 million in 2014 dollars

handed me the phone and said, 'OK, call him right now.' Me? I asked. Why? 'Do it,' she ordered. 'Here's his number.' So I made the call."

Clark then went on to relate his first impressions of the new chairman.

"Casey is inarticulate, a mumbler, but he's also an enthusiast. He had the credentials needed to organize the Reagan kickoff dinner back east. He's well connected in the New York financial world. That's important; Ron and Nancy are concerned about campaign-induced personal liabilities."

Clark's tales astounded me.

He continued. "Casey accepted, and that was that. He'll be the East Coast William French Smith. Mccsc is now supposed to run the campaign."

Not likely, I thought. "Why won't Ron manage his own life?" I asked. "Why couldn't *he* make the Casey call? Ron always folds when Taft or Holmes complain," I added. "I've never seen anyone so averse to bad news."

Clark responded, his voice dropping to a whisper. "Did he ever tell you about his father?"

"Well, yes," I answered quietly. "I think Jack Reagan was an alcoholic. Didn't Ron have to pour him into bed every now and then?"

"Exactly, Tom. Ever know other children of alcoholic parents?" Clark asked.

"Never thought much about it," I answered.

"Some turn to booze themselves," Clark explained. "Some become resentful, but most simply want tranquility in their lives. Trusting others is a challenge. They can't deal with people one on one. They don't want to hear bad news. They need a happy ending to every story. If there's no happy ending, they delete the story from their memory. That's their M.O.," Clark concluded. "That's our man."

"Oh," was my only response.

"Sorry your conversation with Ron did not turn out better," Clark noted as we ended our luncheon.

§§§

Others who knew Reagan well were being more realistic. The day after my lunch with Clark, George Steffes called. For eight years Steffes had served as the governor's strikingly competent assistant for legislative affairs.

"The Reagan campaign is a mess, Tom. It's the Reagan-Meese black hole all over again," he said. "They'll never beat Carter. You worked for Ford. Why don't you organize a Draft Ford Committee? Right now!"

That message was echoed during an evening call from the governor of Texas.

"I've been talking with some of the other governors," Clements reported. "None of us think Reagan can win in the fall. Let's get Jerry Ford back in. The fellows in Michigan, Ohio, and Virginia are all for it. There are a lot of delegates in those states."

On March 2, Clements and I met with the former president at his Palm Desert home. Former Congressman and then Army Secretary Jack Marsh joined us. It was an informal conversation; Ford was dubious, but he also saw the need.

"Let's see who signs up," he offered.

That was the beginning of a serious, if brief, Ford quest for the nomination.

Two days later, I accepted Henry Kissinger's invitation to lunch in New York.

"If Bill Clements won't run, let's give Jerry a try," he said. "We've got to do something."

At the time, Henry had purchased a temporary pass aboard the Ford bandwagon.

During the week that followed, a passel of post-New Hampshire surveys confirmed the spreading conventional wisdom: "Reagan can't win."

In the ABC/Lou Harris Survey noted above, Reagan was losing to Carter while Ford held a 54-44 percent lead over his successor. Lance Tarrance, surveying in Texas, found Carter beating Reagan in that state 56-38 percent, while Ford led 49-45 percent. The Field

Poll in California showed Carter leading Reagan by 7 percent. That was in Reagan's home state.

This flurry of polls, accompanied by Republican establishment concerns, led to a Ford organizing session in Chicago on March 9. Spencer and I met with Dick Cheney, Ford's pollster Bob Teeter, and a handful of other political professionals to consider the possibilities. As always, Spencer was the realist.

"Reagan probably has 1,198 votes, if we include California," he reported. "He only needs 998 to win, so right now he's got it. On the other hand, every poll shows Reagan to be a loser. The party chairmen see another Goldwater debacle coming. They don't like it."

During the previous week, in an effort to bring these discussions to a head, I publicly announced a Draft Ford Committee. Not surprisingly, Ford's old friends Mel Laird, Henry Kissinger, et al., those who had urged a Ford candidacy in private, were nowhere to be seen when it came time to stand up and be counted.

On March 12, the same Chicago group met with the former president in a private office on Lafayette Square in Washington. We summarized our findings: poll support, but no important endorsements.

Ford closed off the discussions with his own summary. "Reagan is not equipped to be president, but I'll support him if he's nominated. The country is in terrible shape, with worse to come. I'm headed home to talk this over with Betty. Let's meet out there, in Palm Desert, on Saturday."

The next day, Ford called me for a personal follow-up. "I think it's wrong for me to get in, but I don't want to say 'the hell with my country,' either. I want your best thoughts, Tom. Please be here on Saturday."

On March 15, the former president gathered his half-dozen counselors in Palm Desert. Ford added two "outsiders," longtime friends Alan Greenspan and Leon Parma, to the group.

As the discussion opened, Spencer and I offered matching advice."The votes are not there, Mr. President, but if you want to go, we're with you."

Ford went around the table, asking all for their comments. In general, they matched the Spencer and Reed assessment. Ford was annoyed that his old pals from the Hill, the men who had said, "We're all with you, Jerry," had vanished when their public support was needed.

Two hours after we started, with the circumnavigation of the conference table complete, Ford voiced his conclusions."This is the most difficult decision of my life, fellows. The Carter presidency is unsound, to put it mildly. Judging by those around Reagan, he would not be much better. I know I could beat Carter; I'm not sure Reagan can. I'd be disappointed if I ran and lost, but that's happened before. On the other hand, collecting a few loyal delegates, a half loaf, would be worse than nothing."

Spencer nodded.

"Besides that, finance would be a problem. We can't kick off a campaign by borrowing money." Ford's pace slowed, his words were now measured. "I've decided not to be a candidate, gentlemen. That's what's best for the country."

We stood for a break and Ford left to put on a jacket.

At 1:00 p.m. I introduced the man who needed no introduction to the press corps assembled outside in the late winter sun.

Ford's statement was concise. "I will not be a candidate," were the key words. "I will support the nominee of the Republican Party with all the energy I have."

That closing phrase was important to all of us. We wanted the air cleared; we did not want to see Jerry Ford pouting for the rest of the year.

With the Ford option behind us, Spencer and I, along with a host of Nixon-era Republicans, put our heads together to address the question of "what next?" We knew Reagan could not win the fall election, but perhaps we could help Carter lose it.

We created an independent expenditures committee, "Americans for an Effective Presidency," which was to raise money and then illuminate the Carter record in a few key states, mainly Texas. The AEP was a forerunner of today's political action committees. (PACs).

During those same months, George Bush enjoyed a modest rebound. He won the primary in his family's home state of Connecticut and then in Pennsylvania, a major industrial state. Another ABC/Harris Poll, conducted at the end of March, once again showed Carter leading Reagan, though by a smaller margin than before. In April, Bush won the Michigan primary, collecting two-thirds of the delegates from the Wolverine State.

The trend was clear. New England and the industrial northeast were showing a distrust of the Western cowboy. More ominously, John Anderson, a former Republican congressman from Illinois, was gaining national ballot access as a third-party candidate. His early poll numbers were comparable to George Wallace's 13 percent showing in '68, though from a far different constituency.

In June, Reagan clinched the nomination with a win in his home state, but his string of victories was hollow. Those primary wins might better be described as "Tea Party triumphs." The hard core in the South and West were providing the delegates. Middle-class independents in the east did not trust the man they saw as the right-winger from California.

A Gallup survey published in June gave Carter a 39-32 edge over Reagan, with a quarter of the voters turning to John Anderson or looking for other alternatives. Reagan was down by seven points. Victory was *not* in the air.

§§§

In mid-June, after the California primary, Spencer got a surprise call from Mike Deaver. "The Reagans want you to come back."

That seemed odd. Spencer was cautious. His skeptical response: "I'll believe that when I hear it from Ron or Nancy."

CH. 21 GETTING IT RIGHT

The call from Nancy Reagan came three days later, during the last week of June.

"You've got to come run this campaign, Stu. It's chaos," she said. "Ronnie is losing it. He's not doing well. We need you."

In response, Spencer reminded Nancy of his own aggressive tactics of '76, the "President Reagan could start a war" ad.

Nancy dismissed all of that. "Just shows you're a pro, Stu. Come on up to the house so we can talk. Ronnie needs you." Her insistent voice was sharp and demanding.

Spencer was appreciative, but cautious. He needed to neutralize those who would be antagonistic to his return. "I need to talk to Ed and a few of the other fellows. I'll get back to you," Spencer told her.

"Soon!" was her imperious closing command.

Three days later, Spencer convened a political peace conference. It was held at Jimmy's, a Beverly Hills hangout adjacent to Chasen's, the Reagans' preferred hideaway. Ed Meese, Mike Deaver, Lyn Nofziger, and pollster Dick Wirthlin were his guests.

After a few medicinal drinks, Spencer advised the group of Nancy's invitation. His message was met with murmurs.

"No hiding out on this one," Spencer proclaimed. His eyes swept the table. "Will you welcome me back into the Reagan political family? I want a clear and unambiguous answer from each of you. Yes or no."

One by one, the grimacing officers of the Reagan entourage went on record with a barely audible "Yes."

Pollster Wirthlin added an authenticating postscript. "Nancy wants the White House so badly she'll put up with anything, Stu. Even you."

Spencer called me on Independence Day, 1980, to advise of his decision to join the Reagan campaign. I believe he called Nancy at the same time. But before meeting with the Reagans, Spencer needed time at his Newport Beach home to think this one through. He was a political professional, but he was also a member of the Greatest Generation. He cared about his country and the presidency. He wanted to do this one right. He knew it would be tough and that it was up to him.

As Spencer assumed these responsibilities, neither Tuttle nor Casey was around to offer a contract. A handshake with Deaver was his only assurance of compensation.

Spencer formally joined the Reagan campaign on Saturday, July 12. On that day, he drove to LAX, met the Reagans at the gate, and boarded their commercial Northwest Airlines flight to the Republican Convention city of Detroit.

The senior Reagan staff was booked in first class, with Ron and Nancy seated together. When the plane reached cruising altitude, Nancy rose. She invited Spencer to take her place, since her husband and his prospective Jedi protector had not talked for almost a decade.

Spencer expected recriminations from 1976, but there were none. Reagan picked up right where he had left off years before. "How's Bill?" the governor asked.

Stu's former business partner, Bill Roberts, had been suffering from diabetes.

"Losing limbs, but gaining weight," was Spencer's realistic response.

The governor smiled. He and his counselor were professionals; they had a job to do.

As they cruised over the Nevada desert, Spencer commented on Reagan's campaign demeanor. "You appeared upset during the primaries, Ron. Uncomfortable."

"Absolutely, Stu. Too much stuff. I'm glad you're here."

In time, the two men turned their attention to convention practicalities.

"Who's your choice for vice president, Stu?" Reagan asked.

"George Bush," Spencer quickly responded. "The obvious choice."

Reagan grimaced. During the primaries, Bush had leveled harsh attacks on Reagan's cherished fiscal ideas. "Voodoo economics," Bush had called them.

"Doesn't matter, Ron. I've said worse things about you, and here we are. George won a lot of big eastern primaries. You'll need those states. And you need balance. Bush is perceived as an eastern moderate; you're the cowboy from the West. Besides that, he's bright. He knows what he's talking about. He'd provide wise counsel once you get to the White House. You need him, Governor."

Reagan's only response was his usual non-responsive, "Hmmm."

After lengthy discussions of other issues, Spencer came to the key question. "Why are you doing this, Ron? Why do you want to be president?"

Without delay, Reagan responded, "It's time to end the Cold War, Stu."

§§§

The two men parted company upon arrival in Detroit. Noisy crowds welcomed the Reagans en route to their suite atop the Renaissance Center Hotel; Spencer was shown to his room in the basement. Mrs. Reagan had invited him to join the inner circle, but the staff was not willing to implement those orders.

Only once did they invite Spencer up to the Reagans' top floor suite, but that was an important elevator ride, taken to cement the VP decision. Others gathered there had some dangerous ideas. RR was cautious.

"Reagan was neither ideological nor proud," Spencer noted later. "He was a pragmatic man. The Bush name made the most sense to him, so that's what he did."

§§§

When both parties' conventions ended, Reagan's standing had improved. The Gallup Poll gave Carter only a one-point lead, 39-38 percent, but third-party candidate John Anderson was providing a worrisome haven for liberal eastern Republicans. Anderson's draw was a reminder of how George Wallace had endangered Nixon's electoral majority in 1968.

After the convention, upon Spencer's arrival in Washington, he found no office space allocated for his use. Propitiously, a key member of the campaign staff had headed off for a two-week golfing vacation. Spencer seized that office, moved the golfer's desk into the hall, and set to work. But doing what? The Reagans were now situated at the former Kennedy compound in the Virginia hunt country, a spacious home known as Wexford.[133] Spencer sat at a desk 50 miles away in Alexandria listening to Casey mumble.

Convergence came via a covert Saturday phone call from pollster Wirthlin. "We're out at Wexford," he whispered. "Campaign planning. Nancy just asked, 'Where's Stu?'"

A Sunday summit followed. Spencer drove out to Wexford where the Reagans and Deaver gave him his commission as commander-in-chief of the fall campaign.

With this now unambiguous authority, Spencer built a tight airborne command post around the candidate. The empowered players were Nofziger, assisted by Jim Brady, handling the press. Martin Anderson was responsible for issues research; Joe Canzeri ran the tours and the advance staff; Ken Khachigian was the speechwriter, i.e., senior policy coordinator. Spencer had exploited Reagan's loose tongue in '76. There was to be none of that in '80. Khachigian, a mid-forties former White House intern and Deukmejian aide, imposed discipline on every Reagan word. Spencer and his aide Deaver rounded out the team.

Meese, Casey, Wirthlin, and a host of others stayed in Alexandria. Phone ties from there to the plane were essentially cut off. Wirthlin was allowed to join the airborne command post when

---

133   By then owned by Texas Governor Clements, who offered its use during the campaign.

he had survey updates to report, but only after Spencer had studied the data.

Knowing of Reagan's aversion to bad news, Wirthlin would only brief Reagan on worshiping demographic groups. After every such spiel, Spencer had to serve as the regent of reality.

"OK, Dick. Now tell him the bad news."

Over Labor Day, Wirthlin's surveys showed Reagan down by seven points. In late September, Spencer noted a stubborn gender gap. Women's antipathy to RR was giving Carter his polling edge. Spencer conceived the historic Reagan pledge that his first appointee to the Supreme Court be a woman. This proposal met with stiff resistance from the (male) lawyers on the plane, but Spencer thought this the right thing to do, not only politically, but morally. The issues experts agreed. When broached to the candidate, there was little debate. Reagan liked the idea, and it worked.

By the end of October, the Wirthlin surveys confirmed that Reagan and Spencer had turned the campaign around, even though published polls claimed otherwise.[134]

As always, RR drove in the winning run with his October 28 debate face-off against Carter. The incumbent president appeared officious and patronizing. Reagan responded with a smile: "There you go again..."

On November 4, Reagan won 51 percent of the popular vote and 489 Electors. Carter received only 41 percent and 49 Electors. John Anderson won 7 percent of the popular vote, but no Electors. His tally did not seem to impact any of the key state races.

Eight historic years followed. Volcker's Fed, accompanied by Reagan's tax reforms, saved and rebuilt the American economy. Reagan's opening salvo, firing the striking air controllers, had a minor impact on most Americans, but it got the attention of the Soviet nomenclatura. "Reagan's tough; he means what he says," they noted.

---

134   On the Friday before the election (Oct 29), the *Washington Post* credited Carter with a four-point margin, leading Reagan 43-39 percent. The next day, on Saturday, October 30, the CBS/*New York Times* poll indicated a race too close to call. Over this same post-debate weekend, Wirthlin's surveys indicated a steady 10 percent Reagan margin. That's the way it turned out.

§§§

Early in 1982, once I had joined the White House staff, President Reagan asked me to codify a plan for prevailing over the Soviet system, for ending the Cold War. A talented and diverse interagency group did the work; I was only the chief clerk, but during the late winter of that year, we devised options for taking the Cold War to the Soviet doorstep. We envisioned a multi-front offensive, to be fought by our oddly-clad Islamic allies, by dedicated clerks with green eyeshades, and by brilliant geeks working in the dark. These troops were to operate from the mountains of Afghanistan to their bunkers underground to the seclusion of outer space.

In April '82, I presented some of our ideas to the president and his National Security Council principals for comment.[135]

Partway through, Reagan interrupted. "Why can't we just push the Soviets over backwards?" he asked. "They're going broke."

Reagan's cabinet, seated at the historic oval table, displayed a collective frown.

"That's a stable system," the secretary from Foggy Bottom warned. "Better be careful."

"You'll annoy our allies," the treasury man cautioned. "Thatcher's your friend, but the Brits and the Germans trade big time with the Russians."

A third cabinet member objected to the president's numbers. "The Sovs are only spending 16-18 percent of their GDP on defense," he said. "Too bad if you're a Russian worker, but the nomenclatura lives well. They won't give up without a fight."

But from the back bench came the voice of Henry Rowen, Chairman of the National Intelligence Council, a group of outsiders drawn from academia and the business community to bring perspective to the often-incestuous CIA findings.

"No, Mr. President," Rowen offered. "With real-world accounting, it is clear the Soviets now spend more than half their GDP on defense. Every road is built to support tanks. Every hospital

---

135   Reagan's diary entry for April 27, 1982, notes, "Strategic plan submitted by Tom Reed. Approved."

caters to the generals. Every factory is a net-value subtractor. My friends and I have been there, Sir. The Soviet-issued numbers are phony. You can push those people over backwards if you want to."

Rowen's associates, seated at his side, voiced their agreement. So did my NSC staff[136] arrayed along the wall in back of me.

Reagan peered over his spectacles as they slid down his nose. The smile I knew so well flashed across the jellybean-laden table. Amidst grimaces from his cabinet, the President of the United States made his intentions clear.

"That's what we're going to do—push 'em over backwards."

§§§

As future SecDef Robert Gates observed in his recent memoirs, "Don't pick a fight, don't go to war, unless you have a clear vision of how it is to end."

Reagan already knew that. Gates was one of his key intelligence advisors during the eighties. As part of the decision directive Reagan signed in May of 1982, Reagan spelled out his vision of the Cold War's end. He did not call for unconditional surrender, nor did he envision American troops toppling statues of Lenin in Red Square. His decision directive drew from Thomas Jefferson and the American Declaration of Independence.

"We wish to convince the leadership of the Soviet Union to turn their attention inward," we wrote, "to seek the legitimacy that comes only from the consent of the governed, and thus to address the hopes and dreams of their own people."

That's how it turned out. At the end of '85, Boris Yeltsin became de facto mayor of Moscow. In the spring of 1988, Reagan's determination to end the Cold War led to his amiable stroll across Red Square with Soviet General Secretary Gorbachev.

In time, an entire class of nuclear weapons was dismantled and destroyed.

---

136   Principally economist Norman Bailey

§§§

During the years that followed the '80 election, Spencer did some lobbying work in Washington. He also turned to the international market, managing campaigns in Greece, southern Africa, and Panama.

The Reagans turned to him again in 1984. For that re-election campaign, Spencer was the undisputed kingpin, promoting a vision of "Morning in America" in the aftermath of a serious recession. As Spencer had discovered in California 10 years before, the re-election of an incumbent is far different than starting from scratch, but Spencer put it all together.

Reagan's first debate with challenger Mondale was a disaster. The aging Reagan had been over-prepared. Spencer demanded a relaxed interlude before the second and final show. Allowed to be himself, Reagan reduced the audience, even his opponent, to appreciative laughter.

When the interlocutor raised the age issue, the 73-year-old president brought down the house. "I refuse to make my opponent's youth and inexperience an issue in this campaign."

Mondale joined in the laughter. He knew it was over; 1984 was a sweep.

§§§

Spencer remained on call. The Reagans asked him to visit the family quarters in the White House whenever he was in town. Once there, he was often called on to mediate intra-family disputes.

In March '83, Nancy was complaining about RR's "Evil Empire" speech[137] to anyone who would listen. "Terrible," she said to her husband. "You can't say those things, Ronnie."

A week later, when Spencer joined the Reagans for supper upstairs, Nancy asked him to weigh in.

---

137   On March 8, '83. Reagan spoke to a meeting of National Evangelicals in Orlando, Florida. He referred to communism as "the focus of evil in the modern world," a remark that emboldened dissidents behind the Iron Curtain.

"It is an Evil Empire," Spencer advised. "Even so, you might scare a lot of people, Ron."

The president's response was typically concise: "Well, thanks Stu, but they are evil people, and we're going to push 'em over backwards. What's for dessert, Mommy?"

That one response confirms, for all time, Nancy's narrow role in Ronald Reagan's life.

§§§

When the just-retired Reagans returned to California on the afternoon of January 20, 1989, they invited Stu Spencer and his wife Barbara to join them aboard the aircraft once known as Air Force One. That was a fitting windup to Spencer's historic role.

With the end of the Reagan and Bush Sr. terms in office, along with the arrival of retirement age, Spencer settled into a new home in Palm Desert where he now lives with his supportive and golfing-partner wife.

Stuart Spencer is one of the most invisible, yet one of the most important, figures of twentieth-century American history. Ronald Reagan may have understood the political stage, and he certainly had the mind needed to compose and deliver the message, but without Spencer providing the direction, Ronald Reagan never would have been elected president of anything. Well, possibly one final term at the Screen Actors Guild.

Nancita

In December of 1980, as Reagan's first inauguration approached, Johnny Carson used the term "Nancita" when labeling Nancy Reagan "The Evita of Bel Air."

Exactly. Eva Duarte Peron, the powerhouse behind Argentina's Juan Peron in the 1940s, is the perfect analogy. Ronald Reagan's rise to the presidency would not have happened without Nancy Reagan's boundless ambition.[138]   Every one of my sources for this book agrees. Without the adoring, striving, and driven Nancy at his side, Ronald Reagan would have spent the eighties as a retired actor and former governor, tending to his horses in the hills above Santa Barbara.

Consider the parallels:

- The biological fathers of both women disappeared early on.[139] Deception was in the air when Nancy was born. One biographer notes, "Only two entries on Nancy Reagan's birth certificate are accurate—her sex and her color. Almost every other family entry was invented." In time, even the baby's name was changed.[140]
- During their younger years, both Evita and Nancy enjoyed multiple close personal relationships with elite men—in Buenos Aires for Evita, in New York and Hollywood for Nancy. Her affair with MGM producer Benjamin Thau assured steady work.[141]
- With similar goals, both women targeted ascenders as potential spouses.
    ◊ Eva Duarte, a 25-year-old radio personality in 1944, targeted the 20-year-older Colonel Peron at the time of his rise to prominence in the wake of Argentina's San Juan earthquake.
    ◊ Nancy Davis, arriving in Hollywood at age 28, compiled a list of "eligible bachelor targets." Reagan, the 10-year-older President of the Screen Actors Guild, topped the list.[142]
- These first ladies were fashionistas. Beautiful clothing was important to both; paying for it was of no personal concern.

---

138   Noted by her classmates at Smith ("Intense ambition"), her colleagues in New York when cultivating theatrically powerful lovers ("her ambition exceeded her affection") to her colleagues in Hollywood (" ... devious... she was so ambitious," Ann Southern).

139   Nancy's parents divorced soon after her birth. Mother remarried eight years later. The daughter was formally adopted by Dr. Loyal Davis and renamed Nancy Davis in 1935.

140   Nancy was born Anne Francis Robbins.

141   "Their affair was well known at the studio." (Kathryn Grayson) "Because she was sleeping with Benny, we had to cast her in our movies." (Gottfried Reinhardt)

142   A list shown to a co-worker at MGM

- Each woman refused to let her man quit when the going got rough.

    ◊ In October 1945, with Peron ousted from Argentina's vice presidency and in prison, Eva and the labor unions organized massive demonstrations outside the *Casa Rosada*, Argentina's presidential palace.[143] These demonstrations, along with Eva's oratory, brought about Peron's release and, four months later, his election to Argentina's presidency.

    ◊ In the mid-sixties, when Ronald Reagan's TV career was on the skids, Nancy insisted that he seek the governorship of California or else.[144] Eight years later, when RR left Sacramento, Nancy was a key agitator in demanding he next pursue the presidency. Reagan was not opposed. His mind was receptive to the idea of such a run; he had long viewed himself as Nixon's logical heir. But it was Nancy who provided the steely ambition.

Paid staffers in the former governor's West Los Angeles office (Deaver et al.) were supportive of RR's seeking the presidency, while, as noted earlier, the Los Angeles Elders were not. Nancy tipped the balance. During the summer of '75, she badgered "the boys" until, by September of that year, many of them had changed their minds and come aboard.

In March 1980, when RR's campaign was once again in Sears-induced shambles, it was Nancy who demanded his firing and then recruited Bill Casey to untangle the campaign's finances. Four months later, with polls still indicating a Reagan defeat, it was Nancy who sought out Stu Spencer, asking him to salvage the race.

Nancy kept the heat on RR. Her presidential ambitions took six years to bear fruit, but during those years Nancy never faltered or failed.

---

143   Crowds estimated at around 300,000 people
144   We know this from family members hearing the shout from the Reagan bedroom in early 1965: "If you don't run for governor, Ronnie, I want a divorce." This was not meant literally, of course, but the remark does confirm Nancy Reagan's determination.

There is one major difference between Evita and Nancy: their political roots. Eva Peron's base came to be known as *Los Descamisados*, the shirtless ones. These were the multitudes of impoverished workers, men from the agricultural, abattoir, and industrial worlds of Argentina, men who could not afford even a full set of clothing.

Nancy's acolytes, numbering only in the dozens, *had* shirts. Some picked them up on Rodeo Drive. Others tried to smuggle their Christian Dior threads into the US as they returned from Paris.[145] Nancy's base continued to be the fashionably dressed, perfectly coiffed wives of the Los Angeles Elders, even as their men died off, though that roster was subject to constant upgrade.

The saddest words Bill Clark and I heard while working in the Reagan White House were uttered by the First Lady's social secretary. Clark and I were discussing the guest list for an upcoming state dinner to honor Great Britain's Queen Elizabeth II. The event was to be held in California, but the name of Reagan's oldest, strongest, and most reliable supporter had not made the cut.

Clark reached for the phone, asking for the First Lady's social secretary. When connected, he inquired about the March event. "Where is Holmes Tuttle's name?"

The gatekeeper cautiously advised us of Mrs. Reagan's exact words: "He's just a car dealer from Los Angeles."

---

145   In September 1976, Betsy Bloomingdale pleaded guilty in federal court to a felony charge: deceiving customs officers.

CH. 22   THE SECRET WEAPON

In July 1980, when newly re-hired campaign strategist Stu Spencer joined Reagan on his flight to the Republican Convention, Spencer asked his candidate about intentions.

"We need to end the Cold War," was Reagan's short-form answer.

To this day Spencer remembers, in crisp detail, the conversation that followed.

Reagan spoke for an hour about Soviet and Chinese oppression and slaughter, about the millions massacred, if only for political sins, as the twentieth century unfolded. Reagan also understood the nuclear sword hanging over the current Soviet-US confrontations. Reagan was a nuclear abolitionist, but he was also a believer in peace through strength. How to reconcile these conflicting perspectives?

"Armageddon could happen on my watch," Reagan offered as the Northwest jet crossed the Great Plains.

The prospective president was a staunch believer, having been raised in the Disciples of Christ Church by his devout mother. The Reverend Ben Cleaver, pastor at the First Christian Church in Dixon, promoted Reagan's attendance at Eureka College, an institution founded in 1848 by the Disciples of Christ. Reagan had studied the New Testament's Revelations 16:16. He feared the final biblical struggle, the cataclysmic showdown between good and evil, might come during his term in office. The spread of nuclear weapons made that possibility all too real.

§§§

In time, the two travelling politicos turned their conversation to more immediate matters: delegate counts, vice presidential alternatives, and campaign strategy. They made it to Detroit. Reagan won the nomination and then the presidency. He spent his first year in office dealing with runaway inflation and the collapsed American economy.

Late in that first year, I met with Bill Clark in the ornate rooms atop the State Department. He wanted to brainstorm priorities in anticipation of his impending transfer to the National Security Council. At the time, he was serving as deputy secretary of state; I was a member of the Defense Science Board.[146]

"What tops your to-do list?" I asked.

"Freeing Eastern Europe," Clark responded.

"That won't be easy. They've just declared martial law in Poland."

"We have a secret weapon," Clark countered.

"What's that?"

Clark pushed back from the historic walnut conference table, reached into his pants pocket, and then pulled out a crucifix. It hit the tabletop with a reverberating "clank."

§§§

In January of 1982, Reagan was able to turn his attention to national security matters. Four months later, he placed his bets on a Cold War trifecta.

- On May 20, Regan issued National Security Decision Directive 32, our six-front strategy for prevailing in the Cold War.
- Two weeks later, Reagan met with Pope John Paul II[147] in the Vatican library. Reagan's intensely Catholic National Security Advisor, Bill Clark, made the arrangements. A year

---

146   A part-time group of scientists appointed by the secretary of defense to advise on technical opportunities and threats in the national security arena.
147   Born Karol Jozef Wojtyla in Poland

before, both men had narrowly escaped death from a would-be assassin's bullet.

Reagan and John Paul II spoke privately for an hour. During their conversation, the pope and the president agreed that God had spared them for a purpose. That purpose was the defeat of atheist communism. John Paul II's Poland, where martial law had been imposed in December '81, was to serve as the lynchpin.

Nancy and Ronald Reagan with Pope John Paul II at the Vatican, June 7, 1982

Six months after Reagan's visit with the Polish pope, General Jaruzelski's system of arbitrary controls and imprisonment was suspended. It was terminated in July 1983. In 1989, a free election entrusted power to Lech Walesa's Solidarity Union.

To me, none of this came as a surprise.

§§§

- From Rome, Reagan flew to London, where he played his third trifecta card. On June 8, as he spoke to the British Parliament gathered in Westminster, the president set out his plans for prevailing in the Cold War. "One of the most important talks I ever gave," RR later told historians. Most now agree. In talking with National Security Advisor Bill Clark, Reagan used simpler language. "God's work," he declared.

§§§

During the spring of '83, Reagan made another Armageddon-inspired move. On March 23, he unveiled his Strategic Defense Initiative (SDI), a planned space-based defense against incoming ballistic missiles. This brought derision from American political opponents and technocrats, but postwar interviews with Soviet insiders suggest a different view. SDI triggered disbelief among Soviet scientists, fear of the unknown in the politburo.

Reagan's SDI initiative went hand-in-glove with his parallel belief in peace through strength. During that spring of '83, his Scowcroft Commission empowered deployment of the Peacekeeper monster missile.

Few of the Washington players understood that Reagan's Strategic Defense Initiative was religion based, but RR thought it simply wrong to accept the possibility of Mutual Assured Destruction, millions of deaths from a nuclear exchange, as a given. At the same time, SDI was a shrewd move on the Cold War chessboard. Reagan and his advisors knew the Soviets could not afford the gate fees required to play in this high-tech ballpark.

At Reykjavik, Gorbachev thought he could sidetrack SDI with juicy counter-offers. The problem was that Mr. Gorbachev came from an atheist society, one that had no understanding of right and wrong, no respect for a higher law. To Reagan, a state believing only in itself was the Supreme Problem. Nothing was going to change his beliefs.

The Soviets finally folded; the American *and* Soviet people won big time as the Intermediate Range Nuclear Forces (INF) Treaty, executed at the end of Reagan's term, removed an entire class of nuclear-armed missiles from the inventories of both sides.

It was Reagan's far-seeing mind and religious beliefs, accompanied by a new Soviet leader's sense of reality, that brought about the INF treaty.

§§§

Dr. Stewart McBirnie, a Glendale radio minister with a substantial following, was one of those present at Reagan's September '65 campaign kickoff. It should come as no surprise that a man of the cloth was present when it all began. Reagan was not a regular churchgoer. He preferred substance over form. He believed in a Higher Being. He found the questions of denomination and place of worship to be inconsequential. Reagan consulted regularly with a series of pastors, from McBirnie to Don Moomaw, prominent in West Los Angeles ecclesiastical circles, and eventually with Billy Graham.

The Washington media made light of Reagan's failure to attend church during his presidential years, but RR had no need for such forays. He recognized the disruption a presidential visit would bring to St. John's, the small chapel across Lafayette Park from the White House. He stayed home, seeking guidance from visiting clerics.

Reagan seldom hosted prayer breakfasts in Sacramento or Washington. He preferred to converse with his God and his pastor in private. But there can be no doubt that RR believed in a divine plan. When weighing any action, Reagan often considered the spiritual dimensions.

During Reagan's post-White House years, as his mental capacity diminished, Billy Graham spent much time comforting both the former president and his wife.

"Reagan was the president I knew best," Graham told a member of the extended family.

At the time of Reagan's funeral in June '04, Billy Graham's son, Franklin, also an ordained minister, spoke with reporter John Gibson.

"Ronald Reagan was a man of deep faith. [Father] and Reagan had a lot of serious theological discussions ... The two had much in common. Both had great senses of humor. [Dad, Billy Graham] stayed in touch until the end."

CH. 23 THE REAGAN WE KNEW

Ten years ago, when pulling together my Cold War history,[148] I convened a former prosecutor, an active rancher, and a retired newsman to join this engineer in developing a broader understanding of the often-discounted man who, by then, had come to dominate the late twentieth century. All of us knew Reagan extremely well, but he presented many faces to his peers. More than one set of eyes were needed to gain the needed perspective.

The four of us, Counselor Ed Meese, Exec Bill Clark, Press Secretary Lyn Nofziger, and I, had worked in politics and government with Reagan for more than 30 years.[149] These Old Sacramento Hands, as we came to be known in Washington, were a different breed from the new friends and gunslingers later encountered in the nation's capital. The latter group thought they had all the answers, that *they* were the bright guys. They saw Reagan as the front man, the spokesman for predigested decisions made by others—a new generation of Battaglias.

We Old Sacramento Hands trusted Reagan's judgment. We believed in the man and his values. We argued tactical issues fiercely, and Reagan often responded to such debates with a legislative veto here or a changed appointment there, but his core philosophy was not negotiable, and that is what we most admired about him. Our gang of four believed in Reagan's ability to articulate his beliefs, make decisions, and, in time, to defeat statist regimes around the world.

---

148   *At the Abyss*, Thomas C. Reed, 2004, Ballantine Books
149   For CVs on the other three gentlemen, see Appendix D

Some journalists invented conspiracy theories to explain what made Reagan tick. Others, historians and biographers, created fictional characters and footnotes. Politicians from the liberal establishment laughed Reagan off as a lightweight movie star; they lost all the elections to which they brought that mindset. The 1980 Soviet analysis of the president-elect found Reagan to be "intransigent, lacking sophistication." Their empire is gone. So, let the four of us offer our conclusions. We lived with the man, day and night, during his politically transforming decade.

Character

There was nothing devious about Ronald Reagan. Recruits to the staffs in Sacramento and Washington anticipated disclosure of Reagan's secret plans, but there were none. To the newcomers' puzzlement, there were no focus groups, no agendas that changed weekly. Over the years, Reagan had developed a set of unshakeable beliefs. He stuck to them with only tactical adjustments. Those of us who knew Reagan well found it easy to support and implement his visions because they never changed.

Reagan believed freedom was worth fighting for and that communism was its antithesis. He understood that communism's grand theories could be implemented only by conspiracy and terror. To him, the Soviet Union was an Evil Empire.

Reagan believed in a Higher Being. He did not focus his Christian faith on any one denomination, nor did he worship in any particular building. His mother, Nelle, was the fountainhead, and visiting pastors lent support, from the opening to the close of Reagan's career.

Reagan believed that the state, that government, was the problem, not the solution. He said as much on many occasions. He was sure that any government, at any level, could and would foul things up. Local councils, regulatory boards, state governors, or the Feds would all turn out to be bumbling bureaucrats if not corrupt cliques when compared to the citizenry making their own free choices.

He believed that in the use of force, the government must have a monopoly, but elsewhere the government should be kept out of the people's lives if at all possible. Reagan believed individuals should be left alone, to spend their own money, to pursue their own dreams, to make their own choices even if their fellow citizens considered them the "wrong" choices. As a consequence, he may have overlooked the plight of those who *did* make bad decisions.

As a youngster, Reagan was hit hard by the Depression. In mid-life, he voted for Franklin Roosevelt. Reagan believed in a safety net to catch those who fell and to protect those who simply could not cope, but he felt strongly that such a net should not become a hammock, nor should it ensnare those who wished to fly free.

He believed that honesty was not negotiable, that truth was absolute; others found Reagan's aversion to bad news a distraction from that claim.

He believed that leaders were to lead, not to poll, their constituents.

Reagan was also a man of the utmost personal integrity. He did not run for office in pursuit of perks and power, nor did he seek those things in Hollywood. He wanted to live comfortably, to enjoy life, and to pass on a better world to the next generation. The Reagan we knew was devoid of political ambition. He had no need to prove himself, no urge to be governor, no burning desire for the presidency. He never achieved superstar status in Hollywood. All he wanted was to do a good job, to support his family well, and then to spend as much time as possible with his Arabian horses. Yet he was the most determined competitor any of us ever met; an odd divergence of focus.

To the best of our knowledge, Reagan had no shady financial dealings. In the words of political pro Stuart Spencer, "Ron was the most honest candidate I ever met." Spencer had seen them all. On the other hand, Reagan seemed oblivious to the details of his personal financial affairs. He may have been careless, too reliant on his theatrical agency as they looked after the practical side of his life.

The financial backers of his campaigns supported him because they believed in him, not the other way around. He was a highly inclusive politician. He lived with a sense of *que será será*. His sense of confidence, tranquility, humor, and inevitability lowered the stress level wherever he went.

Intellect

No one would accuse Ronald Reagan of being an intellectual. His comfortably masculine den was devoid of policy-wonk journals, though its walls sheltered volumes of nonfiction classics. In describing his troubled upbringing, he once remarked to Nancy Reynolds, "If you have a book around, you never lack for friends." During the fifties, when working for the General Electric Company, he steeped himself in serious economic texts. Come the sixties, Reagan wanted full access to the print *and* electronic media. He sought out conflicting views as he searched for the background, the history underlying any bulletin of interest.

"Discussing the issues" with Reagan was an oxymoron. He had long before developed a few beliefs that worked quite well for him. He did not care to spend much time reevaluating them. He was open to new ideas (Star Wars) or information (the plight of hostages), but when addressing contemporary problems, he often relapsed into long-ago movie plots rather than esoteric "what ifs."

This use of motion picture analogies was distracting to newcomers, and detested by his wife. More than once we saw her high heel come down on his shoe, stopping a show-biz story in mid-sentence, but we four understood this system of communication. We could read the code.

A mention of Gary Cooper in *High Noon* meant, "Let's do what's right; deal with the risks; leave the recognition for others." His reference to Grace Kelly in that motion picture reflected his approval of strong women who stood by their man, no matter what.

What set Reagan apart from his peers was his overarching sense of vision; that plus a mental agility that far outpaced all others. He was always 10 moves ahead of any opponent. He understood how things would work out. During press conferences, debates, or confrontations, Reagan was parsing the grammar of his response, adding humor to the close, while his questioner plodded on.

Bulletins that Reagan saw or heard stayed in his memory forever. When long-lost factoids rolled off Reagan's tongue in response to a press query, we looked on in wonderment and surprise. We had to be careful about what data went into Reagan's mental file, to quickly fact-check any reports he found interesting.

Thinking things through to their logical conclusion is what Reagan did with the time freed up by what others called "laziness." The back of a horse, plodding through scrub or surf, is a great venue for reflection. Reagan enjoyed a clarity of thought that gave him the confidence to ignore criticism, media abuse, and countervailing advice. With this farsightedness, he could make decisions quickly, under stress, with the greatest of ease. This is what we meant when we said, "Let Reagan be Reagan." We resisted the bureaucracy's desire to pre-digest every problem into a consensus solution. We Old Sacramento Hands had confidence in Reagan's precepts and his ability to decide.

At the same time, we had to deal with Reagan's unwillingness to accept bad news. In his memoirs and by personal statement, Reagan denied ever seeking the presidential nomination in 1968. Biographer Lou Cannon noted that Reagan erased *every* defeat from his mind, a consequence of being the fiercest competitor of all time. Reagan did not like losing. Stu Spencer offered a broader observation, that Reagan simply deleted *all* bad news, not just defeats. In the face of the Tower Commission's damning Iran Contra report,[150] Reagan continued to declare, "I did not trade arms for hostages. My heart still tells me that's true."

A more recent Reagan biographer[151] coined the expression "genial ostrich" to describe Reagan's antipathy to failure.

An outside observer, Dan Moldea, found these memory lapses all too convenient,[152] noting that Reagan could not tell a federal grand jury why his SAG had bestowed an economic windfall on his theatrical agency. Perhaps, as he was questioned years after the

---

150   Stuart Spencer was called in to help with the Iran-Contra problems in 1986
151   Rick Perlstein, *The Invisible Bridge*, 2014, Simon & Schuster
152   *Dark Victory*, Dan E. Moldea, 1987, Penguin Books

fact, Reagan recognized the MCA waiver as a mistake; bad news he simply wanted to erase.

Distant Background

Our decoding of Reagan's aloof and compartmented nature starts with his upbringing as the adult child of an alcoholic. Dr. Claudia Black[153] notes that "Children of alcoholics don't perceive others as resources; therefore they live their lives alone ... For the majority of such children, trust and trusted persons are not a consistent part of their lives." Thus, for RR, no friends, only compartmented allies. He was, truly, Nofziger's "superb hermit."

The angst-averse nature of such alcoholic-parented children has been studied by others.[154] Kritsberg notes that some such children grow up trying to subordinate their bad memories. Others demand, or at least imagine, happy endings to every story. We believe Reagan followed this latter route. Reagan was a happy man and wanted only happy people around him. He preferred staff that made him feel good, people who were masters at telling the Reagans what they wanted to hear. As a result, RR was willing to accept misfits in his life. He made few managerial demands on his staff since his primary objective was the avoidance of angst, not the search for excellence.

John Sears, a one-time Reagan campaign manager, made this observation in 1990: "As the second son of an alcoholic, Ronald Reagan grew up being a people-pleaser ... That's how he coped."

Placating was Reagan's response to the Elders' criticisms in 1967. It remained as a cornerstone of his relations with staff and supporters for the rest of his career, often with near-disastrous results.

Nancy became the surrogate for his mother, the Saint Nelle who protected Ron and Neil from harsh reality.

---

153   *It Will Never Happen to Me*, Claudia Black, Medical Administration Company, 1982
154   *The Adult Children of Alcoholics Syndrome*, Wayne Kritsberg, 1988, Bantam Books

At Work

Reagan's solidity of beliefs led to a comfortable depoliticizing of any office he held. Whether in Sacramento or in Washington, he seldom asked the impact of some pending decision on his friends, political supporters, or constituencies. While he welcomed survey research in planning his campaigns, he ignored polls and focus groups when setting policy or composing speeches. He often enjoined his staff, "Let's do what's right; the polls will follow."

On the other hand, Reagan was not a competent executive. In his pursuit of a harmonious environment, RR never assigned roles, demanded results, or fired people. He was a ghastly chooser of staff, inevitably turning to the trusted aide outside the door or the nearby loser in need of a job whenever a new problem arose.

As a result of these traits, once in the White House, Reagan's inner office never coalesced, never enjoyed the order imposed by Clark and then Meese in Sacramento. A day in Reagan's West Wing resembled a visit to New York's Bellevue Hospital with the Corleone family acting as orderlies. Reagan's inattention to structure and talent was painful to watch.

Reagan was a product of the Hollywood system where stars could be comfortable only in the company of other stars. To President Reagan, everyone but the political superstars, e.g., Gorbachev, Nixon, and Thatcher, were staff. No matter how wealthy, well connected, powerful, beautiful, or talented the people around him, be it at home or in the office, they were just associates, deserving of the utmost courtesy and concern, but not genuine friendship. He was a master of the stage, but as noted above, he had no friends.

We believe Reagan envisioned Holmes Tuttle as the producer of his political show, the Walt Disney of his life, the man providing the money and making the difficult decisions when needed.

Reagan must have envisioned Stuart Spencer as his director, the Stephen Spielberg of politics, which he absolutely was.

Reagan looked to Mike Deaver as his publicist, not an executive assistant.

For a while, I was the studio chief, his Jack Warner, casting the show, hiring the extras, seeing to it that lighting, sound, and makeup people (schedulers, pollsters, press agents) did their jobs. When it was show time, I was to promote the product while the star held center stage.   When protected by this Sacramento "studio staff," Reagan did well. When captured by outside groupies, trouble often followed.

Nancy, the leading lady, aggravated many in the "studio" by her focus on tomorrow's reviews, not on the long run. As often happens in Hollywood, the leading lady was determined to drive the unkempt, "the overfed and underdressed"[155] from the star's inner circle.

Reagan may not have related well to a desk and telephone, but he was a master of the stage. Pat Brown, Jess Unruh, Jimmy Carter, and Mikhail Gorbachev were not.

The Bottom Line

Reagan was a pragmatic man. He paid attention to the legislators whose help he needed, but overall, his decisions were made on the basis of his central beliefs. Thus, he was determined to end the Cold War, to sheath the nuclear sword, and to silence the screams from Lubyanka prison. As Whittaker Chambers put it, those were the screams that "came from all the citadels of terror [then] stretching from Berlin to Canton, from those freight cars loaded with men, women and children, the enemies of the communist state, locked in, packed in, left on remote sidings to freeze to death at night in the Russian winter."

Ronald Reagan heard those screams. He did what was needed to rescue those in the clutch of the Soviet state and to protect his American brothers and their children from a similar fate.

On December 25, 1991, the Soviet hammer and sickle was lowered from the Kremlin Tower, and Gorbachev turned over his nuclear keys to a democratically elected successor. He then called the President of the United States, by then George H.W. Bush, to extend best wishes.

"You can have a very quiet Christmas evening, George."

Much of the world did just that.

---

155   Nancy Reagan's own words, once used to describe Press Secretary Lyn Nofziger

EPILOGUE

In contrast to the years detailed above, the twenty-first century has delivered "empty suits" to the White House.

A Quinnipiac University Poll[157] of 1,446 registered American voters identified Barack Obama and George W. Bush as the worst American presidents since World War II.

I agree.

That same survey named Ronald Reagan the best.

I agree with that finding as well.

So, what is the message to the political class? What are the county chairmen, convention delegates, and legislators of both major parties to do in their quest for and subsequent exercise of power?

To govern, a candidate must first be elected. I believe the key to that gate is the ability to connect with ordinary people. Specific issues (health care, taxes) engage narrow bands of activists, but the determining factor in each citizen's vote is his/her confidence that the prospective leader will understand their problems when the inevitable crises erupt.

Franklin Roosevelt, Dwight Eisenhower, Ronald Reagan, and Bill Clinton all demonstrated that ability to bond with the voters. Remote nominees, i.e., Adlai Stevenson, Michael Dukakis, Bob Dole, and Mitt Romney, never connected at all.

Stilted candidates (e.g., George W. Bush) sometimes win if their opponents are even more wooden than they are (Al Gore).

An all-encompassing campaign is important in establishing this link. Reagan and Eisenhower understood the need for a big

---

157   Quinnipac University, New Haven, CT. Poll conducted June 24-30, 2014. 1,446 registered voters interviewed nationwide by cell and land lines.

tent; successive Republican candidates were not as perceptive. Obama won in 2008 by promulgating a vision of "Hope." He pledged an end to the divisions of the past, but that is not the way he governs.

Delegates to the 2016 conventions need to select candidates who can and will appeal to broad segments of the American population, not the vocal cells in their own party.

Once elected, what sort of individual makes a good president? I recommend citizens who gain experience in the real world before entering the political arena. That could be wartime leadership, e.g., Truman, the artillery officer worshipped by his men; PT boat skipper Kennedy; or European Allied Commander Eisenhower.

It might be a labor leader, e.g., Reagan, the six-term President of the Screen Actors Guild,[158] or a credentialed technocrat, e.g., Bush Sr., America's emissary to Beijing, and subsequently director of central intelligence.

If we must choose lifetime politicians, elect those who have served as governors, men or women who have displayed executive ability, people forced to make decisions promptly.

Most importantly, once in office our president must cease catering to his political base. Bush Jr. and Obama continued to do so with disastrously divisive results.

Our next president must take the big tent with him into the White House. He/she must serve as president of all the people, willing to share a drink and a joke with the leader of the opposition on a regular basis, e.g., President Reagan and House Speaker Tip O'Neill, President Clinton and House Speaker Gingrich.

This century's post-Reagan, post-Cold War era has yet to be defined. Fourteen years into the previous century, European monarchs envisioned a stable and comfortable Golden Age. Thirty years later those monarchs, their queens, and their archdukes were gone. Their cities lay in ruin. Millions of their subjects lay dead.

As we enter year 15 of the twenty-first century, our dreams of stability and peace seem equally ill-advised. Will this century's

---

158   Soviet leader Mikhail Gorbachev described Ronald Reagan as the toughest negotiator he ever met. "He pocketed each concession, then kept on going."

Sarajevo be a low-tech nuclear device floated into the Ashdod harbor at Tel Aviv?

Domestic decisions avoided, ballooning debt, and/or radicals from the Muslim world will surely deposit heavy responsibilities on the shoulders of the 45th President of the United States

Choose wisely, delegates.

APPENDIX A

Summary of 1964-1968 Ronald Reagan Videos
Available for viewing at <reagan68.com>

A Time for Choosing, **October 27, 1964**   (Edited to 14 minutes)

During the autumn of 1964, Ronald Reagan supported Senator Goldwater's sinking campaign to unseat President Johnson. A handful of Reagan supporters in Los Angeles heard his eloquent articulation of the American purpose. They decided Reagan's talk should be broadcast nationally. *A Time for Choosing* was aired on Tuesday, October 27, one week before the 1964 election. Its closing phrases about preserving this last best hope for mankind in contrast to a thousand years of darkness, captivated millions. An outpouring of year-end enthusiasm propelled Ronald Reagan into his political career.

Eisenhower-Reagan Press Conference   (Edited to 4 minutes)
Gettysburg, PA, June 15, 1966

Ronald Reagan, an FDR-supporting Democrat, first broke with that party in 1952 when endorsing General Dwight Eisenhower's run for the American presidency. In turn, Eisenhower welcomed Reagan's "Time for Choosing" speech of '64. He saw it as a key to rebuilding the Republican Party after the defeats of that year. Upon Reagan winning the California primary in '66, Eisenhower extended an invitation to speak. Reagan accepted, visiting the Eisenhower home in Gettysburg, VA, on June 15, 1966. After office discussions and before lunch, the general and his protégé met with the press. Among Ike's observations: "You can bet he [Reagan] will become a presidential possibility."

Ronald Reagan: Citizen Governor   (29 minutes)
(Biopic shown in Nebraska and Oregon, May 1968)

Reagan's name was to appear on the 1968 primary ballots in Nebraska and Oregon. He would not be able to campaign in those states, so his organization created a "biopic," a video of Reagan's political life. Entitled *Ronald Reagan, Citizen Governor*, the show drew on stock footage of Knowland and Nixon conceding their governorship races to Pat Brown in 1958 and '62, on videos of Reagan as President of the Screen Actors Guild, and on excerpts of his fiery confrontations with Berkeley students. It included endorsements from General Electric chairman Ralph Cordiner and California's Republican Chairman Jim Halley. *Citizen Governor* concluded with excerpts from his talks about Vietnam, the *Pueblo*, and the US economy.

Law and Order, Indianapolis June 13, 1968
(Edited to 18 minutes)
(One week after Robert Kennedy's assassination)

With the coming of the summer of '68, fear hung in the nation's air. Bobby Kennedy had been killed in Reagan's home state. The streets of American cities were awash with crime. College campuses had been closed by rioters. The war in Vietnam ground on, consuming lives with no evidence of a coherent American strategy. Amidst these crises, the Republican Barons had pledged their convention support to Richard Nixon. But Reagan's vote-counters knew Nixon did not yet have the votes to win. If he failed on the first ballot, the Solid South would crumble and a cascade of conservative defections would begin. The Reagan team saw the need for another "Time for Choosing" speech, this one on Law and Order. A large Republican gathering at the Indianapolis fairgrounds on June 13 was the chosen venue.

APPENDIX B

The Solid South, 1865-1964

On April 9, 1865 the bloodshed of the American Civil War came to an end. Wars are never pretty, but civil wars are the worst. Brothers kill brothers, and whole countries are laid to waste. But when the shooting stops, a different cruelty starts. The victors impose their will on the vanquished in very personal and direct ways.

A week after the armistice at Appomattox, Abraham Lincoln was shot by a South-sympathizing actor; he died the following day. The nation fell into leaderless disarray. His well-meaning vice president[159] soon came under attack by the Radical Republicans in the Congress, who wished to visit large doses of retribution on the Southern rebels.

In December 1865, the Thirteenth Amendment to the US Constitution was ratified, liberating all slaves not already freed by Lincoln's Emancipation Proclamation. Black men were given the vote, while those white Southern troops who had sworn allegiance to the Confederacy were barred from voting. Taken together, these new ground rules resulted in a watershed change in ballot-box power.

At the same time, Northern troops and their civilian entourage[160] moved to occupy the South. The era known as Reconstruction began.

In 1868, the Commanding General of the Union armies, Ulysses S. Grant, won the presidency of the United States. Two years later the newly enfranchised citizens of Mississippi elected an eloquent Black minister[161] to the US Senate. During the years of Reconstruction, another 15 African Americans from the South

---

159   Andrew Johnson, a Democrat, a southerner, and a former governor of Tennessee. Johnson was the only US Senator from the Confederate States who did not resign from the Senate when the Civil War broke out. He had been added to the Republican ticket in 1864 for balance, as a gesture toward ultimate reunification.
160   Known as "carpetbaggers" from the makeshift nature of their luggage.
161   Hiram Revels, a 43-year-old minister from the African Methodist Episcopal Church, elected to the US Senate by the Black-dominated Mississippi legislature in 1870.

made it into Congress. Only in 1877, in the aftermath of a very divisive national election, was Reconstruction ended.[162] The South was left to manage its own affairs.

When once again allowed to vote, in 1878, white Southerners immediately turned to a policy of absolute opposition to Lincoln's Republican Party, the party of the Union Army, the occupying carpetbaggers, and the freed slaves. The Southern Democratic Party became the instrument of that white opposition; it soon became the vehicle for a rebirth of Southern political power. Unfortunately, that power came to be exercised by a closed clique who, through a variety of means, steadily excluded their black brothers from the electoral process.

Southerners understood the seniority system in the US Congress. They soon figured out that while they might never have the votes to work their will on the floors of the House or Senate, seniority could give them control of the machinery. Repeated re-election of any given incumbent would, in time, yield to him the chairmanship of his committee or even the leadership of his legislative body.

Thus began an age of one-party rule in the former Confederacy. South of Richmond and east of the Alamo, the Republican Party simply did not exist. The Democratic primaries determined that party's candidates, and once a man was nominated, the party closed ranks behind him. When elected, he usually was re-elected for life. In presidential elections, the Democrats-only game was much the same in the South.

Except for their exclusion during the wartime election of 1864, the Southern states never lost their right to cast electoral votes. The only question was the legitimacy of those Electors. With the Southern soldiers disenfranchised after the war, the Republican candidate, General Grant, was able to win a lopsided victory in 1868 and a unanimous electoral vote in 1872. Once Reconstruction ended, however, the electorate began to shift. In

---

162   In 1876, Rutherford Hayes, the Republican candidate for president, received only 48 percent of the popular vote. Balloting by the Electors was contentious. Hayes was elected to the presidency by only one, perhaps illegitimate, electoral vote. (185-184). In exchange, the South got an end to the Civil War and the immediate removal of all federal troops from the Confederacy.

the South, Ku Klux Klan terror disenfranchised the Blacks, white soldiers regained their vote, and anti-Republican fanaticism ruled.

By 1880, the Southern states had begun an 80-year practice of delivering all of their electoral votes[163] to the Democratic presidential candidate, whoever he might be

In 1932 Franklin Roosevelt, then governor of New York State, took practical note of this anomaly.

For the previous three decades, despite Southern opposition, the Republican Party held a lock on national power.[164] The GOP was an industrial behemoth operating on an axis of railroads running from New York through Pennsylvania and Ohio into the heartland of Illinois. By the 1920s, a string of electoral victories had produced Calvin Coolidge's hands-off style of government, the presidency of a man never before elected to anything (Herbert Hoover), the stock market crash of 1929, and the Depression of the thirties.

By 1932, it was time for a new deal; Franklin Roosevelt figured out how to make it happen. He understood that the Southern states would *always* vote Democratic in the presidential elections—no matter how liberal the Democratic candidate, how incompatible his views with Southern culture. To that base, Roosevelt added a layer of urban poor in the north: the blue-collar and immigrant workers, their union bosses, and minorities, all frightened by the growing Depression. He topped off this loose coalition with a layer of intellectual elites from eastern academia, a community brimming with socialist solutions to the economic crisis gripping America. Together, these votes could give Roosevelt the industrial northeast. He then cemented the Southern vote to his side by the selection of a confederate-state congressman, House Speaker John Nance Garner of Texas, as his vice presidential running mate. With that coalition of urban North and Old South, Roosevelt could win,

---

163   With the exception of the Dixiecrat defection in 1948. In that year, four of those states (AL, LA, MS, SC) delivered their electoral votes to then-Gov. Strom Thurmond, a Southern Democrat from SC. Similar defections reappeared in 1960.
164   Interrupted only by the Woodrow Wilson years, made possible by the third party candidacy of former President Teddy Roosevelt in 1912. Wilson received only 42 percent of the vote in that year, but that was enough to beat the divided opposition.

and he did. In 1932, he carried North *and* South amidst the despair of the Depression, winning 472 electoral votes in the process.

It was a recipe that worked four times for FDR and once again for his successor, Vice President Harry Truman. The foundation of that coalition even stayed in place during the fifties for their would-be successor.

In 1952, Governor Adlai Stevenson of Illinois was a bona fide member of the Liberal Establishment. Even so, he was not able to carry even the heartland of that Establishment[165] against war hero Dwight Eisenhower, nor could he carry his home state of Illinois. What Stevenson did do, with the help of his vice presidential candidate, Senator John Sparkman of Alabama, was to carry seven states of the Old Confederacy[166] plus two of the Border States (Kentucky and West Virginia).

In his second try, in 1956 with Senator Estes Kefauver of Kentucky as his running mate, Stevenson again failed across the nation. Only the Electors from six of the old Confederate States plus contested Missouri[167] stuck with him.

Four years later, in 1960, 15 unpledged Electors from the Old Confederacy signaled a sea change. They cast their votes for Senator Harry Byrd of Virginia, not the Democratic Party's nominee. Byrd had not solicited those ballots; they were protest votes, confirming the fragility of the Democratic hold on the Old South.

Then, in May, 1961, John Tower of Texas broke the ice. He won a special election to become the first Republican senator from the Solid South.

Three years later, in November 1964, the Democrat monopoly ended. The Republican candidate for president carried five of the formerly-Confederate states. For the rest of the twentieth century, those Electors were up for grabs.

---

165   Stevenson lost both New York and Massachusetts.
166   AL, AR, GA, LA, MS, NC, SC
167   AL, AR, GA, MO, MS, NC, SC

Presidential Election of 1952

Presidential Election of 1956

☐ States carried by Dwight Eisenhower 1952 & 1956

■ States carried by Adlai Stevenson 1952 & 1956

Appendix C

Extract of Memorandum from nine staff and former staff members to Governor Reagan, delivered to him and Mrs. Reagan at the Del Coronado Hotel on Friday, August 24, 1967.

August 24, 1967

The Honorable Ronald Reagan
Governor of California
Sacramento, CA.

Dear Governor:

During the spring of this year there occurred several leaks of highly sensitive and closely guarded information which have never been adequately explained.

In May, the Executive Secretary was advised of serious security risks on which no action was taken.

Since that time facts have come to light which indicate conduct which has, and could continue to have, a serious impact on the Governor's office. This appears to involve Phillip M. Battaglia, the Executive Secretary, and his assistant, Richard M. Quinn.

The following is a report concerning the facts now available to us.

These conclusions have been reached jointly and separately by Lyn Nofziger, Communications Director; Thomas Reed, former Appointments Secretary and currently operating as a political field man for the Governor; William Clark, Cabinet Secretary; Edwin Meese, Extradition and Clemency Secretary; Paul Haerle, Appointments Secretary; Arthur Van Court, Travel Secretary; Curtis Patrick, an assistant to Battaglia; Gordon Luce, Secretary of Transportation; and Edgar W. Gillenwaters, your Washington Representative.

This situation is so serious the above named do not believe it can continue any longer without doing irreparable harm to the Governor, both personally and career-wise, to the administration and the goals those in it hope to reach, and to those persons working in the administration at the highest levels.

Allegations have been made and information received which suggests there are persons in the Governor's office or closely connected who are either homosexuals or have homosexual tendencies. These include Battaglia and Quinn, [*eight names deleted*] along with others who do not figure directly in this situation.

[*Nine pages of personal information and supporting documentation deleted*]

This is the situation that faces the Governor today. It is uncertain to what extent this information is known to others, including political opponents. However, it is known that a person closely connected with the national Democratic Party has considerable knowledge of this situation and that there are "whispers" among lobbyists and others close to the Sacramento scene.

We recognize both the tragedy and awkwardness of the current situation. However, because of the potentially serious consequences to the Governor and to his entire administration, we feel an obligation to bring this information to your attention.

/S/	/S/
Lyn Nofziger	Thomas C. Reed
/S/	/S/
William P. Clark, Jr.	Edgar Gillenwaters
/S/	/S/
Paul R. Haerle	Gordon C. Luce
/S/	/S/
Edwin Meese III	Arthur Van Court
/S/	
Curtis C. Patrick	

APPENDIX D

**1968 Republican National Convention
State Delegation Votes**

State	Richard Nixon	Ronald Reagan	Nelson Rockefeller	Other
AL	14	12	-	-
AK	11	-	1	-
AZ	16	-	1	-
AR	-	-	-	18 Gov. Winthrop Rockefeller
CA	-	86	-	-
CO	14	1	3	-
CT	4	-	12	-
DE	9	-	3	-
DC	6	-	3	-
FL	32	1	1	-
GA	21	7	2	-
HA	-	-	-	14 Sen. Hiram Fong
ID	9	5	-	-
IL	50	3	5	-
IN	26	-	-	-
IA	13	3	8	-
KS	-	-	-	20 Sen. Frank Carlson
KY	22	-	2	-
LA	19	7	-	-
ME	7	-	7	-
MD	18	-	8	-
MA	-	-	34	-
MI	4	-	-	44 Gov. George Romney
MN	9	-	15	2 Gov. George Romney
MS	20	-	-	-
MO	16	3	5	-
MT	11	3	-	-

State	Richard Nixon	Ronald Reagan	Nelson Rockefeller	Other
NE	16	-	-	-
NV	9	-	3	-
NH	8	-	-	-
NJ	18	-	-	22 Sen. Clifford Case
NM	8	5	1	-
NY	4	-	88	-
NC	9	16	1	-
ND	5	1	2	-
OH	2	-	-	55 Gov. Rhodes, 1 H. Stassen
OK	14	7	1	
OR	18	-	-	-
PA	22		41	-
RI	-	-	14	-
SC	22	-	-	-
SD	14	-	-	-
TN	28	-	-	-
TX	41	15	-	-
UT	2	-	-	6 Gov. George Romney
VT	9	-	3	-
VA	22	-	2	-
WA	15	6	3	-
WV	11	-	3	-
WI	30	-	-	-
WY	12	-	-	-
PR	-	-	5	-
VI	2	-	1	-
Totals:	692 (667 needed)	182	277	182*

* Some tabulations show John Lindsay, Mayor of New York City, as receiving one vote from this column.

Vote Summary:

Richard Nixon, by region:

Old Confederacy	266	(38%)
Midwest	161	(23%)
Mountains & West	158	(23%)
Northeast	107	(16%)
	692	

Favorite Sons on first ballot:

Reagan, CA	86
Rhodes, OH	55
Romney, MI	44
Case, NJ	22
Carlson, KS	20
W. Rockefeller, AR	18
Fong, HA	14

APPENDIX E

The Old Sacramento Hands

Bill Clark was a rancher and a small-town lawyer when he, like millions of others, heard Ronald Reagan's "Time for Choosing" speech in '64. As Clark put it to me later, "It hit all the right notes."

Clark's grandfather had served as Ventura County sheriff, his father as police chief in Oxnard. During the fifties, Bill Clark served in Germany. It was there that he met, and soon married, Johanna Brauner, a refugee from the German-speaking Czech Sudetenland.

That western segment of Czechoslovakia had welcomed Hitler's 1938 invasion. In retaliation, at war's end, three million German-speakers were evicted from the Sudetenland and shipped off to war-ravaged East Germany with only the belongings they could carry. The Russians were in hot pursuit. The Brauner family migrated to Berlin and then to the west. It was there, in Munich, that 20-year-old Johanna found work for the US Army as a bilingual secretary, and Lieutenant Clark was an officer in the Army's Counter Intelligence Corps. This early exposure of both Clarks to the aftermath of war and the brutality of Soviet forces surely inspired their efforts to close down the Soviet Empire.

In 1966, local Republicans asked Clark to head up the Friends of Reagan Committee then forming in Ventura County. When he connected with Reagan, the two men hit it off at once, not only ideologically but as horsemen and as relaxed Southern Californians. At the same time, Governor Brown's misuse of his judicial appointment powers surely added to the Clark family's desire to bring about change in Sacramento.

After Reagan's '66 election victory, Clark moved to Sacramento with the governor-elect to become his cabinet secretary. In that capacity, Clark administered the policy side of state government, and in the process, he defined a management style for Reagan. After the coup of '67, described in Chapter Ten, Clark became the governor's executive secretary, i.e., chief of staff.

In 1969, Clark transferred to a career on the judicial bench, first as a superior court judge, eventually as a justice of the California

State Supreme Court. After Reagan's election to the presidency, he tapped Clark to become deputy secretary of state and then assistant to the president for national security.

During his two White House years, Clark functioned as Reagan's junior partner in standing up to the Soviet Empire while mapping its end. Clark's opposition to cosmetic summits with aging Soviet figureheads annoyed Mrs. Reagan. Her interests lay in good press every morning; Clark's lay in collapsing the Soviet Empire. Clark was eventually driven from the White House by Nancy and her allies using daily press leaks to denigrate Clark's actions and discount his talent, but while there, he left his mark on history.

Clark wound up Reagan's first term as his secretary of the interior. Clark then returned to his roots as a small-town lawyer and a rancher in San Luis Obispo County, staying there until his death in 2013. Clark's memoirs, *The Judge: Ronald Reagan's Top Hand*[168] were written in the third person by Paul Kengor and Patricia Clark Doerner. His obituary, appearing in the *Wall Street Journal*,[169] figuratively proposed a Clark statue in Washington, DC, "to honor one of the greatest 'generals' in the long twilight struggle of the Cold War ... Judge Clark [was] most responsible for the collapse [of the Soviet Empire] and for the liberation of millions from the tyranny of communism."

Prof. Will Imboden, writing in *Foreign Policy*, put it more concisely: "Bill Clark won the Cold War."

Ed Meese was a product of an Oakland (CA) high school. At Yale he served as president of the Yale Political Union, chairman of the Conservative Club, and captain of the Yale Debating Society. Soon after his 1953 graduation, he entered the US Army as an artillery officer, assigned to a howitzer unit at Ft. Sill, Oklahoma. Meese wound up his active duty tour in 1956 as a battery commander.

Law school at UC Berkeley was next, followed by work in the Alameda County District Attorney's office. By the mid-sixties,

---

168   2007, Ignatius Press
169   John Lenczowski, Wall Street Journal, August 15, 2013, pg A15.

Meese had become a prosecuting attorney, his turf the tumultuous city of Berkeley. Upon Reagan's election in '66, State Senator Don Grunsky urged the governor-elect to hire Meese as his in-house counsel.

At their first meeting, a December '66 interview in Sacramento, Meese was impressed by Reagan's in-depth knowledge of the criminal justice system. Reagan was taken by Meese's careful, balanced approach to every challenge facing California.

"Our ideas always meshed," Meese noted later. "I saw Ron as the best route for securing and improving America's future." On that basis, Meese tied his career to Reagan's star. He joined the team in 1967; two years later he succeeded Bill Clark as Governor Reagan's chief of staff where he served for the balance of Reagan's Sacramento years.

During those years, Meese also remained active in the Army reserves, spending summer weeks as an artilleryman at Ft. Sill. He retired in 1972 with the rank of colonel.

During the mid-seventies, Meese taught law at a California state university before joining the Reagan campaigns for the presidency. In 1981 he became counselor to the president and then, in 1984, attorney general of the United States. Ed Meese brought a sense of calm deliberation to every historic crisis he touched.

Meese wrote his memoirs, *With Reagan: The Inside Story*, for publication in 1992.[170] He now researches policy issues for the Heritage Foundation.

Lyn Nofziger was the oldest and most politically qualified of us four, although decades of work as a reporter took their toll. Nofziger often wore a Mickey Mouse bowtie, seldom a jacket, as he struggled with deadlines, patrolled the bars, and dined nocturnally at the worst greasy spoons across America.

In 1966, Stuart Spencer recruited Nofziger from the Copley Press, a conservative California newspaper chain, to serve as Reagan's campaign press secretary. Nofziger was well respected by an ideologically adverse press corps; his light touch was key to Reagan's massive gubernatorial victory in 1966.

---

170   By Regnery Gateway

In Sacramento, Nofziger was given the fancy title of communications director. He built a solid reputation as an inside Reagan confidant who never lied to the press—until the Drew Pearson episode in the autumn of 1967 (see Chapter Eleven). Nofziger was one of the early Reagan for President sparkplugs.

After the 1968 election, Nofziger went to work for the Nixon White House and then the Republican National Committee. In 1976, he rejoined the Reagan presidential campaign staff as press secretary for that almost-successful attempt to wrest the Republican nomination from Gerald Ford. Thereafter, he organized grassroots groups until the 1980 campaign, when he again handled press matters for Reagan.

Upon the Reagan family's entrance to the White House, Nofziger was denied the job of presidential press secretary, a role to which most of us thought he had been born. His unkempt attire and gruff sense of humor disqualified him in Nancy's eyes.

"Overfed and underdressed," as she put it.

Nofziger displayed his talent on the national stage anyway, if ever so briefly, on March 30, 1981. He handled an unruly press throng outside the George Washington University Hospital after the shooting attempt on President Reagan's life.

Nofziger continued as a columnist and an informal advisor to Republican candidates and officeholders until his death in 2006. He also published his memoirs, simply titled *Nofziger*, in 1992.[171]

Never discussed during his life, and only unearthed with this writing: In June, 1944, at age 20, Nofziger served as a US Army Ranger on Omaha Beach. Scaling the heights of Pointe du Hoc, he lost only one finger to German shrapnel. He was truly a member of the Greatest Generation. Those long-ago events surely played a role in drawing Nofziger to Reagan's "strong America" beliefs.

Tom Reed, your author, served in the US Air Force as a technical project officer and then as a scientist at the University of California's Lawrence Livermore National Laboratory. After turning to work as a high-tech businessman, I became Reagan's Northern California campaign chairman during his first (1966)

---

171   Also by Regnery Gateway

gubernatorial campaign. Upon Reagan's election, I served as his appointments secretary, i.e., chief of personnel. After staffing up the new team, I left Sacramento to become the outside politician, organizing Reagan's 1968 run for the Republican presidential nomination. At the convention that year, I was elected to serve as the Republican National Committeeman for California. I co-chaired Reagan's statewide re-election campaign in 1970 and was involved in national politics until the 1972 end of my term on the Republican National Committee. In '73, I was recruited into the Pentagon, where I became Secretary of the Air Force and director of national reconnaissance in the Ford and Carter Administrations.

During the eighties, I served for two years in the Reagan White House as special assistant to the president for national security policy. My principal contribution may have been the staffing of Reagan's National Security Decision Directive 32, "A US National Security Strategy," his roadmap for prevailing in the Cold War.

After White House service, I returned to California to run my business and to become UC Livermore's expert on nuclear weapons in Ukraine. With the coming of the millennium, I turned my attention to writing history and history-based fiction.

BIBLIOGRAPHY
Listed in chronological order of publication

1. *Witness,* Whittaker Chambers, 1952, Regnery Gateway
2. *Advise and Consent,* Allen Drury, 1959, Doubleday and Company
3. *The Making of the President,* 1960, Theodore H. White, 1961, Atheneum Publishers
4. *Conscience of a Conservative,* Barry M. Goldwater, 1960, Hillman Books
5. "Now the President Must Decide, " Charles J. V. Murphy, *LIFE Magazine,* 12 February, 1962, Pg 71
6. *Suite 3505,* F. Clifton White, 1967, Arlington House
7. *An American Melodrama; the Presidential Campaign of 1968,* Chester, Hodgson, & Page, 1969, Viking Press
8. *The Emerging Republican Majority,* Kevin Phillips, 1969, Arlington House
9. *Ronnie & Jesse: A Political Odyssey,* Lou Cannon, 1969, Doubleday
10. *The Making of the President,* 1968, Theodore H. White, 1969, Atheneum Publishers
11. *Khrushchev Remembers,* Nikita Khrushchev and Edward Crankshaw, 1970, Little Brown
12. *Sincerely, Ronald Reagan,* Helene Von Damm, 1976, Green Hill Publishers
13. *RN: The Memoirs of Richard Nixon,* Richard Nixon, 1978, Grosset & Dunlap
14. *Nancy,* Nancy Reagan with Bill Libby, 1980, Morrow
15. *Reagan,* Lou Cannon, 1982, G.P. Putnam's Sons
16. *It Will Never Happen to Me,* Claudia Black, 1982, Medical Administration Co.
17. *Dark Victory: Ronald Reagan,* MCA & the Mob, Dan Moldea, 1986, Viking Press
18. *Reagan's America,* Garry Wills, 1987, Doubleday and Company
19. *The Adult Children of Alcoholics Syndrome,* Wayne Kritsberg, 1988, Bantam Books

20. *First Father, First Daughter*, Maureen Reagan, 1989, Little Brown
21. *Ronald Reagan: An American Life*, Ronald W. Reagan, 1990, Pocket Books
22. *The Years of Lyndon Johnson: Means of Ascent*, Robert Caro, 1990, Alfred A. Knopf
23. *Operation Anadyr*, Anatoli I. Gribkov and William Y. Smith, 1994, edition q, inc.
24. *The Dark Side of Camelot*, Seymour Hersh, 1997, Back Bay Books
25. *Cold War*, Jeremy Isaacs and Taylor Downing, 1998, Bantam Press
26. *President Reagan; the Role of a Lifetime*, Lou Cannon, 1991, Simon & Schuster
27. *Nofziger*, by Lyn Nofziger, 1992, Regnery Gateway
28. *With Reagan*, Edwin Meese III, 1992, Regnery Gateway
29. *Mutual Contempt: Lyndon Johnson, Robert Kennedy, and the feud that defined a decade.* Jeff Shesol, 1997, W.W. Norton & Co.
30. *Reagan in his Own Hand*, edited by Kiron Skinner et al, 2001, The Free Press
31. Interview with Michael Deaver, Oral History at Miller Center, University of Virginia, September 12, 2002
32. *Governor Reagan; His Rise to Power*, Lou Cannon, 2003, Public Affairs
33. *The Last Tycoon: When Hollywood Had a King*, Connie Bruck, 2003, Random House
34. Interview with Lyn Nofziger, Oral History at Miller Center, University of Virginia, March 6, 2003
35. *At the Abyss: An Insider's History of the Cold War*, Thomas C. Reed, 2004, Ballantine Books
36. *God and Ronald Reagan*, Paul Kengor, 2004, HarperCollins
37. *The Judge: William P. Clark, Ronald Reagan's Top Hand*, Paul Kengor & Patricia Clark Doerner, 2007, Ignatius Press
38. *Going Home to Glory*, David Eisenhower, 2010, Simon & Schuster

INDEX

ABOUT THE AUTHOR

Thomas C. Reed is a former Secretary of the Air Force, having served in that capacity during the Ford and Carter administrations. In the mid-seventies, Reed was the youngest-ever director of the once-covert National Reconnaissance Office, responsible for all US satellite intelligence systems, both photographic and electronic, during the Cold War. During the eighties,  Reed served as Special Assistant to President Reagan for National Security Policy. His technical background includes nuclear weapon design and low-temperature physics.

Reed graduated from Cornell University with a degree in engineering and an ROTC commission into the US Air Force. He began his professional career at the Air Force Ballistic Missile Division in Los Angeles during the 1950s, the years of Sputnik and the "missile gap."

After earning a graduate degree from the University of Southern California, Reed moved to Lawrence Livermore, where he designed two thermonuclear devices fired over the Pacific in 1962. On leaving Livermore, Reed started and ran a successful high-tech company making superconductors, but he also developed an interest in politics.

In 1973, Reed was recruited to manage certain intelligence projects at the Pentagon in connection with the Yom Kippur War then raging in the Mideast. A decade of involvement in national security matters followed. Reed left Washington in 1983 to return to business pursuits, but throughout the years of Soviet collapse, Reed continued to advise the Joint Strategic Planning Staff on policy and intelligence matters.

During the nineties, Reed spent time in Ukraine, assisting with the return of abandoned Soviet nuclear weapons to Russian control. With the coming of the millennium, he turned his attention to writing, documenting the history of the Cold War and its principal players.

His first book, *At the Abyss: An Insider's History of the Cold War*, with an introduction by Former President George H.W. Bush, was published by Ballantine Books in 2004. It delves into the lives of those who fought and ended the Cold War without a nuclear shot being fired.

His second work, *The Nuclear Express: A Political History of the Bomb and Its Proliferation* was co-authored by Danny Stillman, a former chief of technical intelligence at Los Alamos. It was published by Zenith Press in 2009, with a favorable review by William J. Broad, science editor of the New York Times, prior to publication.

In his third book, Reed turned to history-based fiction with *The Tehran Triangle*, written with Sandy Baker and published by Black Garnet Press in 2012. James Schlesinger, former chairman of the AEC, director of central intelligence, secretary of defense and then secretary of energy, wrote that, "*The Tehran Triangle* is a harrowing tale about Iran's quest for the bomb. The story feels real; it could have been written by an intelligence insider and a nuclear weapons expert. And it was."

Reed was born in New York City. He now lives in Healdsburg, California, with his wife Kay.